A CERTAIN BLINDNESS

Paul L. Brady

A
CERTAIN
BLINDNESS

A Black Family's Quest
for the Promise of America

ALP Publishing   Atlanta

*Copyright © 1990 by ALP Publishing, 1185 Niskey Lake Rd.,
Atlanta, Georgia 30331. All rights are reserved.
No part of this book may be reproduced without formal permission.*
94 93 92 91 90   5 4 3 2 1

Library of Congress Cataloging-in-Publication Data
Brady, Paul L., 1927–
   A certain blindness : a Black family's quest for the promise of America / Paul L. Brady.
     p.   cm.
   Includes bibliographical references.
   ISBN 0-9623720-0-5
   1. Brady, Paul L., 1927– . 2. Afro-Americans—History. 3. United States—Race relations. 4. Judges—United States—Biography. 5. Afro-American judges—Biography. I. Title.
E185.61.B788 1990
973'.0496073—dc20
                                               90-5
                                               CIP

What, then, is our neighbor?
Thou hast regarded his thought, his feeling,
as somehow different from thine.
Thou hast said, "a pain in him is not like
a pain in me, but something far easier to bear."
He seems to thee a little less living than thou;
his life is dim, it is cold, it is a pale fire
beside thine own burning desire. . . .
So, dimly and by instinct hast thou lived with thy neighbor,
and hast known him not, being blind.

—William James

Contents

Preface ix
Acknowledgments xi

1.
Masters of Men *1*

2.
Bondman to Lawman *15*

3.
In Pursuit of Equality *37*

4.
"Neither Inferior nor Unworthy" *66*

5.
A Chance to Serve *83*

6.
The Supreme Court Rules for Justice *114*

7.
An Absence of Moral Leadership *139*

8.
The Lawyer: A High and Noble Calling *172*

9.
On Being a Judge *210*

10.
Unequal Justice *243*

11.
The Past as Prologue *279*

12.
A Higher Law *305*

Epilogue 327
Notes 329

Preface

In June 1982 I met privately with Dr. Karl Menninger, the famed psychiatrist and founder of the Menninger Foundation. He pointed out to me that a lecture given in 1892 by the noted Harvard psychologist and philosopher William James was relevant to a view I had expressed on race relations. In that lecture James referred to the blindness of individuals to the feelings and values of others. I chose the title for this book from that lecture, "On a Certain Blindness in Human Beings." My purpose is to show that the white majority has willfully blinded itself to the humanity and worth of Americans of African descent in order to preserve the best portion for itself.

I have written from the perspective of a federal judge who is also the grandson of a slave and the great-grandson of a slave owner. I have, of course, neither been slave nor slave owner, but I have lived in a country that has never recovered from its slaveholding past.

Using my family as the prototype of many other families,

Preface

I place in perspective the roles African Americans have played in the construction of the United States—as well as the roles black men and women have been prevented from playing. Beginning during slavery, my ancestors yearned for human dignity and justice, while the rest of the nation adhered tenaciously to a code of white superiority. I relate the experiences of my great-uncle Bass Reeves, a slave who became a U.S. marshal during America's westward expansion; my grandfather C. R. Wilson, a bright and promising young labor leader during the South's period of reconstruction; my great-grandfather Lewis Slaughter, who walked nine hundred miles from Alabama to Kansas so his family could live in a freer environment; and my aunt Lucinda Todd, whose courageous leadership helped lay the foundation for the historic Supreme Court decision in *Brown v. Board of Education*.

The reality is that black Americans have helped make America what it is today, yet for the most part, white Americans fail to acknowledge them. The burden color adds to the lives of black men and women as they strive to advance themselves is a burden most white Americans simply cannot see.

In my own experience, it has been much more difficult to overcome perceptions about my race than to meet the objective requirements of success. I am acutely aware that my life is not far distant from my foreparents or from those whose lives are presently determined by race and racism. African Americans have rarely received equal protection of the laws and equal justice. To them justice has hardly been more than an illusion, since being treated justly depends on what color their skin is.

Frederick Douglass observed over one hundred years ago that injustice can become so firmly established that the perpetrator cannot distinguish it from justice. Recognizing that such injustice continues to plague our land, I felt impelled to write this book about America's racial blindness.

Acknowledgments

I am grateful to Linda Hollingsworth Johnson, Doris E. Saunders, and two friends who are both deceased, Louis B. Reynolds and Laurraine Goreau, for their journalistic contributions. I include thanks to Rita Johnston and Diane Dowdell, who transferred my handwritten pages to typewritten copy, and to Mavis Edwards for photographic services. My special thanks are due to my sisters and brothers and other family members for their support and encouragement.

I gratefully acknowledge the assistance of Frances C. Locher, who edited the manuscript for publication, and Anne Adamus, who rendered invaluable editorial assistance in the publishing of the manuscript.

Most of all, I am indebted to my wife, Xernona, an outstanding critic who provided significant suggestions. Her patience and support have been most encouraging throughout this undertaking.

1
Masters of Men

It is 1972, and I stand solemnly in a hushed chamber in Washington, D.C., waiting to be sworn in as a federal administrative law judge. The sounds from the street drift into my reverie, which is heavy, introspective. I have achieved a position in American society to determine people's rights and duties according to the Constitution of the United States of America. My thoughts drift naturally to my great-uncle Bass Reeves and to Fort Smith, Arkansas, 1875. Nearly a hundred years before I take my own oath, Bass vowed to uphold the law as a deputy marshal in Judge Isaac C. Parker's court.

Why did Bass want to be a marshal? He regarded the law as the genesis of his own freedom, as I do. And Bass wanted to safeguard that freedom for himself and his family, as I want. But as I become a judge committed to constitutional protection of freedom and justice, I am also acutely aware of the irony, for I am a black man whose forebears, including my great-uncle Bass, were slaves who enjoyed no rights whatsoever.

A Certain Blindness

As I repeat the solemn words during my swearing in, I hear the street sounds again, and I imagine Bass coming down another street in another time. A tall, muscular man sitting astride his big sorrel, Bass rode slowly down the main street of Muskogee in Indian territory. He was delivering two prisoners to the first federal jail to be erected in that territory, and they would later be removed to Fort Smith for trial. Bass had nearly been killed when the three men he had warrants for ambushed him deep in Creek Indian territory, where Bass's pursuit had taken him. He killed one in the ambush and got the other two to surrender. After delivering his prisoners to chief marshal Leo Bennett, Bass was looking forward to a well-deserved rest.

Bennett had another warrant that had to be served, though. He didn't want to assign another deputy to the case, but Bennett was disturbed to have to tell Bass that Bass's own son was charged with the murder of his wife and was a fugitive somewhere in Indian territory. Bass was visibly shaken with Bennett's news. Pacing the floor, he reflected how clearly the law had seemed defined for him, how concerned he had always been with enforcing it. And now it clashed markedly with his love for his own son. But, as the *Muskogee Daily Phoenix* reported, "with a devotion to duty equal to that of the old Roman Brutus, whose greatest claim to fame was that the love of his son could not sway him from justice, he said 'Give me the writ.' "[1] Bass told Bennett it was his son who was wanted and it was his responsibility to bring him in. Two weeks later Bass returned with his prisoner, who was immediately bound over for trial.

Throughout America's westward movement, the frontier lawman has been legendary. No stage better depicts the spirit of America. The Texas Rangers, Wild Bill Hickock, Bat Masterson, and others loom large as heroes, and their names are familiar to young and old alike. Of course we know that many of the tales told about these historic figures sprang from the imagination, but while the story of Bass Reeves is true, few know it, since history has not tended to record the stories of our black heroes. The dedicated, well-liked man was a deputy for thirty-two years, and he served "hanging" Judge Parker for the twenty-one years Parker held court in the territory that became the state of Oklahoma. Yet Bass was born a slave on a cotton plantation near Paris, Lamar County, Texas, about 1840. At that time Texas was still a separate republic, and slavery was legal. Bass and his older sister, Jane (who is my paternal grandmother), spent their early years on the plantation with their mother, Pearlalee.

While Bass was a youth he worked in the fields as a water boy, and he sang constantly about guns, knives, robberies, and killings, and Pearlalee feared Bass would "turn out a desperado and die afore his time." She felt he was too young to be seething with the same rage that had caused her husband to abandon them. A strong-willed, religious woman, Pearlalee believed Bass could find relief in the teachings of Christianity, which she had learned secretly. Like many others held in bondage, Pearlalee had faith that God would set things right. She told Bass and her daughter, Jane, the parables of Jesus, how he was concerned with the lowly and oppressed. These stories gave them hope. Gradually Bass became less agitated and endured his circumstances more calmly, and in addition to making certain there was water available to the slaves working the fields, Bass began watering and tending the mules and horses. His way with animals led to his becoming the blacksmith's helper. Because he was swift with his work at the forge and eager to take on additional duties, the blacksmith never grumbled when Bass spent time with the master's prize horses, and indeed, the horses thrived under his attention.

Bass was selected as his master's "companion," a position of prestige among his fellow slaves. His mother, Pearlalee, was pleased because now each member of her family was an upper servant, able to eat at the "house table." Bass's sister, Jane, had worked inside the house for several years, where her needlework was esteemed. Pearlalee herself had long been her mistress's personal attendant and the household favorite, and she sang on most occasions when her master entertained.

A Certain Blindness

Bass accompanied his master nearly everywhere, serving as valet, bodyguard, coachman, and butler. Compared to fieldwork, smithing, and stable tending, his new duties seemed light. But Bass took advantage of his opportunities to be close to white people, listening to them and trying to understand them. He even asked his master if he could learn to read, because Bass wanted to be able to read the Bible. Like other slaveholders, Bass's master refused this permission, but he did permit Bass, who had quick hands and a good eye, to learn to use a gun. Being himself a poor shot, Bass's master indulged his loyal and trusted slave and appreciated the vicarious prestige when Bass invariably won the turkey shoots and other trials in which Bass was entered, regardless of whether the opponent were black or white.

Nevertheless, like other slaves revolting in the 1850s, Bass yearned for freedom and began to participate in various acts of sabotage and other abolitionist activities. A confrontation with his master was inevitable, and it occurred following an episode one night in which Bass was returned to the plantation by a group of white men, bound, and held in a vacant cabin until the next morning. When his master appeared to deal with his belligerent servant, Bass killed him in the ensuing fight and took the opportunity to escape. Taking provisions, firearms, and a preferred horse, the young slave headed north across the Red River into Indian territory, where he was never caught.

Bass had found the Bible stories of God's deliverance of the Israelites from slavery in Egypt of special significance, and his sentiments were shared by increasing numbers of slaves. And, in fact, all forms of slave protest or armed rebellion were based on the Scriptures. The three major slave revolts in this country were led by men who had known slavery and who stressed the religious nature of their causes. The God-given right to freedom inspired the revolts under Gabriel Prosser in 1800, Denmark Vesey in 1822, and Nat Turner in 1831. Each leader could read and write, was talented, and felt himself ordained to overthrow the system of slavery. Prosser and Turner, in particular, felt

Masters of Men

themselves to be the instruments of God, destined to bring deliverance to their people.

There were also white people who sought to abolish slavery. John Brown was one of these brave people. A descendant of the Puritans who came to America on the *Mayflower,* he abhorred the enslavement of fellow human beings. Brown came into national prominence in the border wars of Kansas and Missouri, and some maintain that Kansas remained a slavery-free state largely through his involvement. He is best known for seizing the U.S. arsenal at Harper's Ferry, Virginia, to obtain arms for a general insurrection. The undertaking was a complete failure, and Brown was hanged following his conviction for murder and treason, but at his trial he stated: "I never did intend murder or treason or the destruction of property. . . . The design on my part was to free the slaves. . . . I respect the rights of the poorest and weakest of the colored people, oppressed by the slave system, as I do those of the most wealthy and powerful."[2] Many viewed Brown as a saint and martyr who gave his life for the liberty of the lowly and oppressed. He had begun his antislavery activities in Kansas in 1855, and beginning in 1856 a vast wave of slave unrest swept across Texas. Despite the incidents of plantation burnings, well poisonings, escape, and murder, the Texas House of Representatives Committee on Slaves and Slavery reported in 1857 that "our slaves are the happiest three millions of human beings on whom the sun shines."[3] Yet the newspapers began reporting what the government refused to acknowledge.

The *Matagorda* (Texas) *Gazette* carried the story of a meeting of slave owners in Marshall at which a local man was convicted of being an abolitionist, and as a result, the slave owners asked Congress to make abolitionism treason.[4] In Fannin County (adjacent to Lamar County, where Bass lived), the newspaper reported three slaves hanged for killing their masters.[5] Fires were allegedly set by abolitionists and slaves in many towns in the area, including Ladonia and Honey Grove, which are short distances from Paris. The *Matagorda Gazette* also stated that a mob of almost five hundred persons hanged a white man "charged with having endeavored to incite the slaves of Wood, Titus and Hopkins counties to an insurrection."[6] Titus and Hopkins counties also adjoin Lamar County.

A *New Orleans Daily Picayune* writer warned prospective buyers not to pay high prices for slaves from northeastern Texas, as he had personally witnessed their "contamination with ideas of rebellion."[7] The *Galveston News* of January 1857 printed this somber note about conditions in the region: "Never has there been a time in our recollection when so many insurrections, or attempts at insurrection, have transpired in rapid succession as during the past six months. The evidence in regard to some of these has indeed proved very unsatisfactory, showing nothing but that the negroes had got hold of some indistinct and vague ideas about obtaining their freedom."[8]

An article in the *Austin* (Texas) *State Gazette* of July 12, 1859, reported that a planned insurrection had been uncovered in the town of Waxahachie, leading to the arrest and punishment of more than one hundred slaves. The Committee of Vigilance, consisting of "the most respectable and responsible men in the country," led a mob in the execution of the three slave leaders— Sam Smith, Cato, and Patrick. Facing certain death, Patrick calmly declared that his actions and those of the other slaves were "just the beginning of the good work."[9]

But the Texas House Committee on Slaves and Slavery reassessed its position on the happy slaves in Texas and concluded: "We have to rely more and more on the power of fear. We must, in all our intercourse with them, assert and maintain strict mastery, and impress it on them that they are slaves. . . . We are determined to continue masters, and to do so, we have to draw the rein tighter and tighter day by day, to be assured that we hold them in complete check."[10]

Determined to be masters over men and land alike, the new men in the New World also had to displace and relocate the indigenous Indian populations. The territory of what is now eastern Oklahoma was set aside for this purpose, and in the

1830s and 1840s some sixty thousand Indians were moved from the South and relocated west to an area far removed from existing American settlements. The reasons for the Indian relocation corresponded strikingly with the entrenchment of Negro slavery in America.

During the Revolutionary War, a number of the eastern Indian tribes, including the Cherokees, supported the British effort. After the American victory, representatives of President Washington met with the Cherokees and forged a treaty requiring the surrender of vast areas of hunting ground in Kentucky, North Carolina, and Tennessee, leaving the Cherokees with large areas in Tennessee, Georgia, and Alabama as well as assurances by the terms of the treaty that they could live on the remaining land "as long as the rivers flowed and the grass grew." But many tribes were forced to give up all their lands. Some of the tribes, however, attempted to thwart the white man's advance. The legendary Shawnee chief, Tecumseh, led the effort to unite the eastern tribes in driving back the settlers so they could continue to live in their own way with complete freedom to enjoy their land. The powerful Creeks of Alabama triumphed in several battles before suffering defeat at the hands of General Andrew Jackson in the Battle of Horseshoe Bend in Alabama. Although Cherokee troops supported Jackson, they soon shared the fate of all the Indians in the Southeast.

Several events occurred that precipitated their removal west. Georgia, largest of the new states, contained within its boundaries land now consisting of Alabama and Mississippi, the home of the Creek, Choctaw, and Chickasaw tribes. Land-hungry settlers, well aware of the rich land occupied by these Indians, were anxious to clear the forest and begin the lucrative business of producing cotton. Textile mills in New England and England would buy all the cotton they could get for the worldwide sale of cloth.

The move to accommodate the settlers began in 1802 when the state of Georgia entered into a compact with the federal government whereby it would give up most of the land in its western portion. The government promised to extinguish all Indian title to the land as soon as it could be done "peaceably and on reasonable terms" with the Indians. The following year the United States purchased the vast area of land known as the Louisiana Purchase. It was to be the most distant point in that wide expanse where the Indians would soon reside, yet their change of residence was accomplished neither "peaceably" nor "on reasonable terms."

The most significant event directly relating to the Indians' move occurred when a Cherokee found a gold nugget near Dahlonega, Georgia. The days of the Cherokees' enjoyment of their land were numbered, as the first gold rush in the United States began. When the hordes of miners swarmed into the area, they drove the Indians from their homes, stole food and livestock, and even killed those who resisted. In addition to not protecting the Indians, which was a violation of the treaties, the state of Georgia even passed laws calling for their forced removal from the state. Subsequently, the United States Supreme Court ruled that the laws of Georgia were void and ordered that troops be sent to restore the land to the Indians. President Jackson indignantly declared, "[Chief Justice] John Marshall made the ruling, let him enforce it." Thereafter Jackson worked tirelessly to have Congress enact his Indian Removal Bill of May 28, 1830.

Over the years the Indians of the Southeast were induced by various treaties, secured by bribes and coercion, to release parts of their land to the demanding whites. After the Louisiana Purchase, the Cherokees had made nine treaties, the Creeks six, the Choctaw four, the Chickasaw three, and the Seminoles one. But the Removal Act meant once and for all that for these tribes "the rivers flowed" no more and the "grass grew" not. When the soldiers came with meager amounts of clothing and provisions, the native Americans left their homelands forever.

In his report to Congress regarding the government's handling of the Indians' removal, President Van Buren declared that it was "just and friendly throughout; its efforts for their civilization constant, and directed by the best feelings of humanity; its watchfulness in protecting them from individual frauds unremitting."[11] But French writer Alexis de Tocqueville witnessed the journey of the Choctaws, about which he wrote in his book *Democracy in America:*

> It was then the middle of winter, and the cold was unusually severe; the snow was frozen hard upon the ground and the river was drifting huge masses of ice. The Indians had their families with them, and they brought in their train the wounded and the sick, with children newly born and old men upon the verge of death. They possessed neither tents nor wagons, but only their arms and some provisions. I saw them embark to pass the mighty river, and never will that solemn spectacle fade from my remembrance. No cry, no sob, was heard among the assembled crowd; all was silent. Their calamities were of ancient date, and they knew them to be irremediable.

The survivors arrived destitute and broken in spirit, as Tocqueville related: "The countries to which the newcomers betake themselves are inhabited by other tribes, which receive them with jealous hostility. Hunger is in the rear, war awaits them, and misery besets them on all sides. To escape from so many enemies, they separate, and each individual endeavors to procure secretly the means of supporting his existence."

Tocqueville's final assessment of the effects of forced migration on the Indians' survival as unique peoples parallels the removal of the Africans to the New World: "The social tie, which distress had long since weakened, is then dissolved; they have no longer a country, and soon they will not be a people, their very families are obliterated; their common name is forgotten, their language perishes; and all traces of their origin disappear. Their nation has ceased to exist except in the recollections of the antiquaries of America and a few of the learned of Europe."[12]

So, in the course of its development, America would destroy part of mankind in the name of advancing civilization. After using all forms of duress to separate the red man from his

A Certain Blindness

land, whips and chains were used to force the black man to clear and develop it for production. The red man was then shunted aside as though he never really counted as a human being, and the black man was allowed to remain, but cast only as inferior, in a totally subservient role. America continues to be plagued by the effects of this inhumanity and yet insists its progress and achievement does, and always has, rested on the premise of equality for all.

Attempts to enslave the red man failed ultimately because the Indian was in his home territory and could easily escape and survive in the wild. But the African was in a strange and terrifying place without knowledge of the country. Separated from his tribesmen, he was even without means of communication. Furthermore, his skin color made him instantly identifiable and thwarted any easy means of escape.

As for the Cherokee, Creek, Seminole, Choctaw, and Chickasaw tribes, their increasing contact with settlers led them to be called "the five civilized tribes." Through their dealings with the white man, they even acquired slaves, some given by the British in payment for assistance during the Revolutionary War, others obtained during raids, still others even purchased as a show of power and prestige. The westward diaspora of the Indians thus included black men and women, some as slaves and some as free people accepted as citizens of the tribes.

Gradually the Indians, living in separate tribal nations, managed to make remarkable adjustment in the West, despite tremendous difficulties. Each of the tribes successfully tamed the wilderness and built towns and established constitutional governments and highly effective court and school systems. The first written constitution was adopted by the Chocktaws, providing for elective government, a court system, and a bill of rights that included trial by jury. The Creeks were pioneers in granting equal rights to women, giving them complete control and ownership of their own property. The tribes of each nation had enormous respect for their laws, which were enforced by mounted rangers known as lighthorse police. When laws were violated, they were enforced swiftly and with certainty. Although prior treaties made by the U.S. government with the Indians had been ruthlessly flouted (altogether the United States had made about four hundred treaties with the Indian tribes, with hardly one being fully honored), the federal government now solemnly guaranteed the permanency of their western home. Even under these circumstances the Indians hoped to live free and peacefully, far removed from the destructive interference of the white man.

In the two decades prior to the Civil War, the relocated Indians perhaps enjoyed the most glorious days of their western existence. It was also the period my great-uncle Bass Reeves began his new life in their country.

Upon his arrival in the territory as a fugitive, he moved about constantly to escape capture and punishment. He made his way deep into the interior of Indian territory to an area controlled by the Seminole nation. The Seminoles had been the last of the tribes to arrive in the West because they had fought seven years resisting forced separation from their homes. Considered the least "civilized" of the five tribes, they were a proud and independent people. Having suffered heavy losses during the war, they harbored considerable animosity toward the white man and viewed Bass as a conquering warrior for successfully resisting the white man's ways, and they willingly shared the land.

Bass's restlessness began to subside when he realized the Indians were his allies against a common adversary. There seemed to be a natural bond between native and black Americans, perhaps because the history of slavery paralleled the Indians' own history of mistreatment and abuse by white settlers. Moving about freely, Bass learned the territory, as he said, "like a cook knows her kitchen." He became fluent in Seminole, Creek, and Cherokee and could converse well in the languages of the other major tribes. He also mastered several lesser tribal tongues and established many relationships of trust and respect with the various tribes.

A Certain Blindness

He developed an especially close bond with Creeks, the most powerful tribe in the territory. Bass found them to be a peace-loving, honest, and orderly people who welcomed him to share their citizenship. Their land was especially attractive to him—beautiful streams, lush bottom land, and rolling hills abounding with game and fish—for it made his new life pleasant.

Living with the Indians afforded Bass the opportunity to learn their ways of hunting and wilderness survival and to understand nature's signs in stalking both men and animals. In all, Bass remained in Indian territory nearly ten years. Great changes were sweeping the country during those years, however, and Bass and the Indians found their lives totally disrupted. As the country moved toward civil war, even those living in Indian territory were sought out to support the abolitionists or those who favored slavery. The Southern influence proved to be a potent factor in causing the tribes to take sides in the war, thereby creating sharp divisions in several Indian nations. Many of the government agents administering Indian affairs were Southern sympathizers, and Southern states sent delegations to the Indians seeking support, which led all of the civilized tribes to make alliances with the Confederacy. Bass early on aligned himself against the Confederacy with dissidents from the Creek, Cherokee, and Seminole tribes under the leadership of Creek chief Opothleyaholo. These anti-Confederates met ultimate defeat at the Battle of Chustenalah in the Cherokee Outlet. Many of the survivors fled into southern Kansas, but Bass remained in northern Cherokee territory on the advice of his friend, Chief Opothleyaholo.

As the Union forces made major gains, the neutral warriors joined them, and as uniformed troops they formed the First and Second Union Indian Brigades. When Union forces took Tahlequah, Fort Gibson, and Fort Smith, major conflict in the territory came to an end. Although legally free since the Emancipation Proclamation of 1863, Bass chose to maintain his close ties with the Indian territory and settled near Fort Gibson.

Cessation of hostilities found members of the tribes widely

dispersed. Many were refugees. Those of the Union, mostly Creeks, Seminoles, and Cherokees, were in the north near the Kansas border, while the Indians who had sided with the Confederacy were located in the south near Texas. The system for handling the Indian territory after the war differed substantially from the way the states of the Confederacy were treated. The federal government claimed the Indians were required to forfeit all their lands and treaty guarantees, and this eventually opened up the land to white settlers as well as Indians of differing tribes. Right of way also had to be granted for construction of the railroad across the territory, and the federal government also promised to develop a unified government for the whole territory and to establish courts to handle matters involving non-Indians, which was how Judge Parker eventually came to have jurisdiction there. Slaves acquired by the Indians were required to be freed and accepted as citizens with full property rights. To quell the ensuing internal disorder and to help stem attacks from Indians hostile to white encroachment, the Ninth and Tenth Cavalry regiments were brought in. These regiments were organized in accordance with an 1866 act of Congress establishing six black regiments in the U.S. Army. These black troops served heroically as major forces in bringing peace and order to America's western frontier. (Congress had stipulated that these regiments were to have white commanders. It is interesting to note that while George A. Custer refused to command such a unit, John J. Pershing, later deemed a hero for his command during World War I, headed the Tenth Cavalry. "It has been an honor," Pershing later declared, "which I am proud to claim to have been at one time a member of that intrepid organization of the Army which has always added glory to the military history of America—the 10th Cavalry.")[13]

The Indian territory in which Bass lived flourished with crime and criminals. "Soldiers of fortune rode the plains," remarked Glenn Shirley in *Law West of Fort Smith,* a history of frontier justice in the Indian territory from 1834 to 1896. "The cattle and horse thief, the prostitute, the desperado, the whiskey

A Certain Blindness

peddler—all sought refuge where there was no 'white man's court' and no law under which they could be extradited to the state or territory where they had committed their crimes." Shirley further claimed that "every white man, black man and half-breed who entered Indian territory was a criminal in the state from which he had come."[14]

With the increase in numbers of outlaws escaping into the territory, Bass sought to assist law enforcement officers. As a result of his knowledge and skill, he was able to make substantial sums as a scout and tracker thoughout the territory. He abandoned an earlier plan to settle in Kansas and instead bought a farm near Van Buren, near Fort Smith, Arkansas, adjacent to Indian territory. Bass relocated his mother, Pearlalee, and his sister, Jane, to Van Buren as well, and married Jinney, a young woman from the territory. An excellent horse breeder and cattleman, Bass established a successful and independent life, and he preferred to minimize contact with the community at large, which still insisted on discriminating against former slaves.

When President Grant appointed Isaac C. Parker as judge of the western district of Arkansas in March 1875, it is said he had a "tough and nasty job" to do fighting the "worst band of desperadoes, murderers, and outlaws to be found in any civilized land." One of his first official acts was to swear in his chief marshal and appoint deputies to enforce the law. Of those fearless men who enlisted in the cause to carry out Judge Parker's mandate to bring them in alive, or dead, was my great-uncle, Bass Reeves, one of the first "who rode for Parker."[15]

2
Bondman to Lawman

Isaac C. Parker was an ideal choice to serve the cause of law and order in the Indian territories. Parker, who had been a judge in St. Joseph, Missouri, from 1868 to 1870, then became a congressman from 1871 through 1875. He sought to improve conditions relating to the Indians by his work on the Committee on Territories and later on the Indian Appropriation Bill of 1872. Another bill Parker introduced was designed to give these original Americans civil government in their territory. President Grant shared Parker's commitment to the Indians' cause and stated in his annual message of 1872: "The subject of converting the so-called Indian Territory, south of Kansas, into a home for the Indian, and erecting therein a territorial form of government, is one of great importance, as a complement of the existing Indian policy. . . . A territorial government should protect the Indians from the inroads of whites for a term of years until they have become sufficiently advanced in the arts and civilizations to guard their own rights, and from the disposal of lands held by them for the same period."[1]

After Judge Parker had served twenty years in the Indian territory, he had definite opinions about the source of the trouble in that land: "This whole evil could have been remedied, and could be remedied now, by the simple performance of this great duty which rests upon the Government to protect the rightful owners of the soil and the rightful inhabitants of the country from the immoral, criminal, and debasing influence thrown around them by the refugee criminal class who have been permitted to go into that country, undisturbed as far as the executive arm of the Government is concerned."[2] In 1895 Judge Parker appeared before the U.S. House of Representatives Judiciary Committee to state his views on the relationship of Indian citizens and crime in the territory. He testified:

> I have for twenty years been judge of the Federal court at Fort Smith. I went there on the special request of President Grant, because he thought I was friendly to the Indians. His desire was that a judge should not go there inimical to their interests, and I want to say here and want to be correctly understood in the declaration that in that land for that time there has been a contest between savageness and civilization. The savageness is not upon the part of the Indians, but the savageness was presented by the refugee criminal classes who have obtruded themselves upon that people from every State in this Union, and who have been doing it from the day that the treaty of Hopewell was entered into to this very hour. . . .
>
> Those in authority in the Indian government have always, in the twenty years I have been there, used their influence and everything in their power to aid the administration of the law. They have respected it; they have sought to uphold it both in their own courts and the Federal courts there. They have made great progress. They are civilized—as far upon the pathway of civilization as we are in the surrounding States. If there is an exception to the rule, that is found largely to exist among the men who have gone in there from the outside, men who have refugeed in there, and men who do not belong there.

Now what is the solution of this problem? In my judgment it is to give them protection, give them security, give them that administration of the law of the United States; they are working out their own destiny, and they are on the road to a final solution of the problem, where instead of having Territorial government it will be Statehood of the Five Tribes. They will come under the flag as a State in this nation. They are not ready for it yet, but they are working toward it. They have every element which is involved in civilization, and they are using those elements from the neighbors and friends of the good people from the surrounding States. They have the confidence and the respect of the people, and I say, let them alone; do not let us add another chapter to a century of dishonor by breaking up their local government.

We all have a pride in our local self-governments. It is the very foundation of patriotism; it is the very policy upon which this great structure of government rests; and the man who has no respect and no veneration for the principle of local self-government is not a good citizen of the United States. Their local governments are as dear to them and as sacred to them as our State governments are to us. Their local governments are better than any Territorial system that we, as a government, can establish over them.

The Territorial system is pernicious, and it has always been so. It creates, and has in almost every western Territory created, a nesting place for adventurers, for speculators, for rings, for men who are looking out for their own interests. These governments stand as the Government of the United States. We have pledged them that we will maintain them; that we will uphold them; and until they get ready, until they feel they are prepared for allotment and prepared for Statehood, I say, Why, in God's name, let them alone.[3]

Then Judge Parker was asked if legislation should grant the Indians full citizenship immediately. He replied:

A destruction of their system of government at this time and the establishment of a Territorial government over them, with free access of white men, would have precisely the same

A Certain Blindness

effect as our action toward the California Indians has had upon those people there, it would send them out as beggars without a dollar.

The man who has a blanket mortgage would rush in there and persuade them that they needed money to build a house or improve their lands, and in six months, if left with the ownership over the soil, they would not have a place to lay their heads in that country. It would be, in my judgment, absolute cruelty. They are protected by their government now. They are shielded by their government. . . .

These nations, as you have heard from the mouths of their representatives, are organized under this great Government of ours just as State governments are. They protect their own people, so that there is not a pauper Indian in the whole Five Civilized Tribes. I wish I could say as much in Arkansas; I wish I could say as much in these other States.

The system has, I think, worked thus far beneficially; but the time will come, and the time is approaching rapidly, when these gentlemen must hunt for a place upon our flag to place their star. They are hunting for it even now. Give them a little time, be forbearing for yet a little longer, and we can clasp hands with the representatives, not of the Indian Five Tribes, but one great State down there which has taken its place in the constellation among us.[4]

Parker's visions of statehood for the residents of the Indian territories were the results of the judge's long experience administering justice in the land that eventually became the state of Oklahoma. A man of high ideals, Parker resigned his appointment as chief justice of Utah at the request of President Grant to become, in 1875, judge of the western district of Arkansas. Parker opened his first term in court eight days after arriving in Fort Smith. Eighteen persons appeared before him that day charged with murder; fifteen were convicted, and eight were sentenced to die on the gallows. When these sentences were carried out, the hangings announced to the world what this court and this judge were all about.

From that day until June 1896 Judge Parker—who came to

be known as Hanging Judge Parker—held court almost continuously, rarely losing a day even for illness. In all he heard 344 cases involving capital offenses. Parker's vigorous administration of justice in a wild frontier covering seventy-four thousand square miles and sixty thousand people resulted in 181 hangings. But it is said that he wept after pronouncing his first death sentence. "I never hanged a man," Parker explained; "it is the law." A *St. Louis Republic* reporter described him as "the gentlest of men, this alleged sternest of judges. He is courtly of manner and kind of voice and face, the man who has passed the death sentence upon more criminals than any other judge in the land."[5] Indeed, Parker claimed, "I have ever had the single aim of justice in view. No judge who is influenced by any other consideration is fit for the bench. Do equal and exact justice."[6] In fact, "I favor the abolition of capital punishment," Parker remarked, "provided . . . that there is certainty of punishment, whatever that punishment may be. In the uncertainty of punishment following crime lies the weakness of our 'halting justice.' "[7] In order to make justice swift, and as a solution to the lengthy appeals process in cases involving capital punishment, Parker believed that courts should be presided over by judges learned in criminal law who, with the full trial record before them, would review each case on its merits and render a final decision as quickly as possible.

When Parker began to organize his force of roving deputies, many who knew the situation in the territory advised against sending unfamiliar and often arrogant white recruits into the area. The territory was like a foreign country to these gun-toting marshals, where the people and their customs were not understood, and where abuse and needless violence often occurred. A hostile, uncooperative Indian population, observers said, would render a white deputy almost completely useless. The problem was especially apparent in the Creek and Seminole nations where the peacekeeping efforts of Parker's deputies were desperately needed.

The Indian attitude notwithstanding, certainly something

had to be done to bring about respect for the law because the interior of the territory had become the hideout for a wild retinue of outlaws. It was clear that a deputy was needed to serve deep in the territory if Parker's court were to be taken seriously and if it were to make headway in its law enforcement mission. A deputy's authority to a great extent depended on his being accepted and respected by the Indians. Since Indians honored courage and honesty above all other qualities, it was the consensus of these officials that deputies should possess these positive traits. Convinced that Bass Reeves was such a man, Parker approached him and urged him to serve an indefinite term with his court at Fort Smith.

When Bass consented, he was the first black American west of the Mississippi to become a deputy U.S. marshal. For a man who had escaped from slavery and had been uncertain about his future in those days, Bass had become an important citizen with valuable expertise about the Indians and their lands. Homesteaders whose farms bordered Oklahoma territory and who had more than a legitimate grievance against roving outlaws could not have been more pleased with the choice. Bass himself felt proud to serve the government whose laws had transformed him from slave to free citizen. At the same time he admitted that mature years and a settled life on his farm in Van Buren had not enabled him to shake off a susceptibility to frontier living, and now he had the opportunity to establish some order out of the reigning chaos in the Indian territory that he had grown to love so ardently. Bass's service as a deputy was to include enforcement of everything from petty misdemeanors to the gravest crimes throughout the Indian territory. In the course of his career he was to ride for the courts of Fort Smith, Arkansas; Paris and Sherman, Texas; and Muskogee, in Indian territory at first and later on Muskogee's police force for two years after Oklahoma became a state in 1907.

Bass was a big man, as my aunt Nettie later described him to me. Considerably over six feet and weighing more than two hundred pounds, Bass had a handlebar moustache and was deceptively stern-faced. His smile, which came easily but not often, was as infectious as the smile of a father at the wedding of his spinster daughter. Bass's voice was deep and resonant and had a typical Southern drawl. Moving with the easy grace of a man accustomed to the great outdoors and with all the stealth and sureness of the natural hunter, he possessed the bearing of one with total self-confidence.

My father's older sister, my aunt Nettie, recalled that, even in retirement, Bass still had the erect posture of his active days, and the focus of his eyes was direct and piercing. His knuckles were large and knotty, displaying the scars that had earned him the distinction of a "rough-and-tumble" fighter. His ability with the six-shooter and rifle was widely recognized, so that he was barred from competition in turkey shoots at local fairs and picnics. His speed, described as fast and sure, included no wasted or unnecessary effort. Faced with dangerous outlaws, he could draw and shoot from the hip.

Regarding his prowess with a rifle, his Oklahoma friends liked to tell about how, on one occasion, Bass rode out to the fringes of the Kiowa-Comanche country over the crest of a hill and interrupted six wolves as they attacked a steer. The predators quickly scattered, but Bass killed all six with eight shots. He broke one wolf's leg and "gut shot" the other, but he stopped both animals with the first shot and used a second to end their suffering.

Bass was fond of horses and became easily attached to his different mounts. Because he was a large man, he needed a horse of majestic size. "When you get as big as me," he used to say, "a small horse is as worthless as a preacher in a whiskey joint fight. Just when you need him bad to help you out, he's got to stop and think about it a little bit." Bass often rode fifty to a hundred miles a day in the performance of his duties, and a small horse could not stand the constant strain of his weight. He was therefore partial to big horses, preferring a bay or sorrel. The speed of a horse had its advantages, but of primary concern to Bass were its strength and endurance. He felt that being sure

A Certain Blindness

he could get where he was going was more important than how fast he got there.

Whenever warrants were issued, deputies went out until they captured their quarry, alive—or dead. Manhunts were conducted without regard for deputies' comfort, and they had to put up with hazardous weather conditions from stifling heat to biting cold. Eventually locating their man, deputies usually encountered mortal danger, for practically everyone carried a weapon and resisting arrest was standard practice; whether there was gunplay or a fist fight depended largely on the criminal charge, since word had gone out that, in Judge Parker's jurisdiction, if convicted of a hanging offense, an outlaw was as good as hung.

Bass Reeves and the other deputies usually worked alone, but assistance was available from possemen who were required to register with the marshal's office before a trip, or guards who could be hired by a deputy along the way. A guard was under no obligation to aid the deputy in his duties if he did not elect to do so. He was hired only to guard the prisoners and drive the wagons to haul them back to Fort Smith for trial, a trip that might involve a number of weeks with as many as twenty prisoners in tow.

From the time he left Fort Smith until he returned, Bass was constantly a target of threats by those he sought to bring to justice. In part this came from the wagonload of chained, surly prisoners who thought only of escape somewhere along the journey to Judge Parker's court, for no matter how capable a man was with his fists or guns, the sheer number of prisoners in a wagonload could overwhelm a careless guard in an instant. Prisoners' relatives were also known to attempt an ambush somewhere along the trail to court. It was certainly an adventurous existence, but it was also one with major occupational hazards and often a short life expectancy. Compensation for deputies was paid in the form of fees and mileage. When on official business they were paid six cents a mile, fifty cents for serving papers, two dollars for an arrest, and a dollar per day for the expenses they incurred. Seventy-five cents a day was allowed to feed each prisoner, but no such provision was made for the deputy and his help. Ten cents was allowed the deputy and each prisoner he brought in. If the fugitive were killed, the deputy earned nothing. There were no provisions for medical costs, disability, family benefits, or burial expenses. In all, sixty-five marshals gave their lives in the line of duty while serving the Parker court.

This court, to which Bass Reeves brought the criminals he had rounded up, was a remarkable tribunal in the annals of jurisprudence, and some court observers have referred to it as the greatest distinctive criminal court in the world. Certainly none ever existed with jurisdiction over so great an area. It was the only trial court in U.S. history from whose decision there was, for more than fourteen years, no right of appeal. And Bass helped build the integrity of this unusual court. While specific records pertaining to Bass as a deputy marshal are sketchy, the accounts that do exist, such as the ones found in D. C. Gideon's book *Indian Territory,* give some insight into his character and motivation. Gideon actually talked to Bass for his book, and Bass's daughter, my cousin Alice, provided me additional materials in support of the same incidents. It was Gideon who declared: "Among the numerous deputy marshals that have ridden for the Paris (Texas), Fort Smith (Arkansas) and Indian Territory courts none have met with more hairbreadth escapes or have effected more hazardous arrests than Bass Reeves, of Muskogee. . . . He fears nothing that moves or breathes. . . . Several 'bad' men have gone to their longhome for refusing to halt when commanded to by Bass; but we will let him tell a story of adventure in his own words."[8] Then followed the perilous arrest of the dangerous murderer by the name of Jim Webb.

Jim Webb was a cowboy who came from Brazos, Texas, to the Chickasaw nation as a foreman for the Washington-McLish ranch. The large ranch was located on Spring Creek in the southern part of the nation and employed forty-five cowboys. Webb, a top cowhand, was also considered a dangerous man because of his quick temper and quick use of his gun.

A Certain Blindness

William Steward, a circuit preacher, had a small farm near the Washington-McLish ranch, which he operated between his preaching jaunts. In the early spring of 1893 Steward set a grass fire on his property, which got out of control and spread to the Washington-McLish ranch. Greatly annoyed by the encroaching blaze, Jim Webb rode over to chastise the preacher, and a bitter but brief quarrel ended with the preacher's death.

Bass was riding for the district court in Paris, Texas, at this time and was given the warrant to arrest Webb for murder. Bass took the warrant, obtained the services of a man named Floyd Wilson as his posse, and crossed the Red River, traveling north and east toward the Chickasaw nation to locate Webb. Several days later, they reached the Washington-McLish ranch in the early morning.

When Bass and his posse approached the ranch house, only three men were present: Jim Webb, a cowboy named Frank Smith, and the cook. Bass had never seen Webb but thought he recognized him from the description provided him before he left Paris. To make certain the man was Webb, Bass and Wilson rode up like any traveling cowboys and asked for breakfast. Webb, however, was immediately suspicious. When Bass and Wilson walked up to the porch, both Webb and Smith had their hands positioned near their guns, obviously prepared for any trouble. Bass wondered how he might arrest Webb without someone getting killed.

Bass and Wilson were led to the kitchen-dining room and told to wait until the cook prepared their breakfast. Bass felt he must do something to ease Webb's suspicions if he hoped to have any chance at all of arresting him. Following a few minutes of conversation, he asked Webb if he could feed the horses while waiting to eat. Webb granted his permission, but he followed Bass out to the barn, watching him every second with his gun still in his hand. Talking easily and steadily with no hint of his uneasiness, Bass fed the horses, loosened their saddle girths, and casually pulled his Winchester from its saddle boot. He leaned it against a corn crib, hoping this would convince

Webb he was honestly a traveling cowboy just passing through the country.

After eating, Bass and Wilson walked out into the dog run. Webb followed and stood directly over Bass as he sat down on a bench; Smith stood by Wilson at the far end of the bench. Both Webb and Smith still had their guns in their hands, and they were watching Bass and Wilson intently. Bass engaged in aimless conversation for a few minutes until a dog from a neighboring ranch began to howl. Dogs throughout the valley followed suit. Webb's attention was drawn from Bass for a second, and when Webb looked away, Bass made his move. Leaping to his feet, he knocked Webb's gun out of his hand, wrapped his left hand around Webb's throat, drew his own gun with his right hand, and shoved it into Webb's face. Webb, with a giant of a man choking the life out of him and looking straight into the barrel of a Colt .45, gurgled out a meek surrender.

In the meantime, Wilson was overwhelmed by the suddenness of the attack and made no attempt to seize Smith. Even as Webb surrendered, Smith whirled and fired two shots at Bass, but both shots missed. With Webb completely controlled by his left hand, Bass turned his attention to Smith and fired one shot. Smith fell to the ground, the fight completely taken out of him by a .45 slug in his abdomen. Never loosening his grip on Webb's throat, Bass ordered Wilson to put the irons on Webb. This done, Bass made plans to return the prisoners to Paris.

Two horses were quickly hitched to a wagon. Webb and the wounded Smith were loaded into it, and the long trip back began. The return trip might be considered uneventful, except that Frank Smith died of his wounds by the time they reached Tishomingo, the Chickasaw capital. Smith was buried there without ceremony, and Bass, Webb, and Wilson traveled on to Paris. Upon reaching Paris, Bass placed Webb in jail and proceeded to forget about him. But Webb and Bass were destined to meet once more.

Webb was given a hearing and bound over for trial. Meanwhile, his friends were hard at work in an effort to free him.

A Certain Blindness

After he had spent nearly a year in jail, two of his friends, Jim Bywaters and Chris Smith, managed to have him released on seventeen thousand dollars bond. But when the time for Webb's trial for murder finally came around, Webb had disappeared and the bail money was forfeited.

Two years passed and nothing was heard of Jim Webb. Bass, rankled by the knowledge that Webb had escaped, continually carried a new warrant in his pocket, hoping someday to recapture his man. Finally, Bass learned that Webb had drifted back into the Chickasaw nation and could be located at Jim Bywaters's general store in the Delaware Bend area across Red River in Indian territory. He set out to investigate, taking John Cantrell as his posse.

When Bass and Cantrell came within sight of Bywaters's store, Bass sent Cantrell ahead to make sure Webb was there. Cantrell rode ahead, slipped up to the store, and sure enough, there sat Jim Webb near one of the windows on the side opposite the entrance. Cantrell motioned for Bass to ride up, but Webb recognized Bass and jumped through the window, wearing a revolver and clutching a Winchester rifle in one hand. The fugitive made a break for his horse about a hundred yards away.

Bass heard the window break and spurred his horse ahead in time to block Webb's path to his mount, calling again and again for him to surrender. Horseless, Webb turned and sprinted from the barnyard toward the nearby underbrush, with Bass in pursuit. After running about six hundred yards, Webb was either completely winded or else convinced his escape attempt was futile. Knowing he faced almost certain hanging if captured, Webb made the outlaw's classic last ditch effort to foil arrest. He turned and fired on Bass. His first bullet grazed the horn of Bass's saddle, the second cut a button off Bass's coat, and the third cut the reins out of Bass's hand.

When the shooting began, Bass's horse got its head down and was doing its best to "jump over the moon," each jump bringing Bass closer to Webb. When the outlaw shot the reins out of his hand, Bass lost control of his animal and dove for the ground. As he rolled to his feet, Webb fired again, clipping the brim of Bass's hat.

Bass drew his gun so fast that Webb never had time to shoot again. Bass fired one shot from the hip, and Webb spun around and started to fall. Before Webb reached the ground Bass fired two more shots, hitting him with both. It was later discovered that all three bullets had hit Webb's body within a hand's width of each other.

By this time general store owner Jim Bywaters and posseman John Cantrell caught up with Bass. They saw Webb lying on the ground, his revolver in his hand, calling feebly for Bass. Advancing a few wary steps toward the gunman, Bass told him to throw away his weapon. Webb hesitated a moment, then pitched it away, and the three men walked to the spot where the wounded outlaw lay dying. Bywaters later wrote down Webb's last words on the back of a freight receipt: "Give me your hand, Bass. You are a brave, brave man. I want you to accept my revolver and scabbard as a present, and you must accept them. Take it, for with it I have killed eleven men, four of them in the Indian territory, and I expected you to make the twelfth."[9]

Bass accepted the gift, and in a few minutes Webb breathed his last. Bass helped to bury him and collected Webb's boots and gun belt to prove he had served the warrant.

Another outlaw who provoked Bass for several years was Bob Dozier, even though they met face to face only once. Bass's daughter, my cousin Alice, said her father considered this incident the high point in his career because he was successful where so many other deputies had failed.

Bob Dozier was a criminal strictly by choice. He had been a prosperous farmer for years, but the wild criminal life appealed to him so strongly that he made a deliberate choice to give up his farm and become an outlaw.

As a farmer, Dozier had been successful; as an outlaw, he was even more successful for several reasons. Rather than specializing in one type of criminal activity, Dozier diversified. He stole cattle, robbed stores and banks, hijacked cattle buyers car-

A Certain Blindness

rying large sums of money, held up stagecoaches, ambushed travelers, stuck up big money poker games, delved into land swindles as well as other confidence game schemes, and was the ring leader of a stolen horse operation. In the course of these pursuits he killed several people, and it was rumored that he even resorted to torture in order to obtain the information his large-scale operations seemed to require.

In many respects, Dozier's theories on criminal operations were remarkably astute. Because of his diversified activities, he never enraged one particular group of people to the extent that they banded together to aid deputy marshals sent out to arrest him. Most people felt that as long as they were not personally involved, there was no point in furnishing information on his whereabouts. This attitude was widespread, no doubt bolstered by knowledge that Dozier always remembered a favor and never forgot a traitor. With this disadvantage, the deputy marshals were completely hamstrung in their efforts to locate and arrest the outlaw. He was able to avoid their every effort for years until Bass took the trail after him.

Bass gathered considerable information about Dozier. He knew what Dozier looked like from the descriptions furnished by his victims, and he understood how Dozier operated to escape capture. Bass theorized that a lone-wolf pursuit, with perhaps a one-man posse to help, would accomplish more than several deputies banded together; one or two men could move about and not arouse any suspicions that might reach Dozier and scare him off.

For several months Bass made no concrete progress in his attempts to arrest Dozier. He never made actual contact with the outlaw even though he did come close enough to keep Dozier constantly on the run.

Dozier eventually learned who was after him and sent word to Bass that, if he did not stop hounding him, he was as good as dead. Bass said Dozier would have to quit running to kill him, and he was ready at any time to give Dozier his chance. Bass eventually caught Dozier's trail in the upper Cherokee nation; this trail was fresh and hot, and he had another man along to help. Deeper and deeper into the hills, Bass knew he could only be an hour or two behind Dozier and his companion. But shortly before dark a heavy, steady rain began to fall, and rain tends to dissolve horse tracks. By sunset all hope of tracking Dozier any further vanished, so Bass and his one-man posse began to look for a dry place to pass the night. They rode down into a wide, heavily timbered ravine, using lightning flashes to pick their way through the treacherous slopes. The instant they reached the bottom of the ravine, a gunshot blast greeted them. A slug whined past Bass's head.

Expecting more shots from the ambush, Bass and his posse dismounted and sought cover in the woods. A few minutes later Bass saw the dim shadow of a man slipping from tree to tree. He waited until the shadow was caught between two trees and then fired two shots. The shadow stopped and fell. This eliminated one of the men, but these two shots had given away his position, and the second man immediately opened fire. Bass jerked upright, took a reeling step away from the protective shield of trees, and fell full length to the ground facing his attacker. He waited with his gun cocked and ready.

For several minutes only the rain and cracks of thunder could be heard. Bass lay waiting in the mud and rain, fully exposed. Finally a man stepped from behind a tree laughing out loud, convinced Bass was dead and that his posse had run away. Bass smiled to himself as the lightning outlined the man's face: the long trail was over; he was suddenly face to face with Bob Dozier.

When Dozier was only a few yards away, Bass raised up and ordered him to stop and drop his gun. Dozier stopped laughing, his eyes wide with surprise. He hesitated for a moment, then crouched down to shoot, but before he could level his gun, Bass shot him in the neck. Thus ended the career of an outlaw who for years had laughed over the deputies' futile efforts to capture him.

Bass did not always have to spend days on the trail to serve a warrant, of course. Sometimes he waited in relative comfort for an outlaw to come to him. This method proved very effective in dealing with Tom Story.[10]

Generally, some of the best horses to be found in the Southwest were located in Indian territory, where they were often accumulated in large numbers to represent tribal wealth. One of the first well-organized bands of horse thieves to operate in Indian territory was the Tom Story gang. Besides Story, the gang had other talented men like "Pegleg" Jim, Kinch West, and "Long" Henry, all experts in the art of stealing and disposing of horses.

From 1884 until 1889 they made their headquarters on the banks of Red River in the Chickasaw nation, a strategic location allowing them to move in all directions, fully covering the Indian territory in their quest for horses they might steal. However, in 1889 they reversed their operation and stole a herd of horses and mules from George Delaney, who lived in north Texas, and drove them into Indian territory in search of a market.

When he missed his herd, Delaney made some inquiries and learned that the Story gang had stolen his horses and mules and was expected to return to Texas in a few days. Delaney contacted the marshal's office at Paris, Texas, and a warrant was issued for the arrest of Tom Story on suspicion of horse stealing. Bass was given the warrant since he was then serving in Paris as a deputy marshal.

Bass convinced Delaney to wait for Story's return. Bass figured Story would cross Red River at the Delaware Bend crossing, and Delaney agreed to go along as Bass's posse. They camped close to the Delaware Bend crossing and even hunted and fished a little while they waited. When Story came riding across the ford five days later, he was leading two of Delaney's finest mules. Bass stepped out of the brush in which he and Delaney were hiding and informed Story he had a warrant for his arrest. Since Bass's gun was still in its holster, Story tried to draw his gun, but before his gun could even clear leather Bass drew his own gun and fired.

Bondman to Lawman

Bass and Delaney buried Tom Story. Delaney left for home taking his two mules and Bass went back to Paris. The Story gang soon disintegrated, never to be heard of again.

Not all of the incidents in the life of Bass Reeves ended with violence. Sometimes his duties as deputy marshal led him into harmless, amusing adventures. This was especially true when Bass was assigned subpoena service duty. As with so many others during those frontier times, Bass had no formal education and never learned to read or write. This complicated matters when he was given a group of subpoenas to serve on the numerous witnesses the courts required during a regular court session because, in most cases, the people who were to be served with a subpoena could not read or write either.

Bass devised a system to get around this problem, however. He would study each subpoena until he could associate the symbols of a written name with the sounds of the name as it was spoken. Then he would have someone read the entire subpoena to him until he memorized which name belonged to which subpoena. When he located a man who answered to one of the names he had memorized, Bass would search through his file of subpoenas until he found the one with the proper symbols; as he thrust it into the man's hands Bass would gruffly command, "Read it." If the man could not read, Bass was forced to locate somebody who could read to insure the right man had been served.

Finding someone who could read was not always an easy task. First, Bass had to keep the man he had located in tow because many of them had a tendency to disappear, having no desire whatsoever to participate in any trial. Appearing as a witness generally entailed making a long trip over rough country, losing several days and possibly weeks of work, and possibly facing reprisals if the man they were testifying against were acquitted. Consequently Bass often had to resort to out and out threats to keep the men he located with him until he found somebody who could read. Secondly, the men Bass sought were usually found in isolated and thinly populated areas of the

A Certain Blindness

territory. Finding someone to read the subpoena sometimes meant riding a hundred miles.

The weather also invariably turned bad when Bass was out in the open on subpoena service; and he would warn the other deputies, "Get ready for bad weather, boys, I got a stack of subpoenas to serve, so Mother Nature is bound to go crazy. Hope I don't drown or freeze before I get back." Nevertheless Bass always served the subpoenas he was issued, and he was proud of the fact that he never made a mistake of serving one on the wrong man. Many of the courts he rode for specifically asked for Bass to serve their subpoenas because of his dependability.

Bass was also known to be incorruptible. As far as duty was concerned, he was beyond temptation or the influence of anyone. There is one recorded story of how an extraordinary Creek medicine man used otherworldly powers in a vain attempt to gain his release.[11]

Bass was completing the last leg of a great swing through the territory from Fort Smith. By the time he reached the North Fork area in the Creek nation he had two wagonloads of prisoners, but he still had one more warrant to serve. After setting up camp around noon and leaving his prisoners in the care of his posse, Bass set out to arrest Yak-kee, a grizzled, old Creek conjurer. Horse thieves liked to buy—for the price of one Indian pony—a medicine Yak-kee made that was reputed to make them invisible. Ironically, two Indians among Bass's prisoners had bought this medicine from Yak-kee yet had been arrested for horse stealing. The medicine man was also known to conjure a spell on anyone who antagonized him. Bass knew all about Yak-kee, but he had a warrant to arrest Yak-kee for horse stealing, so he ignored Yak-kee's threats to conjure a spell that would kill him before they reached Fort Smith. Bass chained Yak-kee, loaded him into the wagons with his other prisoners, and set off for Fort Smith.

By the time they stopped to camp for the night, Bass was feeling stiff and sore and aching in every joint. This struck him as odd because up until noon he had felt wonderful. The next

Bondman to Lawman

morning when they broke camp, Bass was so stiff and sore that he could hardly move. Stranger still, he was riding a good horse that, in spite of its best efforts, could not keep within sight of the wagons. He fell farther and farther behind. By the time Bass caught up with the wagons at noon, all the prisoners had eaten and were sound asleep, shackled together, lying on the ground under some trees.

Bass managed to dismount. He fell forward against a tree, aching in every joint, and his eyes were so swollen he could scarcely see. He couldn't eat and seemed to be dying of thirst. His knees were so weak that he couldn't stand, and he was so sick that Bass was sure he was dying. He began to believe that maybe old Yak-kee had really bewitched him.

Rolling over to face the prisoners, Bass looked over toward his tormentor, Yak-kee. He was asleep, snoring peacefully. But his coat was open and Bass noticed the ragged end of a string dangling out of a concealed, inner pocket. It occurred to Bass that this might be Yak-kee's medicine bag. With the greatest effort, Bass dragged himself over to where Yak-kee was lying. He tugged on the string and a small, moleskin bag filled with bits of roots, pebbles, and tiny rolls of short hair came out of the pocket. Bass threw the bag as hard as he could toward the creek that ran alongside the camp. He watched it fall into the water and slowly float away. From the moment the bag touched the water, Bass began to feel better, his general health improving so rapidly that he felt he would live after all.

Yak-kee awoke with a start. When he saw what had happened, he began to screech at Bass that he had stolen his "conjur-bag." He offered every reward he could think of to bribe Bass to retrieve the bag. But Bass was not about to go after it for any amount of money. Instead he woke everybody, loaded them into the wagons, and quickly broke camp. By the time they stopped for the night, Bass was feeling completely recovered. Later, from his cell at Fort Smith, Yak-kee told Bass that if he had not lost his conjur-bag, Bass would never have lived to see Fort Smith. Bass believed him.

A Certain Blindness

Some accounts about Bass are recorded in the Indian Archives Division of the Oklahoma Historical Society.[12] One person described Bass as "a coal-black negro [who] was a U.S. Marshal during one time and he was the most feared U.S. Marshal that was ever heard of in that country. To any man or any criminal that was subject to arrest he did his duty according to the law. He brought his men before the court to be tried fairly, but many times he never brought in all the criminals but would kill some of them."

I. F. Williams, a former guard with some of the marshals, recalled: "Bass Reeves was a bad negro and wasn't afraid to come out after the bad ones. . . . He would sometimes make arrest alone and bring the prisoners to the wagon in which they would be chained. I saw him one time when he had three prisoners who brought him a reward of $1,000. He tried to hire me to go guard the wagon, but I wouldn't go with him because he was a negro and I didn't think a white man should work under a negro."

One longer account was also found:

> Bass Reeves, a colored man, was a noted and well-known United States marshal. He was a fearless man when it came to fulfilling his duty as an officer of the law. He was a broad shouldered man, standing fully six feet and had very broad hands. He owned and always rode a sorrel horse which he loved next to his duty. He was known in Oklahoma and in the Indian territory for his deeds as U.S. marshal for at least thirty-five years.
>
> It was his custom to hold several prisoners until he had several in the camp when they would be loaded into wagons and hauled off to Ft. Smith. He had a man named Campbell, who stayed all the time in camp with the prisoners, as guard and as the camp cook. All the prisoners were seated on a very large log cut especially for this purpose. The prisoners' feet would be shackled together and the shackles pinned to the ground near the end of the log and the rest of the loose shackles pinned to the log itself.
>
> In his free and spare moments, Reeves would walk up and

down before the prisoners and preach to them for he was a deacon of the church. Reeves hated to think that he took men to prison but it was his duty to carry out the law enforcement so that he would take the time to tell his prisoners and preach to them of right and wrong.

Aunt Nettie said that, during his long career "shooting it out" with dozens of outlaws, my great-uncle Bass was never wounded. At different times his belt was shot in two, a button was shot from his coat, and the bridle rein in his hand was cut by a bullet. He killed fourteen men, but he was never guilty of firing a shot himself until the man he sought started the shooting. And of course he made enemies in the line of duty. The *Muskogee Times-Democrat* reported that an assassination attempt was made on his life on November 12, 1906, when he was riding home from serving papers in the Wybark community near Muskogee.

When the territory was admitted to the Union as the state of Oklahoma in 1907, the role of deputy marshal was assumed by newly created state agencies. The deputies were credited with doing more to prepare the Indian territory for statehood than any other agency. Bass, who had been a deputy for thirty-two years, wanted to continue work on Muskogee's police force, and he served for another two years. But he had spent too many nights sleeping on the ground in the wet and cold and countless days in the saddle, and his health was deteriorating. In 1909 Bass's health collapsed completely. He retired and, after a short illness, died of Bright's disease on January 12, 1910. A great ceremony attended by hundreds of people, Indian, white, and Negro, commemorated his death, and the *Muskogee Phoenix* for January 13, 1910, ran an obituary notice that summed up Bass's place in history:

> In the history of the early days of Oklahoma the name of Bass Reeves has a place in the front rank among those who cleaned out the old Indian Territory of outlaws and desperadoes. No story of the conflict of the government's officers with those outlaws which ended only a few years ago with the rapid filling

up of the territory with people, can be complete without mention of the old Negro who died yesterday.

For thirty-two years, beginning "way back" in the seventies and ending in 1907, Bass Reeves was a deputy United States marshal. During that time he was sent to arrest some of the most desperate characters that ever infested Indian Territory and endangered life and peace in its borders. At times he was unable to get them alive . . . but Bass Reeves always said that he had never shot a man when it was not necessary for him to do so in the discharge of his duty to save his own life.

The role of the early western lawman has been prominent in American folklore. Men like Wild Bill Hickock, Wyatt Earp, and Bat Masterson are acclaimed as heroes, and their names are recognized in every household across the land. When history begins to relate the unique contributions of America's black heroes, the name of Bass Reeves will be widely known as well.

3

In Pursuit of Equality

To improve their political, social, and economic circumstances, many black Americans left the South to head west. Oklahoma seemed especially attractive because of its climate, soil, and resources and because it was described as a place where a black man could enjoy his freedom and exercise his rights as a citizen without fear. There were even groups and individuals who promoted the idea that, if black Americans populated the area in sufficient numbers, they could organize their own state or at least obtain a balance of political power. Their theme was that Oklahoma provided an opportunity for self-help and self-determination in an atmosphere for progressive development, free of the oppressive environment they knew in the post–Civil War South.

During this time there was great public demand that the tracts of land ceded to the government after the Civil War be made available for homesteading. Hordes of real estate and railroad profiteers as well as land-hungry citizens entered Indian

A Certain Blindness

territory illegally and had to be forcibly removed. For this purpose the army sent in the Ninth and Tenth Cavalry, which were all-black regiments. Called "Buffalo Soldiers" or "black white men" by the Indians, these heroic men were described as "the toughest hardest riding organized bodies of troops on the plains."

Mounting pressures in Washington, D.C., resulted in the land being made available for white settlement on April 22, 1889. As the hour of opening approached, great crowds waited on the border while soldiers stood guard to turn back early invaders. At noon guns were fired and bugles sounded to signal about fifty thousand people on foot, horseback, and wagon to commence their scramble for the sixty-acre homesteads. By May 1890 Congress passed the Organic Act, which established a territorial government and named Guthrie as capital of the Oklahoma territory. As other land openings and allotments followed, homesteads were set up on land bordering Indian territory, and homesteaders who failed to secure land legally soon began to encroach on the Indian nations. The legislation making homesteads available specified that the land was for white settlement. Some Negroes, such as some of the "Buffalo Soldier" veterans, were financially able to fight for their legal rights and win, but others were forced to return to their homes in the South. In 1893, in response to the growing demand for homesteads, Congress created the Dawes Commission and authorized it to negotiate for the termination of the Indian nations. The Indians initially refused, but in the face of such odds they were eventually overwhelmed, and Oklahoma thereby did not come into the Union as a state of the Five Tribes, as Judge Isaac Parker recommended when he testified before the U.S. House of Representatives in 1895.

Black citizens of that era, including my great-uncle Bass Reeves, believed that the racial issues of the South would not be felt in these western frontiers. The federal government held some control, and the participation of Negroes in the election of delegates to the constitutional convention under the Enabling

In Pursuit of Equality

Act of 1906 reinforced hopes that black Americans could achieve political, economic, and social equality after Oklahoma became a state. But white Americans feared Negro domination here as they feared it elsewhere. The antiblack sentiments expressed during the convention and the disfranchisement, gerrymandering of voting districts, and illegal rejection of black candidates by the state election board caused widespread concern, so that the Negro Protection League, representing forty-five thousand voters, met in Muskogee on October 3, 1907. The members elected a delegation to meet with President Theodore Roosevelt to prevent Oklahoma's admission to the Union under such circumstances. The appeal at the meeting on October 30 proved futile, however, and on November 16, 1907, Oklahoma became a state.

The first act passed by the Oklahoma legislature, Senate Bill No. 1, which was segregatory and racially oppressive, indicated that the state was to be "for whites only." A prominent Negro, whose sentiments were published in the daily *Oklahoman* of December 23, 1907, protested: "We think it is an unwarranted discrimination against our race and we are going to do all in our power to secure its repeal. We do not intend to adopt violent or radical measures to secure our rights, but will leave it to the courts to decide. We have money to hire competent attorneys and more is coming in every day. It is the principle at stake, and nothing else, which has impelled us to take up this fight."

But the Supreme Court in 1896 had upheld segregation when it established the "separate but equal" principle in *Plessy v. Ferguson*. This decision enabled the white majority to maintain supremacy by suppressing, with force of law, the involvement of black citizens in underhanded ways. At the same time white America welcomed immigrants from foreign countries, and the Statue of Liberty was celebrated as a "prominent symbol of American democracy," representing "the spirit of liberty and equality" for all.

How did it ever come to pass that black Americans received different treatment under the law than their white counterparts? Clearly the racial injustice and oppression my family had known originally developed from the black-white relationship that existed in the Southern states. I had never been in the Deep South. I was born and grew up in Flint, Michigan, and neither my college years nor my military years provided any occasion for me to travel in the South. After becoming a judge I desired a judicial appointment in Washington, D.C., but I chose instead to fill an available position in Atlanta, Georgia, with jurisdiction throughout the area where this black-white, master-slave relationship was rooted. Soon after being sworn in, I left Washington, D.C., for Atlanta, excited about the prospects of living near the birthplace of my maternal grandfather, Charles Richard "C.R." Wilson, who, like my father's mother, Jane, was born a slave.

C.R. was born near Rockmart, Georgia, in 1861, the year the Civil War began. His mother, Cindy, was a slave, and his father, a wealthy Scotsman named Calhoun, was Cindy's owner. Cindy, named for one of Calhoun's ancestors, grew up in the family of her owners in South Carolina and moved with them to Georgia, where they maintained a large farm near Rockmart. Cindy looked after the owner's wife and two sons. Calhoun's wife died shortly before the war after an extended illness. It was during this period that Cindy herself bore a son to Calhoun, and with Calhoun's wife deceased, Cindy attained a position of dominance in the household. The extent to which the relationship between my great-grandmother Cindy and Calhoun differed from the slave-master relationship is not known, but under the Slave Codes, the father of a child born to a slave mother was not recognized, and the rape of a slave woman was no offense. When Calhoun's legitimate sons, one of whom was married, went off to war, Calhoun himself stayed behind to manage his married son's farm as well as his own. C.R. was an infant and toddler during the war years, but he later said he remembered his mother's absence during that time, when she and other slave women went to tend to Confederate soldiers wounded in nearby battles. (These would have been part of Sherman's Atlanta campaign in the summer of 1864.) Cindy later told C.R. she could not reconcile in her mind how white men could go off to war with the express purpose of killing other white men.

The slaves naturally reacted in a manner consistent with the treatment they received, with some being gratified at the suffering of those who had themselves inflicted so much misery.

Calhoun took a keen interest in his new son, C.R., and the two became close companions. C.R. even adopted his father's Scottish brogue. In addition to teaching C.R. about the outdoors and farming, Calhoun helped C.R. learn to read from old school books and taught C.R. to write. Years later C.R. told his own son about a time when as a youth he had gotten into mischief by participating in a shooting spree; this could have had serious consequences for a reckless Negro youth, but local officials knew that Calhoun was C.R.'s father and so refused to act.

My own early education did not depict the origins and course of American slavery in any detail. The formal history I learned was a truncated version, so that I imagined that my ancestors shared as fully as the other figures of history I was reading about. The Declaration of Independence had the ring of biblical truth. The stories about the framers of the Constitution were inspiring, and I was especially impressed with the overriding concerns for human rights and values expressed in this document.

But as I developed my interest in law and delved deeply into family history, I found shocking discrepancies between the high-minded language of these historical documents and the realities of life in our emerging nation. Indeed some of our founding fathers, such as George Washington, Thomas Jefferson, and Patrick Henry, were themselves slaveholders. How and when did America abandon the legal and moral principles it proclaimed and sanction slavery as a matter of law?

America's legal system, like so much of our history,

"grows out of the English tradition." England has never had a written constitution, but its system of laws is contained in Sir William Blackstone's *Commentaries on the Laws of England,* a four-volume work published from 1765 to 1769. The British jurist provided a comprehensive view of the legal system in effect during the period our country was founded and upon whose principles our Constitution was formed. Blackstone stated: "Slavery does not, nay cannot, subsist in England. . . . It is repugnant to reason and the principles of natural law, that such a state should subsist anywhere. . . . The law of England abhors, and will not endure the existence of slavery within this nation. A slave or negro, the instant he lands in England, becomes a freeman; that is, the law will protect him in the enjoyment of his person, and his property."[1]

The early colonists had no intention of creating a slave society in the New World, because the first black men and women arrived as either free or indentured as other settlers did. The indentured servant was bound to a master for a term of years after which he became free, with all attendant rights and liberties. Rights were recognized as belonging to people of Christian status, and in the course of time a distinction was made between Christian servants and heathens, apparently meaning Indians. Initially the purpose for this distinction did not appear to be directed toward the black population, since in 1624 the testimony of a Negro by the name of John Phillip was admitted in court against a white man.

Phillip had been baptized a Christian in England twelve years before.[2] Toward the end of the seventeenth century, a policy gradually evolved whereby Negro settlers were denied the freedoms ordinarily accorded Christians. Gradually, the Negro indentured servant, working in highly isolated areas without means for protecting his rights, saw his term of years extended at the will of his master, in some instances to the end of his life. The courts also became involved, as the case of John Punch indicated. Punch, a Negro, was one of three servants caught in the act of running away. As punishment, the two white servants had four years added to their periods of service, but the court ordered that Punch "serve his master or his assigns for the time of his natural life here or elsewhere," as Benjamin Quarles noted in his book *The Negro in the Making of America.* Soon some statutes appeared that introduced and defined the term "slave."

The Virginia Code of 1705, for example, made it clear that there was to be slavery based entirely on race and color, stating: "that no negroes, mulattos, or Indians, although christians, or Jews, Moor, Mahometans, or other infidels, shall, at any time, purchase any christian servant, nor any other, except their own complexion, or such as are declared slaves by this act." It also required "that all servants imported and brought to this country, by sea or land, who were not christians in their native country (except Turks and Moors in amity with her majesty, and others that can make due proof of their being free in England, or any other christian country, before they were shipped, in order to be transported hither) shall be accounted and be slaves, and as such be here bought and sold notwithstanding a conversion to christianity afterwards."[3]

Thus established moral and legal principles were first violated in America when a line was drawn between Christian and non-Christian persons. When this line was artfully expanded to create an artificial distinction between the rights of certain Christians and persons of specified races and colors, it marked the beginning of many shifting attitudes and techniques for rationalizing the oppression of African Americans in the New World.

The revolutionists' original antislavery position was expressly stated in the first draft of the Declaration of Independence. The draft, approved by the committee, vehemently condemned King George for his involvement in the slave trade:

> He has waged cruel war against human nature itself, violating its most sacred rights of life and liberty in the persons of a distant people who never offended him, captivating and carrying them into slavery in another hemisphere or to incur miserable death in their transportation thither. This piratical warfare, in the

opprobrium of infidel powers, is the warfare of the Christian king of Great Britain. Determined to keep open a market where men should be bought and sold, he has prostituted his negative for suppressing every legislative attempt to prohibit or restrain this execrable commerce.

In England this action was seen as abolishing slavery, and as late as 1788 William Agutler of St. Magdalene College spoke in Oxford: "The western empire is gone from us never to return; it is given to another more righteous than we; who consecrated the sword of resistance by declaring for the universal abolition of slavery."[4]

The final draft of the Declaration, however, failed to specifically abolish slavery even while it continued to assert that all men are created equal. The record of debate in the Continental Congress discloses that all reference to slavery "was struck out in complaisance to South Carolina and Georgia."[5] These two states insisted on their continued practice of slavery if they were to join the Union. Records do not indicate whether Thomas Jefferson argued against slavery. In practice property rights assumed a role superior to the "unalienable rights with which all men are endowed by their Creator." It is a real irony that the colonists would indict England's king for waging a "cruel war against human nature" when they waged it themselves.

Slaveholders wanted to continue exploiting this cheap form of labor, and, in fact, South Carolina and Georgia depended on slave labor for their commercial development. Indeed they declared slaves to be the only humans fit to labor in their climate:

> The utter inaptitude of Europeans for the labour requisite in such climate and soil, is obvious to every one possessed of the smallest degree of knowledge respecting the country: white servants would have exhausted their strength in clearing a spot of land for digging their own graves, and every rice plantation would have served no other purpose than a burying ground to its European cultivators. The low lands of Carolina, which are unquestionably the richest grounds in the country, must long have

In Pursuit of Equality

remained a wilderness, had not Africans, whose natural constitutions were suited to the clime and work, been employed in cultivating this useful article of food and commerce.[6]

In Georgia a group spoke similarly:

> The falling of timber was a task very unequal to the strength and constitution of white servants; and the hoeing the ground, they being exposed to the sultry heat of the sun, insupportable, and it is well known, that this labour is one of the hardest upon the Negroes, even though their constitutions are much stronger than white people, and the heat no way disagreeable nor hurtful to them; but in us it created inflammatory fevers of various kinds both continued and intermittent; wasting and tormenting fluxes, most excruciating cholicks, and dry belly-aches; tremors, vertigoes, palsies, and a long train of painful and lingering nervous distempers, which brought on to many a cessation both from work and life.[7]

The founding fathers in writing adopted the enlightened philosophies of John Locke and Adam Smith. Locke, the preeminent English philosopher, set forth the principles of modern democratic process and the concept of our civil liberties, which included the individual's natural right to "life, liberty and estate" and similar expressions found in our Declaration. Smith, the Scottish political economist regarded as the "father of economics," wrote *Inquiry into the Nature and Causes of the Wealth of Nations,* in which he argued for "a system of natural liberty," and he maintained that any government that interfered with the "individual's right to his life, liberty, and property instead of protecting them was illegitimate."[8] Yet the practice of giving greater weight to property than to life and liberty set in place a complex pattern of continuing exploitation that in one way or another has served to deny black men and women the opportunity to fully develop their productive ability.

The interpretation of this highly contradictory and confusing assertion of "inalienable rights" was tested in the courts. In the *Amistad* case, which came before the U.S. Supreme Court in

A Certain Blindness

1841, John Quincy Adams, former president of the United States, argued for the freedom of African slaves who had mutinied aboard a foreign ship. He referred to a recently published article that discussed slavery in light of the *Amistad* case and attacked the author's assertion that "property in man has existed in all ages of the world and results from the natural state of man, which is war." Conceding that the only condition of slavery is assuming the natural state of man is war, Adams reasoned if that "principle is sound, it reduced to brute force all the rights of man" and no man had a right to life or liberty if he has an enemy able to take them from him. He pointed out that one moment the Africans "are viewed as merchandise and the next as persons. . . . First, they are demanded as persons, as the subjects of Spain, to be delivered up as criminals, to be tried for their lives, and liable to be executed on the gibbet. Then they are demanded as chattels, the same as so many bags of coffee, or bales of cotton, belonging to owners, who have a right to be indemnified for any injury to their property." Adams further asserted: "The moment you come, to the Declaration of Independence, that every man has a right to life and liberty, an inalienable right, this case is decided. I ask nothing more in behalf of these unfortunate men, than this Declaration."[9]

Amazingly the Court held that the slaves were entitled to their liberty, which in effect sustained their inalienable rights over the property rights of others. But slaveholders prevailed at the constitutional convention and, behind every discussion, the pervasive influence of the slavery question could be found. A close examination of the Constitution and the debates that led to its formation shows the framers' intentions to protect the institution of slavery.

Several delegates did not hesitate to challenge the acceptance of slavery. James Madison, "the father of the Constitution," opined, "We have seen the mere distinction of colors made in the most enlightened period of time, a ground of the most oppressive dominion ever exercised by man over man." George Mason declared, "Every master of slaves is born a petty

In Pursuit of Equality

tyrant," and Luther Martin condemned slavery as "inconsistent with the principles of revolution and dishonorable to the American character." But General Pinckney maintained, "South Carolina and Georgia cannot do without slaves."

The final version of the Constitution does not mention the word "slavery," but its implicit protection is found in five different places.[10] Despite Madison's insistence that it "would be wrong to admit in the Constitution the idea that there could be property in man,"[11] there was a sleight-of-hand accommodation to maintaining the slaveholding system.

This action was to be central in the political and legal system; the framers provided that slaves be counted as three-fifths a person each for apportioning representatives and direct taxes. Article I, Section 2, stated: "Representatives and direct Taxes shall be apportioned among the several states which may be included within this Union, according to their respective Numbers which shall be determined by adding to the whole number of free Persons, including those bound to Service for a Term of Years, and excluding Indians not taxed, three-fifths of all other Persons."

Initially the Constitution seemed to be a repository for all human rights. The great abolitionist William Lloyd Garrison even saw it as the fulfillment of the black man's struggle. "Thanks be to God," he declared, "that we have such a Constitution. Without it, the liberties of every man—white as well as black would be in jeopardy. There it stands, firm as the Rock of Gibraltar, a high refuge from oppression."[12] But as a result of the loopholes furnished by the vague and ambiguous clauses, the slave traffic increased, and those questions involving constitutional meaning were more and more resolved in favor of slavery. Garrison prophesied in the militant journal the *Liberator,* "The compact which now exists between the North and South is a covenant with death and an agreement with hell involving both parties in atrocious criminality."[13] (Mark Howe later referred to the intentionally blurred language of the Constitution as "those coward's clauses that dare not speak of slaves but spoke instead of persons 'held to service or labor' and, with something less than candor, contrasted 'free persons,' not with Negro slaves, but with 'all other persons.' "[14])

The three-fifths clause produced great confusion and contradiction in the law. The slave was, therefore, both man and property in the framework of the Constitution. For example, although U.S. Supreme Court chief justice John Marshall, acclaimed as America's most influential jurist, was committed to the inalienability of man's natural rights, he nonetheless found that slaveholders had superior property rights in questions affecting slavery. He wrote in one opinion that "slavery is contrary to the laws of nature. . . . Every man has right to the fruits of his labor," but "a jurist must search for a legal answer."[15] His answer was that slaves were property and the owners had a free and unfettered use of their property.

The court under Marshall's dominance also rejected the common law of England regarding the law of descent and chose to adopt the civil law of continental Europe to hold that a child assumes the status of its mother.[16] A clue to the reasoning behind this decision may well be found in the census of 1850, which showed 246,565 mulatto slaves in the country born of black women and fathered by white men. In the decade that followed, black slaves increased in number by 20 percent while mulattos rose 67 percent. The court opted to protect the interests of the white slaveholders.

Similar proslavery rulings were soon followed by the states. Maintaining that a master cannot be convicted for cruel assault on his slave, Justice Thomas Ruffin of the North Carolina Supreme Court held:

> The end [of slavery] is the profit of the master, his security, and the public safety; the subject is one doomed in his own person and his posterity, to live without knowledge and without the capacity to make anything his own, and to toil that another may reap the fruits. . . . Such services can only be expected from one who has no will of his own; who surrenders his will in implicit obedience to that of another. Such obedience is the conse-

In Pursuit of Equality

quence only of the uncontrolled authority over the body. There is nothing else which can operate to produce the effect. The power of the master must be absolute to render the submission of the slave perfect. I most freely confess my sense of the harshness of this proposition; I feel it as deeply as any man can; and as a principal [sic] of moral right, every person in his retirement must repudiate it. In the actual conditions of things it must be so. There is no remedy.[17]

John Marshall was followed as chief justice on the Supreme Court by Roger Taney, whose *Dred Scott* decision used the judicial branch of government to advance his own oppressive racial views. Chief Justice Taney held as a matter of law the alleged inferiority of Negroes and answered constitutional questions in the decision by simply establishing as law that Negroes, whether free or slaves, possessed no rights which could be protected by our nation's laws.

Dred Scott, a slave, had sought his freedom in an eleven-year legal contest. His master, an army surgeon, had taken him from Missouri to Illinois and then to a part of the Louisiana territory in which slavery had been prohibited by the Missouri Compromise. When brought back to Missouri, Scott filed suit for his freedom. The Missouri Supreme Court repeatedly held that a master who took his slave to reside in a state or territory where slavery was prohibited thereby emancipated him. The U.S. Supreme Court under Chief Justice Taney ruled that Negroes were not citizens within the meaning of the Constitution and, therefore, had no rights before the courts. The decision notably failed to mention Article I, Section 2, which separated slaves from "free persons," and it plainly appeared free Negroes were part of the "people" upon whom our government was founded. When he was attorney general, Taney rendered an opinion that Negroes were not intended to be beneficiaries of the Constitution's provisions. As chief justice, Taney wanted the *Dred Scott* decision to expand on his view and clothe it with the authority of constitutional law.

No cases have been found in which the Supreme Court had

A Certain Blindness

previously dealt with the status of free Negroes; indeed, most history has been written as if these persons did not exist. Notwithstanding Justice Taney's personal views, the vague but artfully drawn clauses of the Constitution made the *Dred Scott* decision possible. The tragic effects of the decision on free Negroes were immeasurable.

For several generations prior to the revolution, free Negroes had flourished and fully realized the fruits of their labors. All Southern colonies permitted them freedom of travel and ownership of land. By 1765 Georgia, threatened by hostile Indians and the Spanish, encouraged free Negro immigration. Following the Revolutionary War, their increased population heightened fears of revolts among slaves. South Carolina and Georgia had argued against their use in the war because in some areas free Negroes outnumbered white settlers.

Upon adoption of the Constitution and enactment of stricter laws governing slavery, their "inalienable rights" took on a strange meaning. Restraints on free Negroes were likewise increased in number and severity. Their zeal in practicing trades, buying property, and exercising all attributes of free people enraged the Southern white populace, who found it expedient to articulate a defense of slavery with less delineation between the free and enslaved Negro.

Southern states curbed the free Negro's mobility, restricted his economic opportunity, and denied him his full civil rights. Taxed for entering some states, barred from professions and trades, he was likewise disfranchised in most states and denied the right to trial. For failure to prove his free status or even if his papers were not in order, an unemployed free Negro could be jailed and his children sold into slavery; more crimes were punishable by death for Negroes than for the white population. The federal government, to suppress "domestic insurrection," revised the fugitive slave law resulting in an indeterminate number of free Negroes being sold into slavery by kidnapping and other devious means.

In Pursuit of Equality

Following the *Scott* decision the federal government even took up the cause by denying Negroes the right to work in certain jobs, including mail carriers. They were also denied preemption rights on public lands. Immediately following the decision, the commissioner of the United States Land Office announced that Negroes could not qualify for public land granted in the West since they were not citizens. One Sylvester Gray, a free Negro, had bought and settled land in Wisconsin in accordance with the Preemption Act of 1841; the General Land Office revoked his claim.

Dred Scott thereafter clearly defined the legal status of Negroes in America, and some scholars believe it focused the issues leading to the Civil War. It left an indelible mark on American constitutional law by diminishing the rights of the Negro compared to the rights of other Americans.

Historical accounts are replete with emphatic denials that the South's primary aim in fighting the Civil War was maintenance of the slave order. Nonetheless, Jefferson Davis, president of the Confederate States, stated in his inaugural address in February 1861 that slavery was "necessary to self-preservation."[18] Confederate vice-president Alexander Stephens, from Georgia, revealed at the time that slavery actually formed the basis of the new government. In a speech at Savannah on March 11, Stephens proclaimed the accuracy of Thomas Jefferson's forecast that slavery was "the rock upon which the old Union would split." He explained:

> The prevailing ideas entertained by [Jefferson] and most of the leading statesmen at the time of the formation of the old Constitution, were that the enslavement of the African was in violation of the laws of nature; that it was wrong in principle, socially, morally, and politically. . . . It was an evil they knew not well how to deal with, but the general opinion of the men of the day was that somehow or other in the order of Providence, the institution would be evanescent and pass away. This idea, though not incorporated in the Constitution, was the prevailing

A Certain Blindness

> idea at that time.... Those ideas, however, were fundamentally wrong. They rested upon the assumption of the equality of races. This was an error....
>
> Our new government is founded upon exactly the opposite idea; its foundations are laid, its cornerstone rests upon the great truth, that the Negro is not equal to the white man, that slavery ... is a natural and normal condition....
>
> This our new government is the first, in the history of the world, based upon this great physical, philosophical, and moral truth.

Stephens pointed out the "errors of the past generation" and further maintained that those "who still cling to these errors, with a zeal above knowledge, we justly denominate fanatics.... They assume that the negro is equal, and hence conclude he is entitled to equal privileges and rights with the white man. If their premises were correct, their conclusion would be logical and just—but their premise being wrong, their whole argument fails."[19]

Stephens and others, of course, did not show how they had arrived at the "great truth," but an article in the *Richmond Dispatch* of March 23, 1861, touched the heart of the matter. Virginia was vacillating between seceding and remaining with the Union, but the *Dispatch,* strongly favoring the Southern states, declared:

> Since the world began there has been no system of labor comparable, in productive efficiency, with the slave system of the Southern States. If we look back through the ages, we shall discover no great achievement of human toil but such as was the product of slave labor.... The commerce and wealth of a country depend upon its surplus products.... The only States of what were the late United States, which produced surpluses for exportation and foreign commerce, were the slaveholding ones.... In other words, the slaveholding section of the Union furnished all the surplus products that constituted the basis of the foreign commerce of the country, while the non-slaveholding section furnished nothing, but consumed all that it pro-

duced. . . . The question is secession or emancipation. It is whether she shall destroy or preserve her slave system of labor—the grandest and most efficient agency of wealth ever enjoyed by any community on the globe.[20]

While it appeared during the revolutionary era that slavery would be completely abolished, it continued and flourished despite the antislavery movement that existed even in the South. This antislavery sentiment caused the legislatures of several Southern states to take up the question of emancipation, and the Virginia legislature of 1831-32 narrowly defeated the emancipation measure by a margin of seven votes. (Constitutional conventions in Tennessee and North Carolina followed the same course.) One element that surely influenced the outcome of Virginia's emancipation question was the slave rebellion that occurred in Virginia in 1831.

In spite of previous revolts under Gabriel Prosser in 1800 and Denmark Vesey in 1822, it was the insurrection led by Nat Turner during the summer of 1831 that caused the entire Southern society to respond. The killing of nearly sixty white men, women, and children signaled the need for establishing a new order in dealing with Negroes, both slave and free.

Every attempt was made to prevent their revolt. Teaching slaves to read or write was forbidden, and they were not allowed to assemble in significant numbers even to worship. Plantations more closely regulated hours of work, rest, and eating and maintained small militias. Owners and overseers banded together and organized "patrols" for enforcing laws as they saw them. Many of the South's military schools were organized to prepare young men in the successful management of their holdings. In the three decades before the Civil War, slave owners realized that, if slavery were to continue, it would be necessary to isolate the black man. The proslavery faction even modified its theology to preserve the system, asserting that Negroes were laborers doing God's work on earth, and if they performed faithfully they would earn a place in heaven.

A Certain Blindness

But all the efforts made to maintain the slave system, including secession from the Union, were ultimately hopeless, and on January 1, 1863, President Lincoln issued his Emancipation Proclamation. Although Lincoln described it as an act based "upon military necessity," the proclamation is recognized as one of America's most outstanding pronouncements of human liberty.

Following the war great hope prevailed among the freed slaves, who assumed, with the ratification of the Thirteenth Amendment by December 18, 1865, that equality and justice were guaranteed. This amendment was seen by its supporters and opponents alike as not only abolishing slavery and involuntary servitude but also guaranteeing equality before the law and the freedom to live, work, and move about in society as one desired.

Congress established the Bureau of Refugees, Freedmen, and Abandoned Lands ("the Freedmen's Bureau") on March 3, 1865, an agency that provided medical aid and distributed rations to displaced and poverty-stricken people, including many white Americans. There was talk of distribution of confiscated and public land, "forty acres and a mule," and Lincoln mentioned compensation for 250 years of unrequited toil. But Congress refused to provide any homestead land or tools. The freedmen, without shelter, tools, or even cooking utensils, were soon reduced to a form of peonage.

The end of slavery marked a radical change in the South's labor system. The Southern aristocrats, who had previously held both property and labor in slaves, now were merely landowners. The former slaves, though free and possessing the ability and experience to work the land, possessed no land. Accustomed to free labor, the former masters employed various means, including fraud, intimidation, and violent assault, to secure the required labor for next to nothing. The intent of the Thirteenth Amendment was soon thwarted, and the American system of law, which tolerated and enforced slavery, was again to deny these freedmen liberty, justice, and dignity.

In Pursuit of Equality

Proslavery state governments were organized under the provisional governors, and the former slave states adopted highly oppressive black codes designed to totally regulate Negro life and thereby impose a new legal form of bondage. Restrictions were placed on the Negro's choice of residence and work. For example, they could not migrate into South Carolina unless a one thousand dollar bond were posted for good behavior; a special license was required for any job other than that of a farmer or servant.[21] In Louisiana a freedman had to make labor contracts within ten days of the start of the year, and he could not "leave his place of employment until the fulfillment of his contract, unless by the consent of his employer." This same law provided that "all difficulties arising between the employer and the laborers . . . shall be settled, and all fines be imposed by the former."[22] Every civil officer in Mississippi, any white man, that is, had the definite authority to arrest any freedman, free Negro, or mulatto suspected of having left the service of an employer. Mississippi denied freedmen the right to own property, and they were not allowed to rent or lease "any lands or tenements except in incorporated cities or towns, in which place the corporate authorities shall control the same."[23]

Widespread terrorism, outrages, and atrocities were allowed, and, although free in a constitutional sense, black citizens remained in a separate and oppressed state. Clearly there was a retreat to the Dred Scott philosophy that they possessed no rights a white man was bound to respect.

Historian Lerone Bennett, Jr., reported the findings of General Carl Schurz, who made a special investigation for President Andrew Johnson:

> "Some planters," he said, "held back their former slaves on their plantations by brute force." Armed bands of white men patrolled the country roads to drive back the Negroes wandering about. Dead bodies of murdered Negroes were found on and near the highways and by-ways. Gruesome reports came from the hospitals—reports of colored men and women whose ears had been cut off, whose skulls had been broken by blows, whose

A Certain Blindness

bodies had been slashed by knives or lacerated with scourges. A number of such cases I had occasion to examine myself. A . . . reign of terror prevailed in many parts of the South.

Throughout this period, and on into the 1870's, hundreds of freedmen were massacred in "riots" staged and directed by policemen and other government officials. In the Memphis, Tennessee, "riot" of May, 1866, forty-six blacks (union veterans were a special target) were killed and seventy-five were wounded. Five black women were raped by whites, twelve schools and four churches were burned. Two months later, in New Orleans, policemen returned to the attack, killing some forty blacks and wounding one hundred.

"The emancipation of the slave," General Schurz concluded, "is submitted to only in so far as chattel slavery in the old form could not be kept up." But although the freedman is no longer considered the property of the individual master, he is considered the slave of society. . . . Wherever I go—the street, the shop, the house, the hotel, or the steamboat—I hear the people talk in such a way as to indicate that they are yet unable to conceive the Negro as possessing any rights at all. Men who are honorable in their dealings with their white neighbors will cheat a Negro without feeling a single twinge of their honor. To kill a Negro, they do not deem murder; to debauch a Negro woman, they do not think fornication; to take property away from a Negro, they do not consider robbery.[24]

The aroused nation sought to clarify what was implicit in the Thirteenth Amendment. By 1866 and 1870, respectively, the Fourteenth and Fifteenth Amendments were ratified, guaranteeing freedmen full citizenship, equal rights before the law, and enfranchisement, clearly placing former slaves on the same level as white persons. Their privileges and immunities could not be impaired by state government, and they could not be deprived of life, liberty, and property without due process of law. The right to vote was explicitly granted, and enabling legislation provided for the presence of federal troops to protect the rights of the freedmen. America had now made the decisive steps to fulfill the promises of the Declaration and the Constitution.

In Pursuit of Equality

Lerone Bennett, Jr., described this period of opportunity:

> Never before had the sun shone so bright. A former slave named Blanche Kelso Bruce was representing Mississippi in the United States Senate. Pickney Benton Stewart Pinchback, young, charming, daring, was sitting in the governor's office in Louisiana.
>
> In Mississippi, South Carolina, and Louisiana, black lieutenant governors were sitting on the right hand of power. A black was secretary of state in Florida; a black was on the state supreme court in South Carolina. In these and other Southern states, blacks were superintendents of education, state treasurers, adjutant generals, solicitors, judges and major generals of militia. Robert H. Wood was mayor of Natchez, Mississippi, and Norris Wright Cuney was running for mayor of Galveston, Texas. Seven blacks were sitting in the House of Representatives.
>
> Nor was this all. Blacks and whites were going to school together, riding on streetcars and cohabiting, in and out of wedlock. An interracial board was running the University of South Carolina, where a black professor, Richard T. Greener, was teaching white and black youth metaphysics and logic.

Bennett also noted: "Never before—never since—had there been so much hope. A black mother knew that her boy could—become governor. The evidence of things seen, the evidence of things heard fired millions of hearts. Black mothers walked ten, fifteen and twenty miles to put their children in school. They sacrificed and stinted. They bowed down and worshipped the miraculous ABC's from whom so many blessings flowed."[25]

My grandfather C.R. Wilson came to Atlanta during this period to begin his formal education, which his father, Calhoun, had promised him and his mother, Cindy, had long dreamed of. After Calhoun died, C.R. returned to his mother, but she decided to leave Calhoun's farm since one of Calhoun's older sons blamed the Negroes for causing the tragic war, and Cindy feared for their safety. She later married an ex-slave named Wilson, whose surname C.R. adopted, and C.R. was able to go to Atlanta to continue his education. This city was

A Certain Blindness

becoming a center of scholarship for black Americans, being the location of Atlanta University, founded seventy-two days after the end of the war, and Morehouse College, founded originally in Savannah, Georgia, in 1867, but relocated to Atlanta. C.R. was enthusiastic about his studies and duly impressed by his various instructors. At this time he also began a lifelong inquiry into the teachings of the Bible. Through his employment by a Jewish merchant and further contact with the Jewish community, C.R. learned some Hebrew and was able to interpret portions of the Old Testament for himself. Yet though he was enthusiastic about the opportunities theoretically guaranteed by the new amendments to the Constitution, in practice C.R. saw little changing in the lives of Negroes.

The Thirteenth, Fourteenth, and Fifteenth Amendments were initially viewed as "a new Magna Carta" in the struggle for freedom and equality for all. The continued blatant denial of basic constitutional rights, however, caused Congress to pass five statutes to implement the amendments (two civil rights acts and three enforcement acts, including the Ku Klux Klan Act). This legislation, intended to meet the responsibility of the federal government as ultimate protector of essential liberties, was not secured or effectively enforced by the executive and judicial branches. President Andrew Johnson vetoed one civil rights bill, and the Supreme Court nullified key provisions of the other laws.

Both Mississippi and South Carolina, where black population exceeded the white, openly denied the Fifteenth Amendment, which specifically guaranteed the right to vote. This failure to protect black citizens and enforce their basic constitutional rights was noted by a federal grand jury in 1872 in South Carolina, which found

> that the Klan, in carrying out the purposes for which it was organized and armed, inflicted summary vengeance on the colored citizens of these counties, by breaking into their houses at the dead of night, dragging them from their beds, torturing them in the

In Pursuit of Equality

most inhuman manner, and in many instances murdering them; and this, mainly, on account of their political affiliations. . . .

That for this condition of things, for all these violations of law and order, and the sacred rights of citizens responsible . . . that large numbers of the most prominent citizens were members of the order. . . .

The jury has been appalled as much at the number of outrages as at their character, it appearing that eleven murders and over six hundred whippings have been committed in York County alone.[26]

Finally, Senator Tillman of South Carolina openly admitted in the second session of the Fifty-ninth Congress that "we stuffed ballot boxes. . . . We shot them. . . . We have not shot any Negroes in South Carolina on account of politics since 1876. We have not found it necessary."[27]

The complete breakdown in federal protection of the new citizens' rights occurred with the political compromise of 1877 under President Rutherford Hayes. While he had served as governor of Ohio, Hayes spoke of equal rights for blacks and his firm commitment to their protection. He believed the presence of troops in the South was necessary to protect both black and white men as he was aware that the states wished "to return to the old state of things—an oligarchy of race and the sovereignty of states."[28] The lawlessness continued, and several years later while running for president Hayes was advised by the attorney general that many states were nullifying the Fifteenth Amendment by various means, including murder.[29] However, as president he removed federal troops, leaving the states to enforce the law and ensure equal rights for all citizens.

Congressman Charles Williams estimated that by 1880, 130,000 Negroes had been murdered in the South for political reasons (seeking to exercise their rights guaranteed by the constitutional amendments).[30] And Frederick Douglass concluded "the citizenship granted in the Fourteenth Amendment is practically a mockery and the right to vote provided for in the

A Certain Blindness

Fifteenth Amendment is literally stamped out in the face of government."[31]

C.R. admired and identified with Frederick Douglass, a self-educated former slave who had become one of the foremost thinkers, writers, and orators of his age. C.R. shared Douglass's view that the Negro should stay in the South, where he had a monopoly in the labor market. C.R. believed that through organizing, Negro laborers, artisans, and landowners could overcome the exploitation they had suffered. C.R. became active in the Noble and Holy Order of the Knights of Labor, a labor movement founded after the Civil War by an abolitionist to organize men and women, Negro and white, foreign and native-born, a union that did not practice religious or political discrimination. A persuasive speaker, C.R., having settled in Warrior, Alabama, was sent to help organize the Negro coal miners in the Birmingham area. These miners were unique in the South because their wages were comparable to those of the white miners.

Membership in the Knights of Labor grew to more than ninety thousand in all-Negro and mixed local unions. C.R. believed that complete assimilation in all aspects of community life would flow from black and white workers associating equally in the workplace, but the presence of organized Negro workers began to provoke the worst fears and prejudices of the white populace. In South Carolina the cotton planters used every means at their disposal to thwart Knights of Labor plantation workers when there were rumors of a strike at cotton-picking time. The planters caused a bill to be passed in the state senate to extend the state's conspiracy laws in order to prevent Negroes from organizing. Some planters were reported to have ordered Negro Knights shot and organizers run out of the state; shortly thereafter the state organizer was slain.

More and more intimidation and violence directed toward the Knights swept across the South. In Florida a Negro store owner and member of the Knights was ordered to leave town;

when he refused he was killed in his store. In Dolomite, Alabama, a suburb of Birmingham, angry white townspeople prevented the members of a recently formed local union from entering their assembly hall.

With the increase in Southern industrialization, a rise was likewise noted in the number of unions with racially exclusionary clauses in their constitutions. Instances arose, as in Nashville, in which black craftsmen outnumbered the white ones in unions, but as more whites joined and became a majority, black artisans were voted out of membership, often after they had trained some of the same white workers. By the late 1880s the Knights were forced to abandon hope of organizing black workers in the South.

Even the American Federation of Labor, which had initially opposed racial discrimination, began admitting white-only unions. Ironically, organized labor itself became one of the main impediments to the black worker gaining equality.

C.R. moved about considerably in connection with his work and he met many people. In Warrior he met his future wife, Estella Jane Slaughter, who lived and worked in the home of a wealthy white family. Estella was the oldest of sixteen children of a sharecropping couple who lived on a plantation near Tuscaloosa, about sixty miles south of Birmingham; her father, Lewis, was a former slave, and her mother, Laura, was an Indian, a descendant of Chief Tecumseh. C.R. married Estella in 1888; they lived in Warrior where their first child, John Lewis, was born a year later. They eventually had twelve children, including my mother, Jessie, and my aunt Cindy.

C.R. was compelled to abandon any hope for his family's future in the South. In Alabama, child labor laws exempted children working in agriculture and domestic service from its protection—Negro children. And the breaking of a contract for service by a farm laborer was a felony punishable by a prison sentence. In addition, C.R. was aware first-hand how Negro laborers were duped out of their land and possessions in total violation of mortgage, lien, and homestead laws. Use of public facilities, such as libraries and parks—like the right to vote—was out of the question.

C.R. was aware of the resettlement of many Negroes in the "free" state of Kansas since the war. Now prompted by overwhelming circumstances, he investigated the possibility of employment in the coal-mining industry of southeastern Kansas. He was offered immediate employment so he moved his family there.

Following their move, my grandparents convinced my grandmother's family, as well as some other miners, to make the move. C.R. settled his family on a large farm near Litchfield, and relations were quite peaceful with the mostly European immigrants who had also settled the area.

The conditions they had had to endure when the family was living in Alabama were described by my aunt Cindy, who explained that with sixteen children in his family Lewis Slaughter found it impossible to feed, clothe, and house his family on a sharecropper's lot. Aunt Cindy related that the owner found it quite easy to keep his tenants always in his debt:

> Each sharecropper was allowed to have only one mule, a dozen chickens, and a small piece of ground on which to raise vegetables for his family. All food, clothing, and medicine had to be purchased from the owner of the farm. There was never a time when they received any money. The owner kept the books and accounts to suit himself. They were so isolated that their world consisted of work and gathering on Sundays at their small church. My grandfather was so hard pressed to make a living for his family that he was forced to deceive his owner by raising an extra hog or two down deep in the woods where no one knew of it.
>
> Finally, my mother, who was a young lady of sixteen at the time, left home to work in Warrior, Alabama. Here she met my father, who was from Atlanta, Georgia. He told of the wonderful plans he had to leave the South and go to Kansas where the coal fields were in need of laborers. This seemed like the "Promise Land" to my uncles who were boys and young men at this

In Pursuit of Equality

time. After my mother married, at the age of seventeen years, she and my father came to Kansas and sent back money to bring grandmother and the children, but they had no money left to pay for my grandfather's transportation. He decided he would follow his family on foot. All of his preparations had to be done stealthily because the land owner would have trumped up some charge, have him arrested, bail him out, and thus he would have my grandfather under his dominion the rest of his life. This happened time and again to Negro families who tried to leave.

My grandfather fried all the chicken and made several sacks full of corn pone and biscuits. He put these in a pillow case and late at night he set out for Kansas on foot. He traveled by day and at night would find a haystack or corn field to sleep in. It took him three weeks to reach Arkansas City. By this time grandfather was ill, hungry, naked, and shoeless. He made discreet inquiries around town and found a family who had participated in the underground railway during slavery days. This family contacted grandfather's family in Hamilton, Kansas, a mining town near Weir City, Kansas. They got together enough money for railroad fare and sent it to my grandfather. This was in the year 1895.

My grandfather had suffered so much exposure and hunger that he was never well again. His feet and legs bothered him till he died at the age of forty-eight years, six months after arriving in Kansas.

This was a terrible sacrifice for anyone to make, but I am convinced that if my grandfather could know what it meant to his descendants he would have considered it not all in vain.

One of my great-grandfather's sons, Uncle Bookter Slaughter, told me how thankful his father had been to see his family arrive safely in a land that offered more freedom. Freedom had an especially deep meaning for my great-grandfather, because when he was young he suffered tremendous grief when his closest brother was sold to a family moving to Texas. Sad and helpless, his family could only watch as the boy, tears streaming down his face, waved until he was out of sight, never to be heard from again.

A Certain Blindness

But Kansas was not utopia either. The work in the mines was hard and dangerous, and C.R. and his older sons worked long hours so that the family could be as self-reliant as possible. The younger children helped maintain their large farm and attended school. Time was also set aside for Bible reading and study. One of Estella's brothers, Holland, was killed in the mines. Bookter himself was once so seriously injured in an explosion that he was not expected to live; his miraculous recovery was attributed to the family's continuous prayers.

Several members of the family chose the most dangerous but best paying job, working as "shot firers," responsible for detonating explosives set after each work shift to blast coal loose for the next shift's work. There were incidents when Negro shot firers were given short fuses by their white bosses, which added unjustly to the dangerous nature of the job.

When my mother was a teenager, she recalled a visit from her uncle Uriah Tolbert, an official in Georgia's African Methodist Episcopal church who was in Kansas City attending a church conference. A prosperous minister who presented each of his nieces and nephews with a silver dollar, Uriah urged C.R. to return to Atlanta, which had a milder climate and a growing Negro community where Uriah felt C.R. could be "a big man." C.R. insisted his children were his only concern, and since they were never accustomed to the Southern way, C.R. feared such a move would result in seeing his "sons hung from trees."

As the mining industry declined, C.R. devoted more time to farming. By this time prohibition was in effect. This interrupted my grandmother's holiday custom of making wine, which even their neighbors claimed to be among the best they had ever tasted, but C.R. declared that Estella would make no more wine "as it is the law." C.R. remained adamant in his deep respect for the law.

My mother was very close to her father, C.R., and she never heard him speak of his disappointing experiences in the South. She was acutely aware that, having begun life as a legal piece of property, he valued the freedom of choice he and his

In Pursuit of Equality

family now possessed. Eventually C.R. moved his family to Girard, Kansas, which was a county seat providing more opportunity for education and employment. C.R. valued education so highly that he required that children who chose to work had to help defray the costs for their siblings who wanted to attend college. Four of C.R.'s children finished college, including my mother, Jessie Lee Wilson, who was the first, followed by Lucinda, Charles, and Lawrence.

4

"Neither Inferior nor Unworthy"

As a girl, my mother, Jessie, worked in the fields with her brothers and was the only girl in the family who could milk cows. During the school year she filled lamps, trimmed wicks, and brought in kindling. Activities like ice skating and swimming were not considered ladylike in the eyes of my grandmother Estella Jane, but Mom was allowed to ride horses, and she loved the black beauty Kentucky coach whip named Dolly. Most of Mom's spare time was spent reading, and even though her mother complained she was reading too much, her father encouraged it. Jessie sometimes read late at night in bed partially under the covers to hide from her mother. In later years, failing eyesight prevented her from engaging in her favorite pastime, and she believed the early eye strain may have had lasting effect.

Recognized as being an excellent student, Mom gained

"Neither Inferior nor Unworthy"

favored treatment from her teachers and was usually called upon to assist in every class. She told the story of when one teacher was transferred and a new teacher from Missouri was hired. Mom was hurt because she was not asked to assist the new teacher, and she was unaware of the new teacher's racial prejudice. It soon became clear, however, as she and her brothers and sisters were reassigned to seats in the rear of their classes and placed at the ends of the lines to drink water, use the bathrooms, and for other activities. Word of the unfair treatment accorded the Wilsons, the only Negro students of the little school, got out to the parents of the other students. A meeting was arranged with the teacher, who was told that members of the community were close and neighborly, and they all shared in each other's misfortunes. It was made clear that fair and equal treatment of all students was required, and anything less would not be tolerated. When the teacher persisted in her previous conduct, she was summarily fired.

After the family moved to Girard, it was necessary for Mom to attend high school in Pittsburg, Kansas, where she resided with Estella's mother and sister, Mom's Grandma Laura and Aunt Sara. Each day Mom read the newspaper to Grandma Laura, a full-blooded Indian. As she sat barefooted smoking her pipe, she loved to rock in her favorite chair and listen to Mom read.

On Friday afternoons Mom's teacher would leave early to return to one of the surrounding mining towns, leaving Mom in charge of the class. And since Estella required Mom to return to Girard each weekend, she had to walk the twelve miles by the railroad tracks, often detouring through woods to avoid hoboes along the way.

Everyone regarded Jessie as bright and promising, and she was proudly seen as being worthy of all the support that could be mustered in her efforts for a higher education, since they all recognized that education was the hope for the family's future. After graduating from high school, Mom immediately enrolled in Kansas State Teachers College of Pittsburg (now known as

A Certain Blindness

Pittsburg State University). She resided with her mother's youngest sister, Beatrice, and her husband, Chris Hunter, both of whom had also made the trip from Alabama; they were proud to have her in their home and treated her as their own daughter. With hard work and inspired by the family's faith in her, she continued the excellent scholastic record she had begun in grade school. My mother was the first member of the family to finish college, and her graduation was indeed a proud moment not only for her but for so many who had contributed to her success. She retained the great beliefs in the importance of education and family unity for the balance of her life.

The pace of her life quickened shortly thereafter when Mom got her first teaching job in Coffeyville, Kansas. This marked the first time she had been so far away from the family, but she soon met two people who influenced the future course of her life—one was the "Honorable Monroe Trotter" and the other was "Luck" Brady, her future husband. Mom kept notes of her activities during this period, detailing events as well as her thoughts and feelings. Not long after arriving in Coffeyville, she became associated with a group that brought in some of that period's outstanding Negro figures as speakers on issues of local and national interest. With the presidential election of 1920 in the offing, the group had invited William Monroe Trotter, editor of the *Boston Guardian,* to speak on racial justice.

A Phi Beta Kappa graduate of Harvard University (in fact, the first black ever elected to Phi Beta Kappa), Trotter was considered "the most persistent uncompromising and unselfish crusader against racial injustice since Frederick Douglass."[1] With W. E. B. Du Bois, Trotter had founded the Niagara Movement, forerunner of the National Association for the Advancement of Colored People. For his topic that evening in Kansas Trotter stressed the importance of educating Negro youth and relentlessly striving for civil rights and equality. Mom was impressed with Trotter's attitude that blacks should never adopt

"Neither Inferior nor Unworthy"

subservient behavior, an attitude she subsequently made her own.

Trotter himself exemplified this attitude during a meeting with President Woodrow Wilson in 1914, which received front-page coverage in both the white and black press. Trotter chaired a committee protesting segregation of federal civil service employees. The *Chicago Defender* reported:

> The committee met the president by appointment after waiting a year for a personal interview with him. Mr. Trotter was the spokesman, and in the fervor of his pleas for equal rights for his people he forgot the servile manner and speech once characteristic of the Afro-American and he talked to the president as man to man, addressing the head of the government as any American citizen should especially when discussing a serious matter. But the president did not like Mr. Trotter's attitude and said that if the committee came to him again it would have to get a new chairman. The president added he had not been addressed in such a manner since he entered the White House.[2]

Trotter pointed out that, in the year since a national petition protesting segregation of federal employees had been presented, segregation of work positions and eating and toilet facilities had not only continued but expanded. President Wilson explained to Trotter and the other committee members that "segregation had been started to avoid friction between the races and not with the object of injuring the Afro-American employees." Trotter responded, "Two years ago you were thought to be a second Abraham Lincoln," and he explained to President Wilson that they did not seek charity or assistance but equal rights that should be respected, and Trotter denied any friction between the races before segregation was begun.

Then Trotter reminded President Wilson of Wilson's pledge that "colored fellow citizens could depend on you for everything which would assist in advancing the interest of their race in the United States." The *Chicago Defender* called Monroe Trotter the man of the hour for his stand during that meeting at the White House. Trotter's outspokenness in defense of civil rights was his hallmark, and my mother emulated him her entire life.

Although Mom did not record the day she met my father, "Luck" Brady, it was one Sunday afternoon following church services in Coffeyville, when her landlady invited her to attend a musical concert. Mom recalled that Dad, singing with his sister Mollie, "sang like a nightingale." As they got to know each other, Jessie expressed amazement at Luck's abilities to attract birds and squirrels with his whistles and chirps.

William "Luck" Brady was a native of Van Buren, Arkansas, the fifth of eight children. Dad's mother, Jane Reeves Brady, had moved from Texas to Arkansas to be close to her brother, my great-uncle Bass Reeves, then serving as a deputy for Judge Parker in Indian territory. Dad's father, John Brady, was described as a mulatto; originally from Tennessee, he had relocated to Texas, where he met my grandmother Jane Reeves. John and Jane's children were quite young when he was killed in a construction accident while building a bridge across the Arkansas River between Van Buren and Fort Smith. Due to his father's death, Dad had to help support his mother and siblings, which cut short his own education.

Dad was especially fond of Uncle Bass and yearned to accompany him into Indian territory, but Bass's missions were known to be dangerous. At the age of twelve my father secretly trailed Bass for several miles, thinking that when he was discovered Bass would allow him to remain—but contrary to his expectations Dad was severely scolded, though only the horse got whipped, taking Dad home at a fast gallop. It was Bass who nicknamed my father "Luck," and Bass also taught Dad how to survive in the wild. Dad became well known as a hunter and fisherman, and he later served as a guide for wealthy sportsmen in the Ozark region of Arkansas. Dad also became an outstanding baker and cook and at one time operated a bakery in downtown Van Buren with his childhood friend Will "Dutch" Miller. Dad later became the main chef for the largest hotel in Joplin,

"Neither Inferior nor Unworthy"

Missouri, where he was working when he and my mother came to know each other.

Mom loved teaching and was offered a position at a school in Neosho, Missouri. Neosho was closer to her family than Coffeyville was, and it was also closer to Joplin, where Dad was working, so Mom accepted the more lucrative offer. A strict disciplinarian, my mother was to have some unsettling experiences from her new job. One day, for example, while she was preparing to discipline a large, unruly, spoiled boy, he jumped out a window and ran home. Mom learned that the boy's parents were on their way to see her at the end of the day. Although frightened, Jessie decided to maintain her ground with the parents in spite of what she expected to be a hostile confrontation. She introduced herself to the parents with a very professional air and clearly but politely explained the problems she had with their son. Though the situation was defused and nothing serious came of it, my mother suspected she was too outspoken for Neosho.

This became even more evident when she asked the school board for supplies. Jessie was told to give school plays and devise other means of raising funds. She felt livid, especially since the white teachers were not expected to raise money when they needed supplies, but Mom forced herself to remain calm and explained to the board that she was employed to educate children the same as white teachers in the district and was not there to raise funds for the school board. The board relented, but Mom left Neosho for Joplin, Missouri, as soon as her contract expired.

My parents were married on Christmas Day 1922 in the home of her parents by her uncle Reverend Reuben Bookter Slaughter. In that year "there were 51 Negro lynchings [nationwide]: 30 of them were lynched after being held by police. On May 6, three Negroes were burned at the stake in the public square of Kirvin, Texas, while 50 whites looked on. All three had been in the custody of police."[3] In 1922 the Lincoln Memorial was dedicated in Washington, D.C., and Negro ticket holders attending the ceremonies were seated in roped-off sections behind white attendees, and washroom and refreshment facilities were closed to them. My parents were determined to find a place to settle where they could have more freedom and opportunity. After Mom's teaching obligations were concluded, the pair traveled to find a place where they could lead better lives.

The first city my parents visited was Detroit, Michigan, which had a rapidly growing automobile industry; jobs there paid well, and my parents liked the city, especially Belle Isle, the nation's largest urban island park, located in the Detroit River between the United States and Canada. They almost decided to settle there when Fred Wakefield, one of Dad's childhood friends, urged them to consider Flint, Michigan, some sixty miles north of Detroit.

Smaller than Detroit, Flint began as a lumber town and later produced carriages, and now it was home to General Motors and was fast becoming a major automobile producer. My parents made the trip to Flint on the electric interurban train operating between Detroit and Flint. The train approached Flint by running north parallel to Dort Highway, then entered the city by turning west into Lippincott Boulevard. Dad did not then imagine that our family home would eventually be built on one of the vacant lots he passed while traveling on Lippincott. Liking Flint's size and appealing countryside as well as its economic promise, my parents chose Flint for their home.

Dad accepted work as a laborer in the foundry at a General Motors Buick factory. The hours were long, and the work was hard, dirty, and hot. Dad believed his advancement would depend on his willingness to work and on how well he performed. He was paid on a piece-work basis; that is, a certain wage was paid for a specified number of units produced, and a bonus was added for all over that amount. Dad noticed the high concentration of Negro workers in the foundry operations, and the white workers who were there were either recent arrivals from the rural South or were European immigrants. Strangely there was a continuous turnover of the white workers while the Negroes

"Neither Inferior nor Unworthy"

remained. Dad learned that the employees who left the foundry transferred to more desirable unskilled work or to semi-skilled production jobs. Dad did manage to get better positions in the foundry, but his requests for transfers were repeatedly denied, until he learned from the plant superintendent that his only opportunity for transfer would be as a janitor.

Within the automotive industry various levels of supervisory personnel had transformed their racial views into plant policy. As union organizer Victor G. Reuther noted in his memoir, *The Brothers Reuther and the Story of the UAW,* "In a sense, Flint was a segment of the deep South transported north, for General Motors has primarily employed white Southern workers, who were lured up during the twenties by the growing automobile industry."[4]

Lloyd H. Bailer analyzed the 1930 census in his article "Negro Automobile Worker" and confirmed racially discriminatory practices in the industry. Negroes were confined to the most undesirable occupations, which included the most hazardous tasks. In his article "Automobile Unions and Negro Labor," Bailer discussed the employment situation by World War II: "The industry's conversion to war production which began in the last half of 1941 threatened to worsen the Negro's already inferior position. . . . The flux of thousands of additional workers, chiefly from the South, weakened the union's grip upon its membership and strengthened opposition to fuller Negro participation in the union and the industry."[5]

My father was never to know that General Motors would become "the largest creation of its kind" and an outstanding success under America's free enterprise system. Through his strong belief in the system, loyalty to the company, and great sacrifice Dad somehow managed to purchase shares of stock in the corporation, which are retained in the family to this day.

Mom recalled that Dad was deeply affected by the disappointment in having his hopes, aspirations, and hard work meet with such complete frustration. He knew he had done his best, and with God's help he would not be deterred from providing

A Certain Blindness

the best possible living for his family under the circumstances. With his good record behind him, Dad cast about for the best employment available. In 1928 my father transferred from the Buick foundry to work as a janitor in the main executive offices at Chevrolet, at that time considered a prize job among the Negro workers. The work was light, clean, and secure, and Dad was well liked. In 1929 my parents bought a new house in the Elm Park area of Flint, two blocks from Thread Lake. Most of the homeowners in this community were also factory workers, though our family was one of only a sprinkling of Negro families, but skin color was not a barrier. Our neighbors also included businessmen, professionals, farmers, and retirees.

My parents eventually had five children. I was their third child, born in September 1927, just prior to the Depression. My brothers, Lindell and Arthur, are older than I, and my sisters, Mary Rose and Wilma Grace, are younger. Dad had steady employment throughout the Depression, so family life was secure; our upbringing emphasized moral values, Bible reading, obedience, and good manners. We attended Sunday school and displayed the flag on national holidays. Dad and Mom stressed the ideals of American life, but they never made us aware of the ways the ideals had failed them. They believed that regardless of the continuing force of racism their children would not be denied because of a lack of strength or worthiness.

Dad was the consummate family man and provider who made sure we ate well, had respectable clothing, and all had something to do. Since he had been a chef, we all looked forward to Sundays and holidays when he prepared feasts, including fine meats and desserts. Periodically he made ice cream, popcorn balls, root beer, and other treats.

We always had at least one dog and cat to care for, and each of us had his own house plant as well as designated chores we were held responsible for. Dad was the magnet around which our activities centered, and he truly delighted in sharing our joys and childish disasters. Because my father had a way of throwing down a gauntlet, we even found the tedious jobs he

"Neither Inferior nor Unworthy"

assigned enjoyable. He often dared us to try some feat of bravery he would invent, such as the challenges he issued to Lind and Art of climbing the back stairs and crossing the attic floor in pitch dark to knock on a certain trunk he knew to be located there. (This same scary route ran through a dark hall in the basement.)

Sunday afternoons when the weather was bad or in the winter, Dad would tell us stories, which included tales about Uncle Bass or his own hunting and fishing trips. He took time to sing interesting songs to us, especially when he rocked my baby sisters. Sunday afternoon walks around Thread Lake were highlights of that period. Most of the neighborhood boys would gather at our house for the hikes, during which we circled the complete lake, crossed over the dam, and walked the woods and open fields. Dad explained the various animals and plants (and would take some plants for use as tea), and he was very safety conscious in helping us learn to appreciate the outdoors.

During this early period in my life, I was provided a valuable experience. While all of my friends were white, there was nothing in my day-to-day life to indicate that I was in any way less because of my color. Although the parents of some of my friends did not want them to associate with others who were poor, skin color never served as a badge of inferiority, which, in later life, so much effort was made to make me believe.

The fabric of our lives was rent when Dad died suddenly in December 1937. His years of foundry work had taken their toll on his health. I remember his deep and extended bouts of coughing each winter until pleurisy and complications ended his life. I was ten; I felt the fun-filled, carefree life of a child ended for me then.

My mother was thirty-seven years old when Dad died. Coming from a family that taught responsibility, duty, character, and integrity, Mom was marked by these virtues which, together with her deep religious faith, helped her overcome her despair. Inspired by the noble women of her race such as Harriet

A Certain Blindness

Tubman, Sojourner Truth, and Mary McLeod Bethune, my mother was determined to raise her children to contribute to making a better society. Trained as a teacher, Mom sought employment in Flint's public schools, but at that time they employed no black teachers. Mom did become one of the first teachers hired in the adult education program of the Mott Foundation. C. S. Mott, a General Motors founder and one of its major stockholders, endowed the Mott Foundation to improve the quality of life in the Flint area. My mother loved teaching and enjoyed her job, but it required her to spend a significant portion of each day away from her children, and in her absence my oldest brother, Lind, was in charge. Twelve at the time of Dad's death, Lind was mature and stable. Gregarious and easy to like, he was a notoriously good storyteller who entertained neighborhood children, for a modest fee, at his Saturday afternoon story sessions.

Lind also raised homing pigeons and had talent for curing the injuries they sometimes encountered during flight, using the medicine and equipment he had access to due to his part-time employment making deliveries for the Flint Medical and Surgical Supply Company. One time some neighbors agreed to release one of his pigeons in Owosso, Michigan, twenty-six miles west of Flint. Contrary to Lind's instructions, the bird was released so it took off into the sun. It struck an electric power line, severing most of its wing near its body. Lind retrieved and saved the bird, as he was able to do for another of his birds shot by hunters.

After finishing high school Lind worked at Buick and attended trade school while waiting for his call to the army. When he left home to report to Fort Custer near Battle Creek, Michigan, he took one of his favorite pigeons, which returned with a message to the family in the capsule attached to its leg. The message read: "Don't worry, I am in God's hands. God bless you all."

My brother Arthur was said to be an extremely brilliant youngster, and the awards and honors he received during his

"Neither Inferior nor Unworthy"

school years were further evidence of his achievement. While he excelled in the academic subjects, especially math, Arthur also kept up with sports. He was an avid baseball fan and followed the Detroit Tigers, keeping batting averages and statistics on each player. He was also interested in college football and was disturbed when Willis Ward, a star player on the Wolverines, the University of Michigan's football team, was barred from playing against a Georgia team. It was reported that the players and officials at Georgia Tech refused to play against a Negro.

This quiet, bookish brother of mine began to be extremely sensitive. When he didn't attend a father-son banquet at our local church where a well-respected member of the congregation was to serve as his honorary father, our own father being deceased by this time, we began to notice other changes in his behavior. Art neglected his hobbies and stayed out late at night and was easily provoked about any perceived unfairness, especially racial matters. He often talked about the difficulties experienced by Paul Robeson, a former all-American football player and internationally known actor and singer. Robeson, elected to Phi Beta Kappa at Rutgers University and a graduate of Columbia University Law School, was acclaimed in the European theater but was ostracized in his own.

When Art learned that the navy was integrating and that he could receive officer's training, he decided to enlist. He scored extremely high on the entrance exam, the highest of any navy applicant in Genesee County, as reported by the recruiting officers, but they didn't know what to do with this promising young black recruit. Only recently had the navy graduated its first black officers from the Great Lakes Training Center in Illinois. Not knowing whether he would join a separate class for Negro candidates or be integrated into a college training program, they told Art to wait at home for word on where to report for training.

But word never came. Art became more and more introverted, convinced that the navy would never let him start officer's training. Mom grew more concerned about Art's withdrawal and arranged for him to be examined by doctors at Hurley Hospital. Much to our shock, the doctors recommended hospitalization. As word got around that Art was hospitalized, some of our relatives blamed the navy's racist treatment of him, but I was not so sure. Having been close to him, I thought about the marked changes in his behavior that started occurring after Dad died. I always felt Art was Dad's favorite, and I began to suspect that Art took the death more painfully than we realized.

Mary and Wilma were quite young when Dad died, Mary a first grader and Wilma a two-year-old. Understanding how much time and attention a toddler required and Mom's mounting burdens, Dad's sister Nettie offered to take Wilma with her to live in Arkansas. Though this did not seem to be an ideal solution, the arrangement seemed to work for a while. When school was out for the summer, Aunt Nettie brought Wilma back for a visit, but after a few days Wilma announced that she wanted to "go home." Mom soon decided that, for better or worse, she had to keep her entire brood together.

Being the middle child between two boys and two girls can often have its perils, but I survived. While Lind, Art, and I had our own circle of friends, we often joined together in fishing, swimming, ball games, and other fun activities. I made it a point to stay close to Art, for I could count on him to know what to do and how to do it, particularly when we explored various avenues of mischief. Although he was bookish and almost perpetually quiet, he always helped his buddies and was among the leading participants in any fight. I was an unwavering supporter and looked to him for leadership; but, when we were candidates for punishment, Mom's leather belt usually fell equally on both of us.

I felt very close to the girls and especially relished the way they looked up to me. Besides, they always came in handy to fill some obscure positions in games with my friends. I often confided in them, though they did not always uphold the trust, as on the occasion when my friend Earl and I were smoking homemade cigarettes in the basement. When Mom, who had been

"Neither Inferior nor Unworthy"

away, returned home, Mary and Wilma led her right down the basement stairs to discover us performing the forbidden act.

During our early years when Aunt Nettie visited us, the older boys were in school and the girls were too young to travel, so I became her constant companion. I would do anything for her—run errands for her, go to the neighbors, whatever she wanted—because she was so pleased with me in return, nicknaming me Jack Rabbit, a name I was proud to have.

My father's influence was immeasurable. He was constantly reassuring when I faced fearful childhood experiences. On one occasion, I had a severe toothache and needed a molar extracted, but I was apprehensive about going to the dentist. The thought of having a tooth extracted gave me the tremors. But after Dad assured me all would be well and accompanied me to the dentist's office, the experience was practically a pleasure. After that, through all the years and into maturity, I have had no problem with being in a dentist's chair.

The summer before I turned ten we were out fishing when Dad's hook caught on some object on the bottom of the lake, and he called on me to untangle the line. As Dad praised how brave and competent I was, I knew I had to suppress my fright, so I waded out to the line, traced it to the bottom, and found the hook snagged on a car spring. My reward for freeing Dad's line—and achieving status in his eyes—was to accompany him to a men's store, where I was outfitted with my first suit. Five months later, in December 1937, I wore it to his funeral.

Dad's brief illness and sudden death devastated us and required each of us to make an indescribable adjustment. After his death, Christmas brought us, not toys, but clothing, books, games, and some money to buy something for ourselves. The local fire department gave dolls and other toys to the girls. Even today I contribute to their neighborhood Christmas campaigns, remembering their generosity and help in those needy years. In her later years Mom expressed her sorrow at being unable to provide toys for her children.

Because our mother felt that "anything worth having is

worth working for" we earned money for bicycles and other things we desired or needed by selling fish we caught and doing yard work and other odd jobs for neighbors. I operated a business of sorts each year after Easter, when I would buy all the leftover baby chicks from a feed store and raise them until they were large enough to sell at a profit to a neighbor who raised chickens.

My elementary school experiences left a positive impression on me. The teachers seemed genuinely interested and were fair and without prejudice. Because there were usually only one or two other black children in my classes—and no black males, at that—my friends were always white boys with whom I spent my time and got into mischief.

Our teachers taught us to emulate the heroes from American history, such as George Washington, Thomas Jefferson, Abraham Lincoln, Henry Ford, or Thomas Edison; we were told hard work was the key to achieving the American dream.

General Motors, the crowning example of success in America, was also born in Flint. While we both had our formative years there, my growth and development did not follow the traditional course to success as promised those in pursuit of the American dream. When I was a junior in high school, Lind was in the service and Art was hospitalized, so I was thrust into the role of man of the house—a position for which I felt inadequate and ill-prepared. It seemed at the time a cruel twist of fate that both of them, better suited to the task, would be gone, leaving me to carry on alone.

However, I welcomed the responsibility and handled it, and Mom was pleased. During this time, I began taking school work more seriously, pursuing each subject with fresh enthusiasm. The effort paid handsome dividends, for my name began to appear on the school's honor roll. Though Michigan schools were considered among the best in the nation, by junior high and high school the teachers were almost stoical, pursuing what seemed to be a policy of benign neglect. Though academically I may have been classified as a promising student, I do not remem-

"Neither Inferior nor Unworthy"

ber any high school teachers expressing a personal interest in me or in anything I did, as they expressed for some of my (white) classmates. And I distinctly recall on two occasions my teachers specifically advised me not to take the college preparatory program but to follow the industrial arts courses instead and learn a trade.

This was a touchy subject with my mother, though. Mom had always emphasized the importance of developing our minds and not allowing others to exploit, manipulate, or misdirect our lives. Mom encouraged me to speak with a black chemist in Flint to do some special work at the Dupont plant. He had a doctorate in chemistry and was a specialist in paints and pigments. It turned out he also had been discouraged from pursuing his field, but he loved chemistry and would not be deterred. I took his attitude to heart.

I am convinced that Mom was trying to erect a buffer against the blind prejudice and hypocrisy we would encounter in the workaday world. Like Monroe Trotter, the newspaper editor she had heard lecture so many years before, Mom taught us that whenever we encountered people who harbored feelings of racial superiority, under no circumstances, she said, were we to adopt an attitude of inferiority or unworthiness. While strongly asserting that we should be responsible for our own conduct, Mom also believed we should distinguish racial problems that were not self-created.

Mom made us aware of the accomplishments of Negroes not mentioned in our school history books, including Frederick Douglass, Booker T. Washington, our great-uncle Bass Reeves, and others who had started their lives as slaves yet still made great achievements. When actor Paul Robeson and prima donna Marian Anderson were prominent on the stage, I once asked a high school teacher, who had told us often that she belonged to the Daughters of the American Revolution, why the DAR had banned Marian Anderson from singing in Constitution Hall. This teacher was annoyed with my question, but she never gave me an answer, and I noticed how our rapport

A Certain Blindness

deteriorated from that time on. Acutely aware that certain valid perceptions could not be discussed between the races, I learned to exercise considerable discipline or else find myself overwrought and agitated. Too often I encountered a blindness or bigotry that could not be penetrated with an alternate point of view.

I never actually experienced overt racial hostility during my high school years—it is possible that people's real attitudes escaped me since I harbored no paranoia. When I attended the thirtieth reunion of my graduating class I experienced the same camaraderie with several of my friends, though with others I sensed a distance or frostiness, as if I were an intruder. When my friend Tony learned through the dinner announcements that I had been made a judge (the only judge in our class), he sought me out to talk. We had been talking only a few minutes when Priscilla, who obviously had imbibed too freely of the drinks, interrupted us to hug and kiss Tony. She was making the rounds, she said, to kiss all the men in the class. Tony made a gesture toward me, reminding Priscilla of my membership in the class. She leaned back, extended an across-the-gulf hand to me, and smiled, saying, "Oh, sure. Hi, Paul."

I supported myself during high school with various jobs. One of my earliest was working weekends at Flint's YWCA. Later jobs included locker room attendant at a country club, janitor and stockboy at a dime store, and porter, bellhop, busboy, and fireman at a downtown hotel and restaurant. The only time I ever violated the family rule "one does not quit a job until one has a better one" was when I quit my hotel job when the desk clerk complained about the dust I raised while performing my duties as a porter. I immediately got another job, washing and polishing cars at the Buick retail store with a friend. After that I became a tire changer at General Tire Company, then I serviced used trade-ins and reconditioned and repaired cars for McDavis Motor Sales.

Once I graduated from high school, however, I longed to join the military service, like my brother Lind.

5

A Chance to Serve

Lind served in the Signal Corps before he transferred to an engineering outfit in the Air Corps. He was variously located in Maryland, Utah, and Florida before being sent to Italy, where he spent most of his service time.

Not having experienced hostile, overt racial discrimination, Lind was totally unprepared for the abuse and humiliation suffered by black servicemen. On most military bases black soldiers lived in segregated areas with inferior facilities and could not eat in certain locations or enjoy recreation as white soldiers could. They often could not purchase items such as shoes or hats that required trying on for a proper fit. German prisoners of war were often accorded better living quarters and preferred seating at eating and recreational halls. The prisoners enjoyed passes off base and could eat and drink wherever they liked, but a black man's presence in that same place provoked immediate arrest.

The number of black servicemen maimed or killed by

A Certain Blindness

white military or civilian personnel for resisting the established order will never be known. In truth Lind's life could have been lost as easily to his comrades-in-arms as to an enemy. In this atmosphere he was denied the opportunity for officer's status on two occasions and was demoted twice because of his inability to accommodate the system.

Although black Americans fought and served honorably in every war in which the nation engaged, the government failed to grant them the same status as other servicemen or extend equal opportunity to them when they returned. Historically black men were initially rejected for fighting, but their participation was eventually necessary to achieve final victory. This relationship between bearing arms and citizenship was summed up by Frederick Douglass after the Civil War: "The negro had been a citizen three times in the history of the Government, in 1776, 1812 and 1865, and in the time of trouble the negro was a citizen and in the time of peace he was an alien."[1]

During the colonial period Negroes were permitted to enlist in the militia of New England and the central colonies. The laws regarding service varied from colony to colony; however, the Militia Law of Massachusetts, as early as 1652, required Negroes, Scotchmen, and Indians to train in the militia. In some colonies where slaves were held, they were set free for "meritorious and courageous action" defending their masters' families against hostile Indians. In the southern colonies, the fear of slave revolts greatly reduced the use of black men in service except in times of emergency, since there were too few whites to carry out a large scale military effort.

Historians have determined that the pattern of racial discrimination in time of war reaches back to America's Revolutionary War and to General George Washington. As commander-in-chief Washington held a council of war in Boston on October 8, 1775, at which time his staff unanimously agreed to reject both slaves and free Negroes who applied for enlistment, despite the fact that, as early as April of that year, black minutemen had fought at Lexington and Concord.

A Chance to Serve

The British, however, were more concerned with manpower and winning the war. The governor of Virginia issued a proclamation on November 7, 1775, which stated, "I do hereby further declare all indented servants, Negroes, or others (appertaining to Rebels), free, that are able and willing to bear arms, they joining His Majesty's Troops, as soon as may be, for the more speedily reducing the Colony to a proper sense of their duty, to His Majesty's crown and dignity."[2]

Fearing the defection of half a million slaves to the British cause, Washington reversed his position and in December authorized recruiting officers to sign up free Negroes "desirous of enlisting." Thus, about five thousand black enlistees fought side by side with white soldiers for American independence—from Bunker Hill to Valley Forge, from Monmouth to the final surrender at Yorktown.

Crispus Attucks, a Negro who led a group of patriotic citizens converging on a British garrison quartered on King Street in Boston, was the first American to die in the war. British Captain Preston, there to help enforce the Townsend Acts, panicked and fired, and the incident left five Americans dead. The British soldiers were later tried for murder but were acquitted.

As historian L. D. Reddick reported, the great orator and statesman Daniel Webster claimed that "Attucks . . . struck the first blow for America's independence."[3] Other Negroes whose efforts significantly aided the patriots' cause included Peter Salem, reputed to have killed British commander Major Pitcairn in the Battle of Bunker Hill; Salem Poor, a hero at Charlestown; and the daughter of a black innkeeper, said to have saved General Washington from an attempt to poison him.

Black men have served the nation's cause in some very unique ways, such as a slave named York:

> During 1804–05, Captains Meriwether Lewis and William Clark explored the newly purchased Louisiana Territory and mapped an overland route to the Pacific Ocean. Clark brought along a slave called York. York soon became an ambassador for the expe-

A Certain Blindness

dition among the plains Indians. They had never seen a black man before and were intrigued. In addition, it was a custom among many of the tribes that warriors returning from a successful raid or battle would daub parts of their body with charcoal to symbolize their bravery. York was seen as a very brave man. His entire body was black and the color would not come off. He was obviously the leader of the group to many, not Lewis or Clark, for only braves led parties such as this. Consequently, many tribes assumed to be hostile by Lewis and Clark were found to be friendly, thanks to York.[4]

My brother Lind reported a somewhat similar experience in how color aided the American cause during World War II. For a period of time the U.S. Intelligence Headquarters near Naples was being infiltrated by Germans posing as American GI's. A plan was devised whereby black soldiers replaced all security personnel and military police at the facility. The plan was highly successful since all access to military secrets and confidential material by the Germans immediately ceased.

Several thousand black Americans fought in the War of 1812, principally a naval engagement, and they were used in all capacities and ratings aboard American vessels. Constituting from 10 to 20 percent of most ships' crews, they performed heroic duty in many engagements. Oliver Hazard Perry, famous naval commander, spoke of his black crew members as "absolutely insensible to danger" after their efforts in freeing the Great Lakes from British control.[5]

It was in the South that black soldiers made their greatest contribution to the war. The Battalion of Free Men of Color was formed in September 1812, but their offer of service was rejected until the British threatened the city of New Orleans. General Andrew Jackson, being short of effective troops, insisted that the offer be accepted. General Jackson's proclamation read:

A Chance to Serve
HEAD-QUARTERS, SEVENTH MILITARY DISTRICT,
MOBILE,
SEPTEMBER 21, 1814.
To the Free Colored Inhabitants of Louisiana:

Through a mistaken policy, you have heretofore been deprived of a participation in the glorious struggle for national rights, in which *our* country is engaged. This no longer shall exist. As sons of Freedom you are now called upon to defend your most estimable blessings. *As Americans,* your country looks with confidence to her adopted children, for a valorous support, as a faithful return for the advantages enjoyed under her mild and equitable government. As fathers, husbands, and brothers, you are summoned to rally round the standard of the Eagle, to defend all which is dear in existence.

Your country, although calling for your exertions, does not wish you to engage in her cause, without remunerating you for the services rendered. Your intelligent minds are not to be led away by false representations—your love of honor would cause you to despise the man who should attempt to deceive you. In the sincerity of a soldier, and the language of truth I address you.

To every noble hearted free man of color, volunteering to serve during the present contest with Great Britain, and no longer, there will be paid the same bounty of money and lands now received by white soldiers of the United States, namely one hundred and twenty-four dollars in money and one hundred and sixty acres of land. The non-commissioned officers and privates will also be entitled to the same monthly pay and daily rations and clothes furnished to any American soldiers.[6]

General Jackson's second proclamation, said to be "one of the highest compliments ever paid by a military chief to his soldiers," stated:

SOLDIERS! When on the banks of the Mobile, I called you to take up arms, inviting you to partake the perils and glory of your *white fellow-citizens, I expected much* from you; for I was not ignorant that you possessed qualities most formidable to an invading enemy. I knew with what fortitude you would endure hunger and thirst, and all the fatigues of a campaign. *I knew well*

A Certain Blindness

how you love your native country, and that you, as well as ourselves, had to defend what *man* holds dear—his parents, wife, children, and property. *You have done more than I expected.* In addition to the previous qualities I before knew you to possess, I found among you noble enthusiasm, which leads to the performance of great things.

Soldiers! The President of the United States shall hear how praise-worthy was your conduct in the hour of danger; and the representatives of the American people will give you the praise your exploits entitle you to.[7]

General Jackson was referring to the black troops' participation in the battle at Chalmette Plains. In that battle the troops "held their portion of the line, then counter attacked. The worst defeat suffered by British arms in years produced a psychological high point for the American people. Ironically, the black role was soon overlooked, as black veterans were not permitted to march in the annual parades celebrating the victory."[8] Thus discrediting and disparaging black fighting men, the Defense Department acknowledged that "the War of 1812 not only provided the capstone of American independence, it also consolidated the slave system of the South. Hopes of black Americans for peace and liberty were dashed when the Treaty of Ghent, which ended the war, provided for the mutual restoration of properties. Blacks who had fled to British lines seeking freedom were returned to slavery or taken to the West Indies, sold, and their American owners were indemnified."[9]

Black men and women saw the Civil War as a struggle to destroy slavery, and their patriotism was viewed as liberation. From the beginning they volunteered for the Union cause, only to be turned back. Lincoln worried about the border states joining the Confederacy, so Secretary of War Cameron informed these volunteers that "this Department has no intention at present to call into the service of the Government any colored soldiers."

By mid-1862, after a period of hard fighting and limited success in new calls for volunteers, newly appointed Secretary

A Chance to Serve

of War Stanton bowed to pressures and approved the recruitment of black soldiers. Various state volunteer units were immediately mustered into service as the United States Colored Troops (USCT). Following Frederick Douglass's appeal to "men of color, to arms," a new war objective had also been established—abolition.

In 1861 and 1862, black soldiers had yet to participate in a major engagement, and many observers were still skeptical about their fighting ability. However, in May, June and July of 1863 black units fought at Port Hudson, Milliken's Bend and Fort Wagner. The blood of black soldiers mixed with that of white compatriots on the battlefield and no one who saw the actions doubted black determination to fight. Yet, doubts persisted, and month after month, black soldiers felt the need to prove their worth, while few asked about the fighting ability of white units.

Bravery aside, most people did not expect black units to serve other than garrison duty—to free white units for combat. Black privates were paid only $10.00 per month in comparison to $13.00 for white privates. In addition, whites received an extra $3.50 per month for clothing while $3.00 was deducted from the black soldiers' pay for clothing. Men of the 54th Massachusetts went without pay for a year in protest.[10]

In all, some two hundred thousand blacks served as Union soldiers and at least that many were laborers in the quartermaster and engineering departments. Following his change of view, President Lincoln wrote General Grant in August 1863 that the black component "is a resource which, if vigorously applied now, will close the contest."[11] By summer 1864 he stated, "No human power can subdue this rebellion without using the Emancipation lever as I have done. Freedom has given us the control of 200,000 able bodied men."[12] In February of that year, Secretary of War Stanton wrote Lincoln attesting to the valor of Negro troops: "They have proved themselves among the bravest of the brave, performing deeds of daring and shedding their blood with a heroism unsurpassed by soldiers of any race."[13]

A Certain Blindness

The Confederate commanding officer at the Battle of Milliken's Bend stated his "charge was resisted by the Negro portion of the enemy's force with considerable obstinacy, while the white or true Yankee portion ran like whipped curs almost as soon as the charge was ordered."[14]

After the Battle of Milliken's Bend the Confederacy apparently adopted a policy of taking no Negro prisoners. Following the surrender at Fort Pillow, Tennessee, nearly three hundred soldiers were indiscriminately slaughtered.

In all Negro troops took part in 499 military engagements, 39 of which were major battles. Their death toll was more than 20 percent of their total troops.

Despite the large number of black troops and units, fewer than one hundred Negroes served as officers. It was assumed that Negroes lacked the leadership qualities necessary to be officers although thirteen black noncommissioned officers received Medals of Honor for their actions at Chapins Farm in 1864. All were cited for assuming command of their units and leading them in the assault after their white officers had been killed or wounded.

The Union Army's recruitment of Negroes was especially offensive to Confederate leaders since, to them, arming black men to fight white men violated a sacred white code. Jefferson Davis retaliated immediately by declaring that Negroes were to be treated as runaway slaves and not cared for according to rules of war among civilized men. He ordered Negroes captured wearing Union uniforms to be summarily shot.

Four years of war and casualties, however, convinced Southerners that slaves offered the only remaining source of military manpower for the South. General Robert E. Lee pleaded for a recruitment of slaves, and Jefferson Davis took the matter to the Confederate Congress, which, in March 1865, authorized the raising of two hundred thousand black troops, offering freedom to each one and his family in return for service. However, this reversal of attitude came too late, for Lee surrendered to Grant at Appomattox within a month.

A Chance to Serve

The Confederacy waited so long to change its policy because, even while watching the Union achieve marked advantage in the war from the emancipation and recruitment of Negroes, the South was being strangled by its "cornerstone" of inequality. The South, where more than 90 percent of all black people lived, could not allow the Negro to fight in a common cause. It reasoned that to be armed like the master is to be free and equal with the master—never to be a slave again. If the Negro is fit for freedom, any justification for holding him as a slave is false and unfounded. The Confederacy was built on the premise of Negro inferiority and was to die on the same notion.

More than thirty-eight thousand black soldiers died for the Union and another thirty thousand were wounded or missing.

> This heavy toll reflected the fact that black units had served in every theatre of operations and in most major engagements, often as assault troops. Some of these casualties were due to poor equipment, bad medical care, and the "no quarter" policy followed by Confederate forces facing them. To the black troops themselves, these casualties reflected their great desire to prove to an uncaring nation their right to full citizenship and participation after the war. They were fighting to be free, not to return as slaves.[15]

Following the Civil War, four black regiments were established and were active in the Indian wars on the western frontier and later fought with distinction in Cuba during the Spanish-American War. Large numbers of ex-slaves enlisted at the outbreak of the Spanish-American War, continuing their record of patriotic sacrifice, heroism, and love of country. The most outstanding record made by black troops in this conflict was with the famous Rough Riders under Colonel Theodore Roosevelt.

But the proven abilities of blacks in military service were quickly forgotten as America entered World War I. Although the army had a pressing need for additional manpower, there was great reluctance to arm large groups of Negroes, and there was no policy for utilization of the black soldier. "As in previous wars

A Certain Blindness

the black community had to agitate and pressure for a role. Integrated units were ruled out as a matter of policy and age-old questions of black fighting qualities were again raised."[16] Two black divisions were formed, the 92nd and 93rd, although neither received its full complement of combat support or support units. Lawrence D. Reddick remarked in the *Atlanta Inquirer:*

> Many of the nation's military units were stationed in the South for their training prior to going overseas. This was true of black as well as white units of the segregated army. But black soldiers found themselves targets of white police and civilians in the surrounding towns who subjected them to no end of harassment. The very idea of blacks with guns was considered by some southerners as "dangerous." Movie houses, beaches and "good time" areas that were open to whites were declared "off limits" to blacks.[17]

For both black divisions there was trouble from the beginning. This included serious problems from within the military itself. Part of the 92nd Division trained at Camp Funston, Kansas. While there, a black soldier tried to enter a theater in nearby Manhattan and was denied entry, even though Kansas law prohibited discrimination. When General Charles C. Ballau, the division commander, learned of the incident, he issued a bulletin in which he chastised his soldiers for starting trouble. He also said, "The division Commander repeats that the success of the Division, with all that success implies, is dependent upon the good will of the public. That public is nine-tenths white. White men made the Division, and they can break it just as easily if it becomes a trouble maker."[18] An uproar of protest flowed from the black community. Two months later the division hurriedly left for France, poorly trained and poorly led.

The 93rd Division, which was one of the first American units to arrive in France, also left the States prematurely, for reasons Reddick described:

> Once when a northern-born black soldier, who was also a popular band leader, went into a white hotel lobby to buy a copy

A Chance to Serve

of his hometown newspaper, the *New York Times,* he forgot—or meant to forget—to take his hat off. Several white men in the lobby—with their hats on—surrounded him and demanded that he remove his. When he declined to do so, one of them knocked his hat to the floor. When he stooped to pick it up, another man kicked him. When he got back to his unit at the training camp, the soldier told his buddies what had happened to him. They got their guns and started to town. Somehow the white commander of the unit heard of their intentions and intercepted the men before they got to town. He pleaded with them and finally persuaded them to call off their planned assault. The commander also telephoned and telegraphed the War Department that the situation was likely to explode at any time. To ease that situation, the War Department immediately ordered the 93rd Division overseas.[19]

Colonel Howard Queen identified the soldier as Noble Sissle, stationed in Spartanburg, South Carolina.[20] He was serving the 15th National Guard Unit from New York City. The 15th was later designated the 369th Infantry Regiment of the 93rd Division.

Controversy arose over what to do with the black troops upon their arrival in France. Eventually they were "loaned" to the French where they received rifles, helmets, rations, and other gear except uniforms. Many of these American soldiers received their entire training in France without as much as seeing a gun stateside.

Within three months of its arrival, the 369th joined the French 4th Army at the front and were welcomed as "liberators." The 369th stayed in the trenches for 191 days, the longest front-line service of any American regiment. The regiment, as a unit, and well over 170 of its men, were awarded the French Croix de Guerre or Legion of Honor for gallantry in action. Known as the "hell fighters" by the Germans, this black regiment received elaborate praise from Marshall Foch, commander-in-chief of the Allied Armies, who declared:

A Certain Blindness

> After having boldly stopped the enemy, you have attacked them for months with indefatigable faith and energy, giving them no rest.
>
> You have won the greatest battle in History and saved the most sacred cause, the liberty of the world.
>
> Be proud of it.
>
> With immortal glory you have adorned your flag.
>
> Posterity will be indebted to you in gratitude.

The 370th, 371st, and 372nd followed the 369th, and all saw extensive action and acquired many awards. General Goybet of the French army honored the Afro-American soldiers of the 371st and 372nd Infantry regiments who had been brigaded with his division, the 15th (Red Hand) Division:

> For seven months we have lived as brothers-at-arms, partaking in the same activities, sharing the same dangers, and the same hardships.
>
> Never will the Red Hand forget the indomitable dash, the heroic rush of the American regiments up the Observatory Ridge and into the Plains of Monthois. The most powerful defenses, the most strongly organized machine gun nests, the heaviest artillery barrage, nothing could stop them. These crack regiments overcame every obstacle with a complete contempt for danger; through their steadfast devotion the Red Hand Division, for nine whole days of severe struggle were constantly leading the way for the victorious advance of the 4th Army.[21]

The 370th Infantry also participated in action on the western front and were the first Americans to enter the fortified city of Laon. The Germans called them the "Black Devils." Other black units participated in the Battle of the Argonne, Chateau Theirry, St. Mihiel, Champagne, Vosges, and the Rhone.

The 92nd Division saw less extensive combat because it fought as a unit with the American Expeditionary Force. In all more than 450,000 blacks served and over one-half of that number were sent overseas. Nevertheless Colonel Queen recorded:

> We sailed from our POE aboard the USS *George Washington* under totally segregated conditions. We hoped for some respite

A Chance to Serve

on foreign soil, but once in France our troubles really began. American authorities spent considerable time watching Negro soldiers and French women. Brigadier General James B. Irwin issued an order which forbade Negro soldiers speaking to French women. American MPs would arrest soldiers of color caught disobeying this order. The whole anti-Negro campaign reached its height, rather its depth, with an order from General Pershing's headquarters 7 August 1918:

> TO THE FRENCH MILITARY MISSION STATIONED
> WITH THE AMERICAN ARMY
> *Secret Information Concerning Black American Troops*
> We must prevent the rise of any pronounced degree of intimacy between French officers and black officers. We may be courteous and amiable with the last but we cannot deal with them on the same plane as white American officers without deeply wounding the latter. We must not eat with them, must not shake hands with them, seek to talk to them or meet with them outside the requirements of military service. We must not commend too highly these troops particularly in front of white Americans. Make a point of keeping the native cantonment from spoiling the Negro. White Americans become very incensed at any particular expression of intimacy between white women and black men.[22]

L. D. Reddick, in the *Atlanta Inquirer,* further described the situation:

> At any rate, the black soldiers, who served overseas got a taste of human relations that only a precious few of them had experienced in their native America. They responded so positively to the openness of public places and the hospitality of French families, that they behaved as though "social equality" was the new order of human relations. Most black men seemed to have . . . enjoyed their stay in France.
> Meanwhile, there was some apprehension that these blacks upon returning to their homes in America—especially if they were from the South—might bring their new behavior patterns with them. Dr. R. R. Moton of Tuskegee Institute, successor to Dr. Booker T. Washington (who died in 1915), was dispatched

A Certain Blindness

to France by the War Department to caution the black soldiers that when they returned home, they should remember that "Mississippi is not Paris" and would be expected to behave themselves accordingly.[23]

When the black veteran returned home, he expected to share in the spoils of winning the war to preserve democracy, but in many instances he was not even allowed to enter his hometown in uniform. Instead he was met with a bloody period in 1919 when seventy-six Negroes were lynched and eleven black men—some of them soldiers in uniform—were burned alive. Twenty-five race riots occurred in American cities. James Weldon Johnson, then executive secretary of the National Association for the Advancement of Colored People (NAACP), dubbed it the "red summer," and noted that between 1889 and 1918 some 3,224 men and women were lynched and an unknown number disappeared without a trace.

W. E. B. Du Bois, one of the founders of the NAACP, advanced the concept of a society totally open to both whites and blacks, and the NAACP worked actively toward it under the leadership of its executive director, Walter White, and chief counsel, Charles Houston. Equal treatment for military personnel was one of its target issues brought to the attention of the Roosevelt administration in the early 1930s. In correspondence with Chief of Staff Douglas MacArthur, Houston related the need for "a more united nation of free citizens." In a 1937 editorial the NAACP asked why black and white men could not fight side by side as they had in the Continental Army. Walter White told President Franklin D. Roosevelt in 1939 that, if democracy were truly to be defended, discrimination must be eliminated from the armed forces.

On September 27, 1940, a meeting was arranged with President Roosevelt attended by White, Arnold Hill of the Urban League, and A. Phillip Randolph, head of the Brotherhood of Sleeping Car Porters. The group outlined for the president the important phases of the integration of the Negro into all

A Chance to Serve

aspects of the national defense program. The president assured them further policy changes would be made to insure fair treatment for Negroes. The central theme was that segregation is unacceptable in a democratic society and hypocritical during a war fought in defense of the four freedoms. The *Pittsburgh Courier* introduced the "Double V" slogan as the rallying cry demanding victory against fascism abroad and discrimination at home.

As a result the army announced plans for the mobilization of Negroes, and Congress amended the Selective Service Act of 1940 to increase their training opportunities. The Fish Amendment provided that in the selection and training of men "there shall be no discrimination against any person on account of race or color." Determined to maintain the segregationist policy of World War I, however, the army submitted its plan to the White House providing for black units in each major branch, both combatant and noncombatant, but strict separation of troops. When the policy, endorsed by Roosevelt, was bitterly attacked, the president appointed a black, William H. Hastie, dean of Howard University Law School, as a civilian aide to the secretary of war. Hastie, who later became a U.S. Court of Appeals judge, was a brilliant lawyer long associated with the black cause. Morris J. MacGregor, Jr., in his book *Integration of the Armed Forces, 1940–1965,* stated:

> Hastie was confident that he could demonstrate to War Department officials that the Army's racial policies were both inefficient and unpatriotic.
>
> Judge Hastie spent his first ten months in office observing what was happening to the Negro in the Army. He did not like what he saw. To him, separating black soldiers from white soldiers was a fundamental error. First, the effect on black morale was devastating. "Beneath the surface," he wrote, "is widespread discontent. Most white persons are unable to appreciate the rancor and bitterness which the Negro, as a matter of self preservation, has learned to hide beneath a smile, a joke, or merely an impassive face." The inherent paradox of trying to inculcate

A Certain Blindness

pride, dignity, and aggressiveness in a black soldier while inflicting on him the segregationist's concept of the Negro's place in society created in him an insupportable tension. Second, segregation wasted black manpower, a valuable military asset. It was impossible, Hastie charged, to employ skilled Negroes at maximum efficiency within the traditionally narrow limitations of black units. Third, to insist on an inflexible separation of white and black soldiers was "the most dramatic evidence of hypocrisy" in America's professed concern for preserving democracy.

Although he appreciated the impossibility of making drastic changes overnight, Judge Hastie was disturbed because he found "no apparent disposition to make a beginning or a trial of any different plan." He looked for some form of progressive integration by which qualified Negroes could be classified and assigned, not by race, but as individuals, according to their capacities and abilities.[24]

When the War Department failed to implement any effective new policies, Hastie resigned.

The records of hearings concerning the 1940 Selective Service Act conclusively show that neither house of Congress was committed to equitable training and opportunity for black Americans serving in our armed forces. America boldly protested anti-Semitism abroad but was blind to the humiliation it imposed on some of its own citizens, as a writer for *Crisis* magazine succinctly pointed out: "It sounds pretty foolish to be against park benches marked 'Jude' in Berlin, but to be for park benches marked 'Colored' in Tallahassee, Florida."[25] Despite the efforts of the NAACP and other black organizations, the Senate killed a federal anti-lynching bill, and the War Department announced it would not allow Negroes and whites to serve in the same regiments. Racially America followed the same discriminatory course in World War II as it followed in World War I.

The segregated 92nd and 93rd Divisions were activated. During an Allied offensive in Italy, there were reports of poor fighting quality in the 92nd Division. These reports were based on actions which occurred in late 1944 and early 1945 when certain battalion-size units failed to seize or hold their objectives, but the soldiers in the 92nd still performed admirably. Over twelve thousand decorations and citations were eventually awarded to individuals in this division, including two Distinguished Service Crosses, sixteen Legion of Merit awards, ninety-five Silver Stars, and nearly eleven hundred Purple Hearts. The 92nd also suffered over three thousand casualties in six months of fighting.

In addition, in any assessment of performance, it is worthwhile to consider the training and morale of the men. On many stateside bases these soldiers did not enjoy the same rights and privileges that white soldiers did, a condition that raised questions about exactly who the enemy was.[26] Commanding officer Colonel Queen related that when the 366th regiment joined the 92nd he was informed his regiment would occupy the battle line "equipped or not equipped." The commanding general explained: "I did not send for you. Your Negro newspapers, Negro politicians, and white friends have insisted on your seeing combat and I shall see that you get combat and your share of casualties."[27] Queen reported that the general "most certainly kept his word." Lieutenant Colonel Marcus Ray, commander of the 600th Field Artillery, made this summary:

> The 92nd was doomed to mediocre performance of combat duty from its inception. . . . I do not believe enough thought was given to the selection of white officers to serve with the 92nd, and further, the common American error was made of assuming that Southern white men understood Negroes.
>
> In white officered units those men who fit the Southern pattern are pushed and promoted regardless of capabilities and those Negroes who exhibit manliness and self-reliance and self-respect are humiliated and disgraced. . . .
>
> In the main I don't believe the junior officers guilty of faulty judgment or responsible for tactical failure. Soldiers do as

ordered, but when plans sent to them for execution from headquarters are incomplete, inaccurate, and unintelligible there is inevitable confusion.

Racially we have been the victims of an unfortunate chain of circumstances backgrounded by the unchanged attitude as regards the proper "place" of the Negro.[28]

German officers captured during the Italian campaign provided their perception of the 92nd Division to Special Investigation and Intelligence, which is as near to an objective appraisal as we can get:

> The 92nd Division forces were plan-bound. They would adhere strictly to plans formulated before the attack, never deviating from them. The Germans found that the scout and shock undertakings of the division were well prepared and carried out. . . . The front line troops of the 92nd were vigilant and in readiness for the defense, but the German command considered the division, whose combat efficiency and training it judged inferior to that of other American divisions, to have made poor use of terrain, to have irresolute command.[29]

Defense Department records indicated that the 93rd Division, assigned to the Pacific, never fought as a whole unit and saw little combat. The 2nd Cavalry Division, which was created in 1943, was sent to North Africa, where it was deliberately disbanded—its members were reassigned to laborer units. These records also described the 761st Tank Battalion: "Small, nondivisional units, were also created. Perhaps the most well known was the 761st Tank Battalion which fought in the European Theatre of Operations. It was the only all-black unit to win the Presidential Unit Citation. Fighting for 183 continuous days, the unit conducted over 30 major assaults. Although nominated for an award six times, between 1945 and 1976, it did not receive the award until 1978."[30]

There was a remarkable contrast between the training and morale of the 761st and the 92nd. The 761st was attached to General Patton's 3rd Army. Mary Penick Motley records in *The*

A Chance to Serve

Invisible Soldier that from the beginning this well-trained unit was inspired by Patton and respected his style. When Patton asked for more tankers, he was told that the best available tank unit was black. Patton demanded: "Who the f—— asked for color. I asked for tankers."[31] Upon first meeting his new unit, Patton made his position clear:

> Men, you are the first Negro tankers ever to fight in the American army. I would never have asked you if you were not good. I have nothing but the best in my army. I don't care what color you are as long as you go up there and kill those Kraut sons-of-bitches. Everyone has their eyes on you and are expecting great things from you. Most of all your race is looking forward to your success. Don't let them down, and damn you, don't let me down! If you want me you can always find me in the lead tank.[32]

Black combat units fought all across Europe capturing towns, liberating concentration camps, and finally meeting the Russian troops, but neither these troops nor the black combat units in the Pacific theater of operations received the credit they deserved. Such was the case with the Patton museum in Fort Knox, Kentucky, which initially failed to mention Patton's black tankers, though the matter was rectified when the new museum opened in 1972.

The Germans' final assault in Europe and breakthrough at the Battle of the Bulge caused the American military to desperately reach out for all available troops for immediate combat. Defense Department records reported that "as a result of the German Army's offensive in late 1944, some 2,500 blacks were organized into separate platoons and assigned to all white companies in the First and Seventh Armies. This was the only example of integrated units in the Army during World War II."[33]

The efforts of the all-black and integrated units received some attention, as when General Maxwell Taylor, commander of the 101st Airborne Division, wrote to the commander of the 969th Negro Field Artillery Battalion in January 1945: "The

A Certain Blindness

officers and men of the 101st Airborne Division wish to express to your command their appreciation of the gallant support rendered by the 969th Field Artillery battalion in the recent defense of Bastogne, Belgium. . . . This division is proud to have shared the battlefield with your command. A recommendation for a unit citation of the 969th Field Artillery Battalion is being forwarded by the Headquarters."[34] And Colonel John R. Ackor of the 99th Infantry Division reported on the use of Negro platoons attached to white units to replace lost white soldiers: "The Negro platoons performed in an excellent manner at all times when in combat. These men were courageous fighters and never once did they fail to accomplish their assigned mission. They were particularly good in town fighting, and [were] often used as the assault platoon with good results. The platoon assigned to the 393rd Infantry is credited with killing approximately 100 Germans and capturing 500. During this action only 3 of their own men were killed, and 15 wounded."[35] Victory in Europe was thus achieved with black and white Americans for the first time fighting side by side.

Though there were a few modest gains made for black servicemen it was another matter entirely for black workers, who, stateside, faced serious problems of employment even when attempting to serve the war effort. When a Wright aviation plant hired two unskilled Negro workers, all its white workers went on strike. "While we are in complete sympathy with the Negro," declared the president of North American Aviation Company, "it is against company policy to employ them as aircraft workers or mechanics . . . regardless of their training. . . . There will be some jobs as janitors for Negroes."[36] Protesting this and other incidents, the NAACP, along with several other organizations, joined with A. Phillip Randolph in his plan for a 1941 march of one hundred thousand Negroes on Washington, D.C. The goal was to protest employment discrimination in war industries and to open up jobs in defense plants for Negroes to be employed other than as janitors. The march was canceled when President Franklin D. Roo-

A Chance to Serve

sevelt issued Executive Order No. 8802 on June 25. His order forbade employment discrimination in government and defense industries, and the Fair Employment Practices Commission (FEPC) was established to implement the order. At first the order was hailed as a second emancipation proclamation, but employers openly violated it with impunity.

For example, conversion of the automobile industry to war production did not convert the discriminatory employment policies of the manufacturing plants. When the Chrysler Corporation tank arsenal opened in 1941, white workers transferred from Dodge, passing over black workers with more seniority. Despite protests, by the end of 1941, out of 5,000 workers there were 170 blacks, all janitors. The same year, two black employees were transferred to war production at the Packard Company plant touching off a wildcat strike until the black workers were withdrawn. In 1942, a black worker was upgraded at the Timken-Detroit plant, but he was returned to his former status following a wildcat strike. Strikes likewise occurred at Chrysler's Highland Park plant and the Dodge Truck plant in response to the transfer of black employees to war production.

The most serious strike in protest of Negro employment occurred in the spring of 1943. Twenty-six thousand white workers struck the Packard airplane motor plant when three black workers were promoted to work on the final motor assembly line. Feelings ran so high among the striking workers that Walter White of the NAACP reported hearing one shout, "I'd rather see Hitler and Hirohito win the war than work beside a Nigger on the assembly line."[37] Many believe it was this strike that helped ferment the trouble that culminated in the Detroit riot that year, the nation's most devastating disturbance to that date. On the hot, muggy Sunday evening of June 20, 1943, perhaps a thousand people were on Belle Isle and on the bridge connecting it to the city. In the slow traffic and heat, tensions exploded and fighting began. Before six thousand troops could restore order, thirty-four people were killed. Twenty-five were Negro. One young white man, cruising the streets, bragged: "We killed eight of 'em. . . . I saw knives being stuck through their throats and heads being shot through, and a lot of stuff like that. . . . They were turning cars over with niggers in them, you should have seen it. It was really some riot."[38]

The Negro press covered racial injustice extensively both stateside and in the military. Black newspapers were actually banned from some military posts for a period, and some publishers had difficulty purchasing newsprint. The Justice Department reportedly considered sedition charges against some of these newspapers, since the Negro press was seen as the cause of racial unrest rather than for its role as chronicler of policies and events.

When I first became interested in joining the military service, I talked with servicemen home on leave, trying to determine which branch was most likely to eliminate racial discrimination. Aaron McGee, a sailor and a close family friend, believed that, in spite of many drawbacks, the navy would provide improved opportunity for me and gave me a copy of the *Blue Jackets Manual,* known as the "Sailor's Bible." An official navy pamphlet on race relations that I obtained stated, "The Navy accepts no theories of racial differences in inborn ability, but expects that every man wearing its uniform be trained and used in accordance with his maximum individual capacity determined on the basis of individual performance." In addition the pamphlet declared: "The idea of compulsory racial segregation is disliked by almost all Negroes, and literally hated by many. This antagonism is in part a result of the fact that as a principle it embodies a doctrine of racial inferiority. It is also a result of the lesson taught the Negro by experience that in spite of the legal formula of 'separate but equal' facilities, the facilities open to him under segregation are in fact usually inferior as to location or quality to those available to others."[39] The local navy recruiting office also informed me that the navy had abandoned its practice of segre-

A Chance to Serve

gated training camps as well as segregated sea-going assignments, so I decided to enlist in this branch of the service.

Historically, however, the navy has as inconsistent a track record as the army regarding the use of black personnel. During the War of 1812, black sailors served in all capacities aboard America's fighting ships. A Defense Department publication described the situation during the Civil War:

> Suffering from its long-standing shortage of manpower, the Navy began enlisting blacks as early as September, 1861. Blacks who early sought service, flocked to the Navy as entry into the Army was barred to them. . . .
>
> Blacks, however, were confined to the position of servant, cook, or Powder boy. By 1862, the regular seaman ranks were opened to blacks, and by war's end, some 30,000 blacks had served of a total Naval enlisted strength of 118,000, a much higher proportion than the Army. . . .
>
> Perhaps the most famous incident involving seafaring blacks occurred early in the war. In May 1862, Robert Smalls, a black pilot, and seven slave crewmen seized the Confederate ship *Planter*. Making their way through the defenses of Charleston harbor, they turned the ship over to Union blockade forces. As a reward, Smalls was appointed to a position in the Union Navy and after the war was appointed as a general officer in the South Carolina militia.[40]

Historian Lerone Bennett, Jr., described the *Planter* incident for *Ebony* magazine:

> Smalls was only 23 at the time, and his story reflected the contradictions of the slave system and the absurdities of racism. A native of South Carolina, born in slavery in Beaufort on April 5, 1839, he was one of scores of slave seamen who were impressed into service on Confederate ships at the beginning of the Civil War. Many of these seamen were better sailors than their masters. Smalls, in fact, was said to be one of the best pilots on the South Carolina coast. It was said he knew the location of every reef, shoal and torpedo in the Charleston harbor and that

A Certain Blindness

he could almost navigate the South Carolina coast with his eyes closed.

This is how Bennett described the crucial scene:

> As the *Planter* passed under the walls of Fort Sumter, Smalls stood in the pilot house "with his arms folded across his breast, after the manner of the captain," his head and face shielded by "the huge straw hat which Captain (Relyea) commonly wore on such occasions." Turning his back slightly to the sentinel, and shielding his face, he pulled the cord of the steam whistle, giving the countersign—three shrill sounds and one hissing sound.
> There was an electric moment of silence, a moment that aged Smalls and his crew, and then came the magic words of freedom:
> Pass the *Planter!*
> The sentinel added:
> Blow the damned Yankees to hell, or bring one of them in.
> Under the broad-brimmed hat, Smalls smiled and said softly:
> Aye, aye, sir.

The *New York Tribune,* as Bennett found, "said it was ironic and significant that 'a slave has brought away from under the very gun of the enemy, where no fleet of ours has yet dared to venture, a prize whose possession a commodore thinks worthy to be announced in a special dispatch.' "[41] Smalls received prize money and was named captain of the *Planter* for the duration of the war. He subsequently served in the U.S. Congress during Reconstruction.

During the balance of the nineteenth century, Negroes served in an integrated U.S. Navy averaging between 20 and 30 percent of the enlisted strength. They were, therefore, at the guns of ships that defeated the Spanish at Manila and Santiago. In the early twentieth century, due to legalized segregation, there was a cutback in the number of black sailors. In *Black Americans in Defense of Our Nation* the Defense Department ac-

A Chance to Serve

knowledged: "Blacks were prohibited from enlisting in the Navy after World War I. It was not until 1932 that blacks were permitted to enlist and then only in the messman's branch which was filled predominately with Filipinos. Only in 1942 did the Navy decide to accept volunteers for general service in all branches. Even then, blacks were prohibited from going to sea and were restricted to assignments ashore or in small harbor coastal craft."[42]

Strangely, during the period they were denied enlistment, black sailors were not barred from re-enlisting. As a result, there were black gunners, machinists, and other rated black sailors well into the 1930s. When enlistments were allowed to resume in 1932, black sailors were limited to subservient roles such as stewards and messmen, who prepared and served meals and maintained both the living and dining areas. However, as the Defense Department noted, "Despite the fact that their enlistment contracts restricted their training and duties, stewards, like everyone else aboard ship, were assigned battle stations, including positions at the gun and on the bridge. One of these stewards, Dorie Miller, became a hero on the first day of the war at Pearl Harbor when he manned a machine gun on the burning deck of the USS *Arizona* and destroyed two enemy planes."[43] Mess attendant Leonard Harmon, serving aboard the USS *San Francisco,* and cook William Pickney both received the Navy Cross for extraordinary heroism. Dorie Miller and Leonard Harmon both gave their lives in service to their country.

Reflecting the mood of the times, Secretary of the Navy Frank Knox announced in 1941 that the navy could not take Negroes into the general service because men live in such intimacy aboard ships, a decision that provoked loud protests from the Negro press and civil rights organizations. The situation did not escape notice by the national press, particularly when black boxer Joe Louis donated his entire purse from the Louis-Baer fight to navy relief and when Republican presidential nominee Wendell Wilkie condemned the navy's practice as a mockery of democracy. On April 7, 1942, Secretary Knox was forced to

A Certain Blindness

reverse his policy. Thousands of black volunteers hastened to join, feeling at long last that color would not be a factor in service to their country, only to discover the navy's plan for segregation in training and assignments. An isolated section of the Great Lakes Training Center was set aside for their training and renamed Camp Robert Smalls, after the Civil War hero.

In 1944, under Secretary of the Navy James Forrestal, a small number of these sailors were integrated on sea-going ships. It was soon thereafter that the navy announced it was abolishing all segregated training and assignments, and I enlisted, confident that my career in the "New Navy" would be based solely on my conduct and ability.

Recruitment officers recommended me for machinist school with special training in diesel engineering. They assured me I would receive this training since many reservists were being separated from the service, creating openings for regular navy men in this position. Upon completion of my physical examination, swearing-in, some testing, and orientation at the regional center in Detroit, I joined a large group of recruits to await assignment to boot camp. I did not know any of the others, nor did I see any other black faces anywhere. At this point I was called into a room where I was interviewed by a chief and two other petty officers. The chief asked if I was flat-footed; I said no, and this apparently agreed with the record on his clipboard. He mumbled that there must be a mistake because "all Niggers are flat-footed." At his request, I removed my shoes and socks and walked on some sensitized paper. The print showed that I was not flat-footed. I was too stunned to question the chief's motives, but perhaps I should have inquired because at that point I would have gladly confessed to having flat feet if I could have returned home. This was my introduction to the blemishes and foibles of this "New Navy."

The next morning we boarded a train, and I got to know several other recruits from Flint, especially Bob Anderson, whom I especially liked. During the afternoon each sailor was called into another car to receive his orders. As one by one the recruits returned from their interviews, I was able to examine several of their orders. Each sailor was designated an A/S (apprentice seaman), assigned to Camp Peary, Virginia, for basic training. My friend Bob Anderson learned he was to become a yeoman, as he had requested. When I was called, the officer handed me my orders: STM 2/C (steward's mate second class), bound for Bainbridge, Maryland. I asked the officer why I was being classed as a steward when my friends were rated as apprentice seamen going to Camp Peary. Surprised I would ask, he explained that apprentice seamen would have to go to boot camp, whereas, based on my test scores, I would go directly to school. Determined not to be placed in a subservient role, I assured him I had been told my test scores qualified me for machinist training, and I did not want to be a steward. The officer did change my orders to apprentice seaman and assigned me to Camp Peary, but he claimed I was denying myself training that could be valuable to my future. (I later learned that at that time nearly 95 percent of all black personnel in the navy were stewards, many of whom were diverted to the messman's branch when they thought they were joining the general service.) I also noticed that the officer giving me my orders wrote "Colored" on the cover of my file.

I was the only black seaman in Company 104, which numbered almost 150 men, but that posed no particular problem for me. The problem came when our company won the competition with the other area companies to score the most points for drills, inspection, and general efficiency. We earned a day off for sightseeing in historic Williamsburg, Virginia. The morning of the trip a lieutenant came to our barracks to see me. He said that since I was from Michigan I was probably not aware of "how things are down here" and that as a Negro I would not be served in Williamsburg's shops and restaurants.

While I was somewhat prepared to deal with individual prejudice, I was stunned to encounter widespread, institutional bigotry and greatly disappointed that the navy endorsed it by accommodating it. I refused to visit Williamsburg that day and

A Certain Blindness

was further dismayed when the other seamen in my company, some of whom I considered buddies, showed no concern or support. I felt totally isolated, especially since being abandoned was in such sharp contrast to my childhood when my white friends always showed their loyalty to me during difficulties.

A short time later we concluded our training and waited for our next assignments. Bob Anderson was transferred to Washington, D.C., for yeoman training. My orders were to report to a new ship stationed in Norfolk, Virginia, not to machinist training school as I had expected.

While stationed in Norfolk, I encountered, again, laws and customs that applied specifically to black Americans. On one occasion, after visiting the segregated black USO in town, I decided to take the local streetcar into the downtown section and remain aboard as it came to the end of the line and make the return journey to the naval station. In this way I would be assured a seat, as it was usually full of sailors. Approaching the downtown section, the streetcar stopped and two police officers came aboard. To my surprise, they approached me and asked where I was going. Startled at their interrogation, I proceeded to explain what I had planned to do. They said they supposed it was all right, especially if I did not get off, as "niggers are not allowed downtown after 10:00 P.M."

When I joined the ship's crew my initial duty was as a fireman tending boilers in the fireroom—the hottest, most miserable job I ever had. While most of the petty officers and enlisted personnel in the firerooms were basically easy to get along with, one, a chief petty officer from Mississippi, was clearly angry at my friendly association with the others. Working with him one morning on the four to eight watch, I operated the super heaters, which produced steam for accelerated speed. When the ship abruptly reduced speed, the safety valves went off briefly since it was nearly impossible to cut out enough burners to reduce the pressure so quickly. The chief petty officer ordered me to clean bilge plates for the next twelve hours. I eventually managed to transfer to the division maintaining and operating the auxiliary diesel engines aboard ship and the small diesel craft that transported personnel from ship to shore.

During my stint in the navy I traveled to sixteen countries on five continents. The most serious problem I had came near the end of my tour of duty in the Mediterranean, when we revisited Naples, Italy. The townsfolk here were especially friendly to black servicemen, since the troops of the 92nd Division had liberated the area from German occupation not long before. I hoped to contact a friend I had made on a previous visit but learned from her relatives that she had not yet arrived from her home in southern Italy, so I returned to the ship early, hoping to earn additional shore leave. That evening another boat operator came down to our compartment during his break to show us an Italian-made gun he had bought as a souvenir. While displaying it he accidentally discharged the gun, shooting himself in the hand. I took over his boat duty for the remainder of the night so he could get his hand treated.

The next day he and I were called before the ship's captain, who wanted to know who owned the gun and why I had operated the boat without permission from the duty officer. The boat operator never admitted that he owned the weapon, and I explained that I neither owned nor at any time handled it, but only saw it briefly before it was discharged. I also remarked that boat operators frequently exchanged duty, but not shore leave, without permission, and my only involvement was to help my fellow boat operator when the accident occurred.

Satisfied with my explanation and seeing no wrong in my conduct, the captain added that since we were not at sea but subject to the command of the European theater of operations, I would have to make a statement to some other officers regarding servicemen possessing illegal war souvenirs. Since the boat operator had been injured, the captain saw no further need for him to participate.

The other officers, however, charged me with bringing the gun aboard ship and ordered me to be court-martialed. Although there was no testimony or evidence that I committed the

A Certain Blindness

act, I was nevertheless found guilty and sentenced to serve time in the ship's brig. While I was later absolved and my record cleared, the suffering and distress associated with this entire matter were not so easily overcome. To make matters worse, a white marine sergeant told me my case was used as an example for other black servicemen, since there was great anxiety over black servicemen arming themselves aboard ships and on military bases.

Before the Uniform Code of Military Justice was enacted in 1950, it was unclear what constitutional rights, if any, were available to service members. In the highly racial atmosphere of those times I came to understand that for a black American to obey the law was no assurance of his protection, since the legal process itself could be used to prosecute and punish an innocent individual. It also left me with an indelible perception of the dichotomy between law and justice. Prior to this ordeal I believed that the law protected the rights of citizens and that only those who violated it were subject to prosecution and punishment. Having experienced what it was to be a victim I determined never to allow myself to be defenseless before the system again.

On July 26, 1948, President Truman ordered "equality of treatment and opportunity for all persons in the armed forces," strikingly similar to the wording contained in the Selective Service Act of eight years earlier. Segregated units took another six years to be dismantled. In 1949, 62 percent of the Negroes in the navy were in the stewards branch.

After Truman's order to integrate, army chief of staff General Omar Bradley made a speech in which he remarked that the army would have to retain segregation. One critic commented that "General Bradley's statement, subsequent to the President's orders, would seem to indicate that the President either did not mean what he said or his orders are not being obeyed."[44] Despite executive orders and legislation requiring integration and equal treatment, the military did not allow black servicemen "to break into a club that doesn't want them."[45]

A Chance to Serve

So sensitive were the armed forces to the subject that the State Department banned the motion picture "Home of the Brave" from being shown in Japan. It was the first film to depict racial prejudice in the armed forces, and the military government reasoned that the Japanese were "not sufficiently oriented" to understand this side of American life. On the other hand, the movie "PT-109," the dramatization of John F. Kennedy's wartime experiences, showed the navy as being racially integrated, when actually segregation and discrimination were the order of the day.

More than thirty years following my stint in the military, the U.S. Navy acknowledged that the promises of opportunity it made did not apply to me. A recruiting poster from the late 1970s aimed at attracting black recruits into the service asked: "Does a black man have a chance in the Navy? Twenty years ago he didn't. These days, a chance to go as far as his brains and dedication will take him." When the navy was hit by a sexual harassment and bias report in 1986, forcing it to open up assignments to women, it volunteered in 1987 that it has not done well in terms of black and Hispanic opportunity either. A study it requested in mid-1988 revealed widespread but subtle bias against minority sailors, pointing to little effort made by the navy "to educate officers in their responsibilities to promote racial equality, counsel black and Hispanic officers on how to succeed in a military society dominated by whites, and ensure that minority officers are given a fair share of prestigious positions."[46] Chief of naval operations Admiral Carlisle Trost instructed naval officers "to maintain a climate in the Navy that provides the opportunity for our people to perform and achieve realistic goals."[47]

My paternal roots—five generations (*left to right*): My great-grandmother Pearlalee, grandmother Jane, aunt Nettie, cousin Ethel, and Ethel's son, Lee Curtis, in 1904.

Uncle Bass Reeves, Deputy U.S. Marshal.

Bass Reeves (*second row, left*), pictured with the Federal Official Family (including U.S. Marshals, U.S. Commissioner, and U.S. District Attorney) on November 16, 1907, in Muskogee, Oklahoma.

Uncle Bass's daughter, Alice Spahn, a Muskogee, Oklahoma, public school teacher.

My maternal grandparents Charles Richard ("C.R.") and Estella Wilson on their wedding day in 1887.

The Wilson family (*first row, left to right*): uncle John, grandfather C.R., uncle Laurence, grandmother Estella, uncle Charles, and uncle George; (*second row, left to right*): uncle Harold, aunt Lucinda ("Cindy"), uncle Hughie, mother Jessie, and uncle Bob.

My father pictured with his English Setter, Tobe.

My father and his childhood friend "Dutch" Miller pose with one of their bird dogs.

My parents with their first child, my brother Lindell.

A family picture, taken a year after my father's death (*first row, left to right*): Mary Rose, Mother, and Wilma; (*second row, left to right*): Arthur, Lindell, and me.

Me and my cousin Adrienne during our preschool years.

The house on Lippincott Boulevard in Flint, Michigan, where I grew up.

My mother and one of her many civic groups, the YWCA youth group, in Flint.

Mother, with another civic group, the Blue Star Mothers, a veterans' support organization.

My graduation photo, Flint Central High School, 1945.

Me, with my company, during U.S. Navy boot camp training.

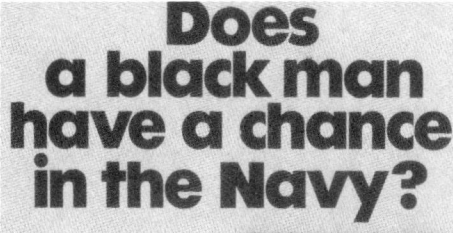

Does a black man have a chance in the Navy?

Twenty years ago, he didn't. But things have changed a lot since then.

Today the Navy has black lieutenants flying jets, black captains commanding ships, black admirals holding down key positions. In the enlisted ranks, black Navymen are rising in every specialty from advanced electronics to nuclear propulsion. It's a different Navy, and a better one.

Ask your Navy recruiter or call **800-841-8000** toll free. (In Georgia, 800-342-5855.) Does a black man have a chance in the Navy? These days, a chance to go as far as his brains and determination will take him.

NAVY

In 1974, some thirty years after my enlistment in the navy, this recruiting poster appeared in newspapers and magazines across the country.

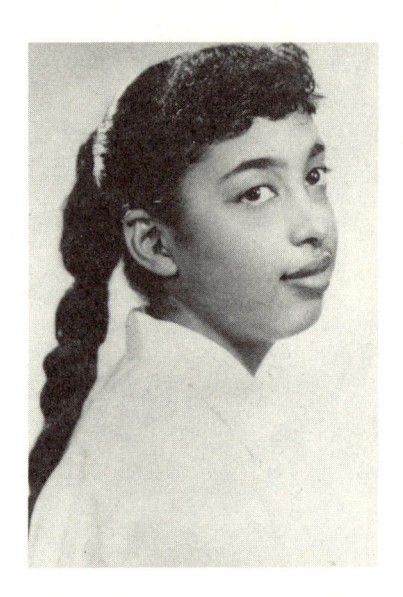

My cousin Nancy Todd, plaintiff in the landmark case *Brown v. Topeka Board of Education*.

My graduation from the Washburn University School of Law, Topeka, Kansas, summer class of 1956.

The wedding party of my marriage in Atlanta to Xernona Clayton, June 1974.

My mother, Jessie Brady, is introduced at my wedding reception, along with my brother Lind, his wife, Peggy, my brother-in-law Henry Watts, and his wife, my sister, Wilma Watts.

Me; my son, Paul, Jr.; my daughter, Laura; and my wife, Xernona, during the children's college years.

My mother is honored on her seventy-ninth birthday with a party and special public citations. Looking on are me, my sisters Wilma Watts and Mary Rose Holland, and my brother Lind.

My former law partners in a Chicago firm, attorneys Frank A. Anglin and William C. Starke.

Me and Leroy Day, my long-time friend from my navy years.

Cousin Howard Wilson, Aunt Cindy, and Uncle Alvin enjoy a family occasion in Atlanta.

Xernona and I chat with Mrs. Rosa Parks.

I share a smile and a handshake with Judge Elbert Tuttle, former chief judge of the Fifth Circuit Court of Appeals.

At a National Judicial Conference in St. Thomas, Virgin Islands, with (*left to right*) Doris McCree, U.S. Solicitor General Wade McCree, U.S. District Court Judge Horace Ward, Mrs. Luis, and Juan Luis, Governor of the Virgin Islands.

My cousin Dr. John Brooks Slaughter, chancellor of the University of Maryland.

My sixtieth birthday celebration, attended by more than four hundred friends and family members. Atlanta Mayor Andrew Young presents a proclamation as C. Delores Tucker, former Pennsylvania Secretary of State, looks on.

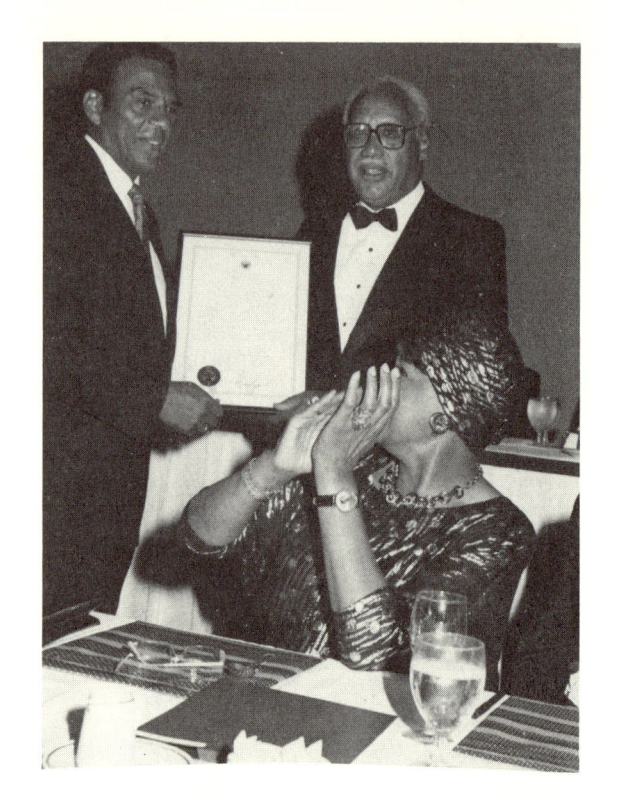

My brother Lindell and my sisters Wilma and Mary Rose make me a presentation.

Noted civil rights leaders who helped me celebrate (*left to right*): Congressman John Lewis, Dr. Ralph David Abernathy, Coretta Scott King, and Rev. Hosea Williams.

Judges make their presentation (*right to left*): Judge H. T. Lockard, Judge Thelma Wyatt Cummings, and Judge Horace T. Ward—all past national presidents of the National Judicial Council.

My son, Paul, Jr., and daughter, Laura Kathleen Brady.

6

The Supreme Court Rules for Justice

Brains, merit, and determination did little to enhance my experience in a racially discriminatory navy. After I was discharged from the service in 1947, I returned home to Flint, Michigan, where I enjoyed being close to family and friends again.

I fished and hunted with my brother Lind, who had several English setters, including Bruno, which Lind had trained in Italian. When Lind's military service was over, he returned to his job at Buick, where he was to become one of the first black skilled tradesmen. He attended college part time and was engaged to marry Peggy Harris, a former classmate of mine. My brother Art was working in Pontiac, Michigan, and he joined us often when we fished and hunted. My sisters, Mary and Wilma, were in their teens and still in school. My mother, Jessie, worked at the city library and was active in church and commu-

The Supreme Court Rules for Justice

nity organizations, notably the National Association for the Advancement of Colored People, the Urban League, the Blue Star Mothers, and the Young Women's Christian Association.

My future seemed to be taking shape and the outlook appeared bright. The preliminary paperwork having been completed, I was now awaiting the next term of the General Motors Technical Institute in Flint to begin training in auto engineering. I was excited when I was notified to report for an enrollment interview and orientation. The interview ended quickly when I was told I could not be enrolled because of my race. The facts that I met entrance requirements and was a veteran and that my family owned General Motors stock did not matter. At that point another man entered the office and offered me a factory job. When I asked what I would do and where the job could lead, he could not say, so I turned down the offer. I had known of many promising young black men whose ambition had been stifled after being forced into dead-end factory jobs. I bitterly considered that my white friend Bob Anderson had already found an office job at a Chevrolet plant since his discharge from the navy.

Shortly after that disappointing encounter my former shipmate Leroy Day learned that the Chesapeake and Ohio Railroad had opened a diesel plant in Grand Rapids, Michigan. Though our experience was limited to working with diesel-powered generators and engines for small naval craft, we were hired, and we were elated about the new training and opportunity we would get. Our excitement proved to be short-lived. Except for janitors, Leroy and I were the only Negroes employed in the plant. Several weeks after beginning our jobs, the company informed us we could not continue working in the engine service department. We were told that the conversion from steam to diesel engines resulted in the displacement of some employees and that the company faced the threat of strike by hiring new employees rather than first granting seniority preference. The railroad official acknowledged that Leroy and I were better qualified for our positions than the displaced workers, and he

A Certain Blindness

did not know if anyone had actually attempted to gain our positions.

At the time we had no way of determining whether racial considerations entered the picture, but I later learned that the four major operating railroad unions had maintained a strict prohibition against Negro workers. As late as 1943 these unions had been cited by the Fair Employment Practices Commission for impeding the war effort by excluding Negroes from membership and for their hostile acts against black workers.

In any case, at this point I felt totally defeated in my attempts to advance myself. On the one hand I couldn't enroll in school because of my race, and on the other hand I couldn't receive training on a job either, ultimately because of my race. In neither case was consideration given to my intelligence, determination, ability to learn, or any other aspects of worthiness.

Leroy and I were transferred to the coach yard to work as janitors for the Chesapeake and Ohio. Reflecting on my options, I considered how displeased my mother had been when during high school I was advised to learn a trade and not go to college. Mom's theme had always been to acquire education and knowledge for the purpose of advancement. Although I had completed the college preparatory program in high school, I had not yet pursued college; now it seemed my wisest course. I believed it could serve as protection against the type of vulnerability I had known.

I worked nights and attended the Grand Rapids branch of the University of Michigan during the day. I decided to quit work before the fall term to attend school full time, but first I wanted to take advantage of a reduced-fare special available to railroad employees. En route to see the western United States, I made a stop in Topeka, Kansas, to see my uncle and aunt, Alvin and Lucinda "Cindy" Todd, who were already entertaining my mother and sisters. Aunt Cindy and Mom had obviously been discussing me, because I had scarcely put down my bags on her steps before Aunt Cindy began a strong campaign to convince me to move to Topeka and enroll in college there.

The Supreme Court Rules for Justice

Learning of my interest in law, justice, and individual rights because of my personal experience and my attraction to the field of psychology due to my brother Art's hospital stays, Aunt Cindy reminded me that Topeka was the home of the famous Menninger Foundation, a center that embraced all areas of the psychiatric discipline including treatment, education, and research. Also within walking distance was Washburn University, known for its outstanding law school.

Since Aunt Cindy's advice was sound, I put off the rest of my trip to see the West (for nearly twenty years!) and enrolled for the fall 1949 term at Washburn University in Topeka. (Years later, looking back on my visit at that particular time, Aunt Cindy claimed: "If Paul had gone to California, he might have gone the wrong way. This was the turning point. Too much potential to waste his life.")

Topeka, the state capital and third largest city in Kansas, was in the days after World War II an attractive city with wide streets lined by mature shade trees. Located about sixty-five miles west of Kansas City in the fertile Kaw Valley, Topeka was an important distribution point for the rich farming community. Since the end of the Civil War Kansas had grown and prospered due to settlers being granted 160 acres by the Homestead Act of 1862. Once the grasslands were tamed, corn and wheat flourished, and Kansas became the granary of the nation by the century's end. Though it endured economic factors similar to the agricultural South, Kansas was more prosperous because, not relying on a single product, it produced other crops as well, including livestock, and it also processed the fruits of its soil in its own grain mills and meatpacking plants. Kansans increased the yield of their soil by mechanizing, and they improved their railroads and highways to get their produce to market.

When I began school at Washburn in 1949, the second largest grain elevator in the world dominated Topeka's skyline. The railroad was a dominant force in this city, too. The Atchison, Topeka, and Sante Fe Railroad rarely employed fewer

A Certain Blindness

than three to four hundred people in its principal Topeka offices and machine shops. The city also housed many hospitals, the best-known of them being the Menninger Foundation. With some ten thousand people employed in this medical community, the hospitals had long been the biggest industry in town. The sophisticated and enlightened people of Kansas had abolished capital punishment near the turn of the century, and, during the period of U.S. slavery, several underground railroad stations could be found in Topeka alone.

The enlightenment would seem to be a longstanding pattern. The entire Kansas Territory lay north of the line designated by the Missouri Compromise of 1820 to be the northern limit of slavery, so slavery was to be outlawed there. But when the territory applied for statehood, the antislavery Kansas Constitution denied the vote to any free Negroes residing there. Separate-but-equal schools were established during the state's first legislative session, and while segregation was abolished in 1876, it was reinstated in 1879. The desegregation laws of 1876 also prohibited racial discrimination in any licensed place of public accommodation or amusement or public transportation, laws which were violated by countless hotels, restaurants, and theaters. But by the time I began attending school in Topeka, Topeka had been a Jim Crow town as long as any of its black residents could remember. Since the white residents of Topeka wanted little to do with the Negro population, the few black businessmen and professionals were limited to serving their own kind, and the rest had to make do with menial work. But they perceived that things were worse for Negroes living elsewhere, so few wanted to rock the boat.

However, the very notion of keeping the Negro apart by law and custom was discriminatory, and the white population knew it. In the late 1800s, when black refugees from the South swelled the Negro population, Kansas, which had abolished school segregation in 1876, reinstated it in the elementary schools. As Richard Kluger observed in his remarkable book *Simple Justice,* "A specific exception was made for high schools, 'where no discrimination shall be made on account of color.' The wording of the law itself thus made it clear that Kansas knew that the establishment of separate schools was an unmistakable act of discrimination."[1]

But during World War II blacks served honorably both at home and abroad. After the war, they resented their inferior status more poignantly. They knew more than ever that their hopes were in the hands of the courts. When Negroes began to challenge the system, the National Association for the Advancement of Colored People was there to help. Recognizing that assistance in the legal arena was desperately needed, the NAACP, born only five years before, had by 1915 authorized a lawyer to represent its members before the Supreme Court in cases that would demonstrate violations of the Constitution.

By the time I started classes at Washburn University, trouble was already brewing in Topeka. Washburn itself maintained an atmosphere conducive to study and learning, and there was a sizable number of Negro students who seemed to fit in well. From fellow classmates Samuel C. Jackson, who later became assistant secretary of the federal Department of Housing and Urban Development, and Arthur Fletcher, a football hero who became assistant secretary of the Labor Department, I learned that Washburn had a tradition of welcoming Negro students. Nationally syndicated columnist Carl Rowan, who had served with an officer-training unit stationed at Washburn during World War II, described the campus as an "oasis of democracy set in a community of many social contradictions." He noted that the strict policy of segregation in theaters and restaurants somehow did not apply in the use of local buses. The elementary schools were segregated but the high school was not.

My education about these matters was not limited to what I heard on campus. Back in Flint, Michigan, my sister Mary had decided early in her life that she wanted to become a nurse. In high school she joined a group of other girls who shared her aspirations. When the group toured Flint's Hurley Hospital

A Certain Blindness

School of Nursing, Mary was told the school would not accept her because of her race. A student of high scholastic standing, Mary enrolled at Homer G. Phillips Hospital School of Nursing in St. Louis. She completed her nurse's training at Phillips, a large, segregated medical facility named for a prominent black physician. Having received all her previous education in Flint in completely integrated schools, Mary was ironically forced to obtain her career training in a totally segregated environment. She later received her undergraduate degree at Rutgers University and her graduate degree at Seton Hall University.

The ferment was also taking place right where I lived, in my aunt and uncle's home. In his book *Simple Justice* Richard Kluger recorded some events of my Aunt Cindy's early fight against discrimination in Topeka:

> In the black community, a few enlightened discontents began to emerge, like Lucinda Todd, an ex-schoolteacher who had been forcibly retired by the then common rule that married women could not teach. Mrs. Todd was especially sensitive to the education her daughter, Nancy, received and was increasingly disturbed when she found that it was not as rich as that offered white youngsters. She had wanted her daughter to play the violin, for example, but there was no musical instruction at any of the black schools. Then one day she saw a notice in the newspaper about a concert by the grade-school orchestra representing all eighteen schools in town, and she exploded. "I got on the phone to the music supervisor," she remembers, "and told him there were twenty-two grade schools in town, not eighteen, and why weren't the black children offered music instruction?" She was directed to the coordinator of black schools in Topeka, who assured her that colored folks did not want music instruction and could not afford to buy the instruments. She brought her case to the Board of Education and won it. There was another time—in 1944, she places it—when Mrs. Todd bought a ticket to the Grand movie theater, the one that admitted Negroes to a section of the balcony, and when she climbed up there the two dozen or so seats reserved for colored were filled, so she took a seat right across the aisle in the white section. A police-

The Supreme Court Rules for Justice

man came and told her that she could not do that and would have to sit in the colored section or nowhere. They gave her her money back. "They did things like that all the time," Lucinda Todd recalls. Soon she became active in the NAACP, was elected secretary of the branch, and once had Walter White as an overnight guest in her residence.[2]

The week after Aunt Cindy met with school officials, music supervisors came to the Negro schools and began organizing orchestras and bands. Of course Nancy participated in the program—and eventually majored in music, receiving a degree in music therapy at the University of Kansas.

Generally regarded as good schools, the black schools of Topeka did produce success stories—such as Frank Peterson, whom I knew at Washburn. Frank later served heroically as a marine fighter pilot during the Korean and Vietnam wars; he became the first black U.S. Marine Corps general. My cousin John Brooks Slaughter eventually earned a doctorate in engineering science; he has served as director of the University of Washington Applied Science Laboratory, as chairman of the National Science Foundation in Washington, D.C., and is now chancellor of the University of Maryland.

Nevertheless, the system of maintaining racially separate schools was a drain in many ways, and it hampered the schools from serving the notion of American unity. Any historical justification for their existence was—by now—completely outmoded. A few years before I arrived in Topeka, Mr. V. A. Graham successfully sued the Topeka Board of Education to admit black seventh- and eighth-graders into its junior high schools. Kluger recounted in *Simple Justice* how Topeka fought back:

> Eight black teachers were promptly fired. . . . The brief uprising that led to the integration of Topeka's junior high schools did not please the dominant white-supremacist element in the community. In 1942, a new superintendent of schools was brought in who would shortly spellbind the city's civic and commercial establishment with his silver tongue, ambassadorial smoothness, and the iron hand he clamped on the school system. He also

A Certain Blindness

made it unmistakably clear that he favored the continuing separation of the races in the elementary schools, and his agents moved forcefully to squelch interracial chumminess at the junior-high and high-school levels. For the black teachers and students of Topeka, the coming of Kenneth McFarland was a dark day. That he would soon become a nationally known and ceaselessly traveling evangelist of four-square Americanism, speaking to Rotary Clubs and Chambers of Commerce across the land under the sponsorship of *Reader's Digest* and later the General Motors Corporation, was an irony no harder for Topeka blacks to swallow than the pledge of allegiance their children offered every morning to the land that brought liberty and justice to all.[3]

Black teachers who challenged him in any way were fired, and dealing with the NAACP was considered just such a challenge. McFarland brought with him an effective weapon to control dissent: Harrison Caldwell, a black teacher he appointed director of Negro education. Outside the classroom, the policies Caldwell implemented kept the races separate, since his superintendent was of the mind that "black children aren't ready to go to the same schools as whites,"[4] as Caldwell said in a speech he delivered at the Rotary Club.

One of Caldwell's first acts was to remove the black elementary teachers from the Topeka Teachers Association. He then organized them into a black association cut off from the original group, with no contact or administrative recourse except through him. At lunch time he appeared in the cafeteria of the integrated Topeka High School to insure that black students sat together at the same tables; many were forced to move when there was an overflow of white students from other tables. Further, at assembly time, two bells were rung—one for white students to gather in the auditorium, and another for black students to assemble in a classroom for a talk that Caldwell would give. He also initiated a policy to segregate the senior proms; black members of the graduating class were turned away from the Meadow Acres Ballroom and told their prom was scheduled for Monroe grade school, where they were to

The Supreme Court Rules for Justice

dance to recorded music. To their credit, the white students stopped their dance in protest.

Aware of the dangerously backward movement in the education of black children, the Topeka branch of the NAACP entered the battle. In 1948 McKinley Burnett, a fifty-two-year-old stock clerk at the Veterans Administration hospital who had just become NAACP branch president, and his co-worker Daniel Sawyer petitioned the Topeka Board of Education, attacking McFarland-Caldwell policies. The petition detailed specific requests: that black teachers be involved in the junior and senior high schools; that women teachers, when qualified by training and experience, be eligible for principalships; that Negro students be able to participate in all branches of high school athletics and other extracurricular activities; and that a course in Negro history be taught in high school.

Nothing came of the meeting with the school board. My aunt Lucinda Todd, who was NAACP branch secretary, told writer Richard Kluger that the school board members "were just as insulting as they could be.... I remember Mr. Burnett standing up at our meeting and saying that we paid taxes just like everyone else—and that he paid the same twenty-five cents for a loaf of bread—and that he was entitled to the same rights as anyone else. This got one of the board members so angry that he jumped up and said, 'Let's go outside and settle this matter right now.' And Mr. Burnett, just as cool and dignified as could be, said, 'I don't settle these matters that way. I settle them by legal means.' "[5]

My involvement in the NAACP cause began with talks to students and various community groups regarding the Ramblers, the high school's black basketball team. The Ramblers, which competed with other teams in Kansas, Missouri, and Oklahoma, had long been a source of pride in the Negro community, and it provided a social outlet as well. But in order to ensure that students, teachers, and other personnel had access to every aspect of school life, the NAACP felt the segregated basketball team would have to be sacrificed. I discovered a lot of

A Certain Blindness

opposition to the proposal, and some members of the black neighborhoods branded me as an outsider. The issue at stake was important, though, and I, too, was caught up in the efforts to end school segregation.

The NAACP decided its next move would be to present a protest petition to the school board. The task of obtaining signatures proved to be monumental for the relatively small group of workers. I worked when time permitted, and my aunt Cindy was busy day and night. Since she did not drive, she traveled on foot, by bus, and whenever she could hitch a ride. Often she joined with a neighbor, Mrs. Daniel Sawyer, another tireless worker who had a small truck, and they rambled throughout the city in search of signatures.

The petition, signed by nearly fifteen hundred people, requested that the school board abolish racial segregation in all schools commencing with the 1950 fall term. Denying the request, the school board claimed that Negro children were "not ready" to be enrolled with white children. Moreover, the board told the group its position would not change until the law changed. In his lament over the decision, NAACP branch president McKinley Burnett declared, "Words will not express the humiliation and disrespect in this matter." The school board of Topeka never explained its assertion that Negro children were "not ready" for enrollment with white children, nor did they address the detrimental effects of segregation on Negro children.

The thoughts of many small Negro children were similar to my cousin Nancy, who recalled "being downtown and seeing white people eating at lunch counters in the five-and-dime stores and wishing I could do the same thing" or "going to Gage Park and asking to watch white kids swim in the huge fancy pool and wishing I could go into the water."

The Jim Crow lines were so tightly drawn that even half brothers and sisters, living in the same house, could not attend the same school if they were racially different. Expressing the mood of the white majority, Paul Wilson, the assistant attorney general for Kansas, remarked: "Most people involved probably

The Supreme Court Rules for Justice

thought segregation was okay. At least there was no pressure to change the state laws."

Famed psychiatrist Karl Menninger vigorously opposed the prevailing order, however. Discrimination had no place anywhere in the Menninger Foundation's facilities, which also included Winter Veterans Administration Hospital, reputedly the largest psychiatric institution in the country, and Topeka State Hospital.

Not long after becoming settled in school I was hired as a psychiatric aide, working under the auspices of the Menninger Foundation's tri-hospital plan. But Menninger personally refused a group of society women who volunteered their services to Winter Hospital, because they would not admit Negro women as members. An NAACP member himself, Menninger was a man of high ideals who encouraged foundation staff and employees to work for the NAACP cause as well. As a result, some of the aides and interns helped solicit signatures for the petition presented to the school board.

Menninger wrote to school superintendent Kenneth McFarland, as the psychiatrist later recounted in his autobiography *Sparks*. McFarland's answer assured Dr. Karl that those responsible for Topeka's schools were "earnestly striving to improve racial relations in Topeka and do everything possible to assist every citizen to realize the full measure of the rights that are constitutionally and morally his." Menninger responded:

> Thank you so much for taking the pains to write me at such length as you did on February 9th. I am glad to know that you and others in the school system are, as you say, "earnestly striving to improve racial relations in Topeka." I am not personally able to see that improvement taking place very rapidly and it is encouraging to know that you and others are working on it. I think it is a shame that a community which paid in blood and sorrow for the principle of freedom from 1860–1865 should now be guilty of as many Jim Crow practices as you and I know exist.
>
> I think I would be very discouraged were I a teacher of young people trying to talk about democracy and freedom and

A Certain Blindness

other ideals in the face of such a situation. And if I were a superintendent I think I should be very heartsick about the necessity of having to expect my teachers to be either hypocrites or be silent.[6]

By 1950, when meetings with the school board had produced no results, the NAACP decided to take the matter to court. On August 29, 1950, Aunt Cindy wrote to Walter White, executive secretary of the NAACP's national office in New York, requesting for the first time assistance in formulating legal action against the inequities found in Topeka schools. Both White and Thurgood Marshall, the NAACP's special counsel, had visited Topeka previously, where they had been guests in my aunt's home since Negroes were not accepted in the local hotels. They were generally familiar with the problems in Topeka and assigned Robert Carter and his assistant Jack Greenberg, both from the national office, to help John and Charles Scott and Charles Bledsoe from the Topeka branch prepare the case for trial. The Scotts, with their brother Elisha, Jr., also an attorney, had been Aunt Cindy's students when they were in elementary school. Their father, Elisha, Sr., known around Topeka as Mr. Civil Rights, had been an outstanding and courageous attorney over the years, and he helped found the local NAACP chapter.

Bob Carter immediately responded to the request for assistance and indicated the importance of winning cases "in both areas and states like Kansas where the pattern [of segregation] is not as definitely and rigidly set as it is in the deep South." Carter, who later became the NAACP's general counsel and then a federal district court judge, had experienced his own share of racial discrimination and prejudice. Raised in the North, he served in the army as a lawyer and was almost court-martialed himself following his successful defense of a black soldier charged with raping a white woman.

Carter announced the legal plan to attack the 1867 statute that first permitted the city to segregate the races. This tactic

The Supreme Court Rules for Justice

would entitle plaintiffs to an early trial, and they could bypass the U.S. Court of Appeals and go directly to the Supreme Court. It was agreed that there would be as many plaintiffs as could be obtained, representing various grades in schools throughout the city. The plan was to show that the students were being damaged by the practices of the school board. Also, specific relief would be requested by the plaintiffs for orders requiring their immediate enrollment in their all-white neighborhood schools.

Many problems confronted the relatively small group of overburdened workers who sought equality in Topeka public schools. Some local black citizens feared only the loss of their favorite basketball team, the Ramblers, and a possible worsening of conditions if an adverse ruling were entered. Others offered support but feared their personal involvement would result in a wave of reprisals, economic and otherwise. Some groups were openly hostile and favored segregated schools. No teachers outwardly supported the cause; of course, most of the black teachers were mindful that following the desegregation of the junior high schools, eight black teachers were immediately fired.

Throughout these very difficult times, the inspiring efforts of a relative outsider cannot be overstated. Esther Brown had lived comfortably with her husband and family in a suburb of Kansas City, Kansas. One day in 1948, while driving her maid home to nearby South Park, she saw the rundown school for Negro children. The school was without plumbing, had improper heating, and had only a tiny basement room to serve as a cafeteria. Shocked, but unaware the school district was in violation of the Kansas statute permitting segregation only in cities of more than fifteen thousand, Esther Brown began her crusade. Determined to do something about the conditions at the school, she almost single-handedly initiated the legal action that brought about the school district's compliance with the law and the Negro children's enrollment in the newly constructed white school. Her subsequent efforts in Topeka and across the state

A Certain Blindness

were an insipiration to all who sought justice in Kansas schools. The *Los Angeles Times* reported that in referring to Esther Brown, Aunt Cindy (the "most knowledgeable witness to that period") stated that her participation was immensely helpful in the struggle.

One of the most difficult jobs for the NAACP was the recruitment of plaintiffs. Some, like Aunt Cindy and Lena Carper, the mother of Nancy's close friend Kathy, readily stepped forward (some of Aunt Cindy's longtime friends thereafter feared to visit her). Others agreed only reluctantly, while some required great efforts to convince them the suit was in their own best interests. NAACP branch president McKinley Burnett was the driving force in this effort and spent long hours persuading Oliver Brown to become a participant. Although Brown was not a member of the NAACP, he was sought as a plaintiff because he was a minister, which gave him influence and credibility, and, with a union job at the Santa Fe Railroad, he was less subject to reprisals. Brown lived in close proximity to public schools for whites while his children were required to walk a long distance under hazardous conditions to reach the bus for the trip to their school.

Oliver Brown served as assistant pastor for St. John AME (African Methodist Episcopal) Church, where E. Woody Hall was pastor. I got to know Brown when I served as a Sunday school teacher and superintendent there, and I found him to be a quiet and deeply religious man. On more than one occasion he indicated to me how pleased he was in deciding to join the suit. Oliver Brown's name unintentionally was placed at the head of the list of plaintiffs by attorney Charles Scott's secretary when typing the complaint, which was officially filed as *Brown v. Board of Education of Topeka*. Neither Brown nor the other parents suspected the far-reaching effects the case would eventually have.

In the early stages of preparing the case, an in-depth survey of the elementary schools was needed, and Esther Brown promptly volunteered to search for someone qualified to per-

The Supreme Court Rules for Justice

form the study. Her range of contacts led her to Hugh W. Speer, an experienced school administrator and professor of education at the University of Kansas City (now the University of Missouri at Kansas City). Various local officials attempted to dissuade him from undertaking the task. One school administrator told Speer that "the NAACP group in Topeka were not the kind of people he wanted to get mixed up with." (This individual also indicated to Speer that he was leaving Topeka to take a position in a large city where he had bought a suburban home. "He was pleased to find a large new church nearby . . . and 'there was not a nigger or a Jew within ten miles.' ")[7]

Speer's study revealed that, with some exceptions, the schools for black children were on par with white schools. The attorneys therefore devised a legal strategy conceding the physical equality of the education facilities, and they would present the case on the theory that, socially, segregated schools were inherently unequal. Assistant general counsel Bob Carter had the feeling that this case could be one of the most important that the NAACP had handled. A little over a week before the trial in Topeka, he wrote Thurgood Marshall, "The more I think about this case, the more importance I think it will have on our main objective of securing legal support for our attack on segregation."[8]

The NAACP forces had generally believed that the school board would have gone along with its pleas had it not been for Superintendent McFarland's stiff resistance. Nearly three months before the scheduled trial date, three of the six members of the board that hired him were up for re-election. A strong campaign was waged by a slate of candidates organized to oppose McFarland, and there was some hope that the school board would reverse its position before the trial started. In a related matter the *Topeka Daily Capital* reported that a bill was moving through the state legislature that would deny citizens the right to inspect the financial records of boards of education in the state. A follow-up inspection of the Topeka board's records revealed that "thousands of dollars of Topeka public school money . . . have

A Certain Blindness

been spent in a manner considered improper by official auditors and repeated recommendations for tightening controls over these funds have not been followed by administrative officials."[9] The *Capital* reported that McFarland's secretary, who also served as clerk for the school board and business manager of the Topeka schools, had made purchases in violation of state law. In the wake of the scandal three new members were elected to the school board, and, although McFarland was not charged with any illegal acts, he resigned two days after the election. The election did not affect the school board's position regarding the lawsuit, however, and the trial began in the U.S. District Court in Topeka as scheduled.

The case of thirteen plaintiffs seeking immediate relief from the segregated conditions imposed by the school board under the state's permissive statute was now on its way into history. Several parents, such as my aunt Cindy, offered evidence about the conditions under which their children traveled to the four Negro schools from various parts of the city. Lena Carper testified about the distance her daughter Kathy had to walk to the bus stop and then often wait for the late bus. Ten-year-old Kathy, my cousin Nancy's close friend, told the court that often the bus was overcrowded and the children sat on each other. She also spoke of her white friends and playmates who attended school a short distance from her home. There were actually two all-white schools much nearer to her home than the Negro school. Oliver Brown related that his daughter Linda left home at about 7:30 A.M. in order to reach school by 9:00 A.M. It was necessary for her to walk through the Rock Island switching yard to reach her school bus. Many times she was required to wait for the bus in the cold, the rain, and the snow, and after the thirty-minute ride to school she sometimes had to wait another half hour outside the school for it to open. The nearest white school was about seven blocks from their home and did not entail any hazardous travel.

Next came the expert witnesses. Hugh Speer testified that

The Supreme Court Rules for Justice

the Topeka curriculum or any school curriculum cannot be equal under imposed segregation; this included the total school experience of a child in developing his personality and social adjustment. Horace English, full professor of psychology at Ohio State University for thirty years, pointed out that there is a tendency to learn what people say we can learn; thus legal segregation has the effect of depressing the Negro child's expectancy and is, therefore, prejudicial to his learning. The testimony of Louisa Holt, a sociologist who taught at Menninger's and at the University of Kansas, proved to be significant as some of her language was adopted in the ultimate decision. She stressed that enforced separation of children inevitably is interpreted by both races as denoting inferiority of the Negro group. Holt reasoned: "A sense of inferiority must always affect one's motivation for learning sense. It affects the feeling one has of one's self as a person." She did not believe that the joining of the races at the junior high school level would correct the traumatic effects of the earlier experience.

The Topeka school board in its defense did not refute the testimony of the plaintiffs. It showed, rather, that district schools were safely and regularly operated in compliance with pertinent regulations: similar books, supplies, curriculum, and teacher salaries were provided. School superintendent Kenneth McFarland maintained furthermore that there was "no objective evidence that the majority sentiment of the public would desire a change" in policy.[10]

When all the testimony was in, the three-judge panel delivered its unanimous decision on August 3, 1951. The judges stressed that since there were only four colored schools compared with eighteen white schools in the Topeka school district, colored children traveled much greater distances than their white counterparts and indeed traveled much greater distances than they would if they attended the white schools. Adopting the language of the expert witnesses brought in by the NAACP, particularly the testimony of Louisa Holt, the court stated:

A Certain Blindness

> Segregation of white and colored children in public schools has a detrimental effect upon the colored children. The impact is greater when it has the sanction of the law for the policy of separating the races is usually interpreted as denoting the inferiority of the Negro group. A sense of inferiority affects the motivation of a child to learn. Segregation with the sanction of law, therefore, has a tendency to restrain the educational and mental development of Negro children and to deprive them of some of the benefits they would receive in a racial integrated school system.

The court unanimously decided: "We are accordingly of the view that the *Plessy* and *Lum* cases, *supra,* have not been overruled and that they still presently are authority for the maintenance of a segregated school system in the lower grades. The prayer for relief will be denied and judgment will be entered for the defendants for costs."

Though the NAACP lost the case at the local level, the district court was clearly inclined to accept the contention of the plaintiffs but knew the Supreme Court would have to overrule itself on the issues at stake in the *Plessy* and *Lum* cases. In *Plessy v. Ferguson* (1896) the Supreme Court upheld a Louisiana statute that commanded railway companies to provide separate cars for Negro and white passengers. Homer Plessy, white by color and seven-eighths white by blood, was arrested and convicted for refusing to leave a whites-only car. The Court ruled that "separate but equal" laws did not violate the equal protection clause of the Fourteenth Amendment, and thus the concept became established in American law. In 1927 the Court reaffirmed its position that segregation did not violate the Fourteenth Amendment in *Gong Lum v. Rice* (1927), when a girl of Chinese ancestry sought and was denied admission to a white school in Mississippi. Although a number of decisions over the years granted relief to Negroes under the Fourteenth Amendment, the Supreme Court avoided deciding whether the *Plessy* formula was still constitutionally valid, thus leaving intact the issue of segregated public education.

But pressure was mounting from several arenas at once for

the Court to grapple with the issue directly. There were four other school segregation cases making their way to the Supreme Court, and a majority of the justices voted jurisdiction in them. *Brown* was set for hearing in the Court's 1952 term with the four other appeals. Since the issues were similar, the Court sought the benefit of argument from different aspects and settings. The other cases were *Briggs v. Elliott,* South Carolina; *Davis v. County School Board of Prince Edward County,* Virginia; *Belton v. Gebhart* and *Bulah v. Gebhart,* both Delaware; and *Bolling v. Sharpe,* District of Columbia. Justice Tom Clark remarked that *Brown* was to lead "so that the whole question would not smack of being a purely Southern one."[11]

As in *Brown,* the Delaware cases also established clearly that black students were penalized by segregation. Before reaching his decision, Collins Seitz, chancellor of the Delaware Chancery Court, personally observed the schools for black and white students and found the differences overwhelming. Seitz's decision was searing:

> Defendants say the evidence shows that the state may not be "ready" for non-segregated education and that a social problem cannot be solved through legal force. Assuming the validity of the contention without for a minute conceding the sweeping factual assumption, nevertheless, the contention does not answer the fact that the Negro's mental health and therefore his educational opportunities are adversely affected by state-imposed segregation in education. The application of constitutional principles is often distasteful to some citizens, but that is one reason for constitutional guarantees. The principles override the transitory passions.[12]

Chancellor Seitz went beyond the decision made by the district court in Kansas and ruled within the separate but equal doctrine that the plaintiffs were denied equal protection of the law by their inferior school facilities. He believed the concept in *Plessy* should be discarded but reasoned that it was the Supreme Court's place to overrule itself. Viewing the right to relief in

Belton v. Gebhart and *Bulah v. Gebhart* to be personal, however, Seitz ordered the immediate admission of the Negro plaintiffs to the superior white schools in their communities. This marked the first time in America a segregated white public school was ordered by law to admit Negro students.

Meanwhile, in Kansas the Topeka school board—under the sway of the newly elected members—was insisting the state attorney general step in to defend the early Kansas statute that permitted school segregation. Indeed, several weeks before the *Brown* case was scheduled for argument the board announced it would not defend the case before the Supreme Court. The Topeka school board filed a brief, stating that, "having resolved to terminate segregation in the elementary schools," it "no longer has an actual interest in the controversy over the constitutionality of segregation in such schools."[13] The state attorney general for his part was of the view that, since the school board was the defendant and the school board's policy was at issue, he as attorney general need not make a defense on behalf of the state. Reversal of the board's policy indicated that it no longer chose to exercise its authority under the permissive statute. But the Supreme Court intervened and ordered Kansas to participate: "Because of the national importance of the issue presented, because of its importance to the State of Kansas we request that the State present its views at oral argument. If the State does not desire to appear, we request the Attorney General to advise whether the State's default shall be construed as concession of invalidity."[14]

In response the attorney general of Kansas pointed out that he would not concede the invalidity of an act passed by his state legislature, as such an act is presumed to be constitutional until declared otherwise by the Supreme Court. He therefore filed a brief and appeared for argument. The exchange between the Supreme Court and the state of Kansas indicated some confusion on both sides; while one extended itself in seeking help, the other simply did not want to be involved. In any case the rights of the plaintiffs were becoming more blurred in the overall picture.

In Kansas there appeared to be another type of official

action taking place. According to the *Topeka State Capital,* a "statewide survey of first-class Kansas cities which still have segregation revealed a mass unannounced weeding-out of Negro teachers is taking place" as school boards failed to renew the contracts of its most recently employed Negro teachers. "The boards have anticipated the end of segregation for several years by filling all vacancies with white teachers." The article was clear that these decisions were made at executive sessions of the school boards and not in open meetings.[15]

On June 8, 1953, the Supreme Court ordered the five cases to be re-argued on October 12 and asked litigants to provide evidence showing whether or not they could determine if the framers and ratifiers of the Fourteenth Amendment understood it would abolish school segregation or allow future congresses or courts to do so. The five questions posed by the justices required a gargantuan amount of research, which was made even more imposing because many scholars had already committed themselves to other study projects for the summer.

Before the school segregation cases came before the Court, however, Chief Justice Frederick M. Vinson died, on September 6, 1953. President Dwight D. Eisenhower appointed Earl Warren, then governor of California, to head the Supreme Court. The new chief justice did not rush the decision on *Brown,* partly because he wanted a unanimous decision and partly because it took five months for the Senate to confirm his appointment, which it did unanimously. Once Warren obtained the support of all the justices to end school segregation, he decided to write the opinion himself in a manner that would be clear even to the lay reader.

On May 17, 1954, the entire Supreme Court of the United States proclaimed racially segregated public schools to be illegal. "In the field of public education," Chief Justice Warren declared as he read the *Brown v. Board of Education* decision, "the doctrine of 'separate but equal' has no place. Separate educational facilities are inherently unequal." In a non-accusatory fashion, the document relied on the equal protection clause of the Fourteenth

A Certain Blindness

Amendment of the Constitution and dismissed the relevance of applying *Plessy* to contemporary public education. Thus while not directly overruling the 1896 concept of "separate but equal" established by *Plessy,* the Court upheld the contention of the plaintiffs that separate educational facilities are inherently unequal even if comparable in physical accommodations. The Court left no doubt with respect to the constitutional right of every American child to public education—unsegregated by race—and their chance to learn and grow and be treated as full citizens of the society into which they were born.

Yet, recognizing the great variety of conditions throughout the country, the Court scheduled further input in how the decision was to be implemented. Thurgood Marshall, chief counsel for the cases and now himself a Supreme Court justice, stated that he believed segregated schools would be eliminated within five years and that segregation of any kind would be unknown within ten years, coinciding with the 1963 centennial of the Emancipation Proclamation. The feeling was that the Court had finally made good on the Constitution's promise as uttered in the Fourteenth Amendment, that no state could deny to any of its citizens equal protection of the law.

Louis H. Pollack, dean of the Yale University Law School, called the *Brown* decision "the most important American governmental act of any kind since the Emancipation Proclamation."[16] It certainly went on to affect the entire fabric of American society, as newspaper columnist James J. Kilpatrick recounted:

> In any list of the Supreme's Court's greatest cases—great in terms of their impact upon our country and its institutions—the several cases lumped together as "Brown" would rank near the top. By that opinion, the Court put an end to school segregation in 17 states, but the Court did far more: It set in motion the dammed-up moral and political forces that would produce a social and legal revolution.
>
> Everything flowed from Brown. The resulting flood wiped out state sanctioned segregation in parks, theatres, restaurants, libraries and public transportation. The decision led to the Civil

The Supreme Court Rules for Justice

Rights Act and the Voting Rights Act to equal opportunities at law in housing and employment. The decision changed the population patterns of cities across the country. In any metaphor—landmark, watershed, earthquake, tidal wave—the Brown decision had cataclysmic effect.

I vividly recall the great joy in my aunt and uncle's household, and my cousin Nancy Todd remembered that "the telephone never quit ringing." In addition to great optimism, I felt relieved that the decision served notice that the injustice, humiliation, and abuse black citizens were daily forced to endure were no longer sanctioned by law. Customs that held us as inferior would have to be abandoned.

By this time I had decided on a career in law and had entered law school. I had been greatly inspired by the tireless efforts on the part of the black lawyers and wanted to play a role myself in seeking justice for all under the objective rule of law.

The year before the decision in *Brown,* I had married Mary E. "Betty" Lee of Pittsburgh, Pennsylvania. Betty had come to Topeka to do field work at Menninger's as a graduate student from Smith College. We lived on campus in housing provided for veterans and, although we had no children at the time, I was active with various groups of young people, helping to prepare them for a future that loomed so brightly. Members of my family in Michigan were all doing well. My brother Lind and his wife, Peg, had two children, Linda and Steve; my sister Wilma was about to finish high school; and my sister Mary finished nursing school in St. Louis and had married Clay Holland, Jr. They lived in Washington, D.C., where Clay, a University of Michigan graduate in engineering, worked for the navy and attended law school.

I contemplated how "ordinary" people had been instrumental in bringing about the *Brown* decision. Ordinary, midwestern Topeka had seemed an unlikely environment to produce a landmark desegregation case. "Why Kansas?" was exactly the question Paul E. Wilson posed. Professor of law at the Univer-

A Certain Blindness

sity of Kansas who, as assistant attorney general of Kansas, had participated in the argument and re-argument of *Brown* before the Supreme Court, Wilson wondered how a quiet, conservative town like Topeka could earn a reputation for discriminatory acts against its black citizens. In an article Wilson published in the *University of Kansas Law Review* ten years after *Brown* was decided, he remarked: "For nearly a hundred years Kansas had boasted of its tradition of freedom. Kansas had started John Brown on his road to Harper's Ferry and glory. Kansas was firmly aligned with the Union during the Civil War and during the early years of statehood Union Veterans determined the State's policy. To many, it seemed indeed strange that Kansas should be aligned with South Carolina and Virginia and Delaware in defense of a twentieth century vestige of slavery." Kansans "are like most other Americans," he wrote. In the years since the Emancipation Proclamation their social attitudes "have experienced . . . the same growing pains that have been felt elsewhere." Wilson admitted, however, that the Kansas approach to Negro equality "has been characterized by inconsistency and indecision and often by injustice."[17]

Yet the *Brown* decision was not voted the top news story of 1954. The Associated Press placed the desegregation story second on its top ten list, after the censure of Wisconsin senator Joseph R. McCarthy. That year the French were defeated in Indochina, and Americans were assured that the United States would not be pulled into an Asian land war (but the U.S. Navy sent a ship to Southeast Asia to "win friends for the United States"). In 1954 Roger Bannister broke the four-minute mile in England (time 3:59:4); Jonas Salk, a University of Pittsburgh physician, developed a trial polio vaccine; and Bruce Catton won the National Book Award as well as a Pulitzer Prize in history for his book *A Stillness at Appomattox*—the Civil War was ended at the Appomattox Courthouse in Virginia when General Lee surrendered his army there to General Grant.

7

An Absence of Moral Leadership

Following the May 31, 1955, Supreme Court decisions that legal scholars have dubbed *Brown II,* Thurgood Marshall acknowledged that "desegregation will become a reality only if Negroes exhibit real militancy and press relentlessly for their rights."[1]

The initial elation experienced in Topeka's community after the Supreme Court announced its ruling faded by September 1955 when nothing changed. My cousin Nancy Todd was never admitted to the nearby white school, and neither were any of her black friends. The Topeka school board said their desegregation plan was not ready to be implemented, and the federal district court determined that the delay was permissible because the school board had at least made a "good faith" start. This was, of course, the same school board that declared to the Supreme Court prior to argument for *Brown I* that it "no longer has an

A Certain Blindness

actual interest in the [school desegregation] controversy" since it was already (in 1953) making plans to desegregate its schools. The original order to desegregate the Topeka schools remains in effect—more than thirty years later! Although Nancy's constitutional rights were vindicated, she was never permitted to walk the few blocks to attend her neighborhood school, and even today the burden falls on any plaintiff to prove that illegal segregation exists.

The delay in granting equal justice to the nation's African-American citizens is business as usual. A writer for the February 1973 *American Heritage* magazine observed: "Since the Constitutional Convention of 1789, the issue of race had either been compromised or evaded, except during Reconstruction. No branch of government had been willing to confront it squarely and, as Justice Jackson commented during the oral argument of *Brown,* 'I suppose that realistically the reason this case is here is that action could not be obtained from Congress.' "

Congress had not passed any civil rights legislation since 1875, and the few laws that were on the books were not enforced. As a whole, the United States had not been willing to take the necessary steps to ensure that its Negro citizens could enjoy the same rights as its white Americans. And when a Negro looked to the federal courts for protection, he was just as likely to be frustrated.

The 1857 *Dred Scott* decision was just such a case in point. One of the earliest attempts on the part of a black man to realize racial justice, its outcome was tragic. Post–Civil War amendments and Reconstruction raised Negro hopes, which were dashed again when the 1896 *Plessy* decision revealed the judicial perception that black Americans weren't fit to associate with white citizens. In spite of the equal protection clause of the Fourteenth Amendment, most court decisions reflected the view that Negroes were inherently unworthy of the rights white people could enjoy without question, without litigation. As an example, of the twenty-eight cases involving the Fourteenth Amendment brought before the Supreme Court between

An Absence of Moral Leadership

1868 and 1911, twenty-two were decided adverse to the Negro's rights—and the Fourteenth Amendment was adopted for the benefit of the Negro!

The Supreme Court issued no decision granting full equality until *Brown,* which seemed to remove black citizens from the special and inferior category to which they had been relegated. On May 17, 1954, the Court stated unequivocally that segregating Negro children in public schools deprived them "of equal protection of the laws guaranteed by the Fourteenth Amendment." But instead of specifying that relief was to occur immediately, the Court invited segregating states to offer input on how desegregation might be implemented. When Chief Justice Earl Warren read the *Brown II* opinion of the unanimous Court on May 31, 1955, he explained:

> Full implementation of . . . constitutional principles may require solution of varied local school problems. School authorities have the primary responsibility for . . . solving these problems; courts will have to consider whether the action of school authorities constitutes good faith implementation of the governing constitutional principles. Because of their proximity to local conditions and possible need for further hearings, the courts which originally heard these cases can best perform this judicial appraisal. Accordingly, we believe it appropriate to remand the cases to those courts.

Warren concluded that the courts were to enter "such orders and decrees consistent with this opinion as are necessary and proper to admit to public schools on a racially nondiscriminatory basis with all deliberate speed the parties to these cases." Making the constitutional rights of the plaintiffs dependent on the vague, immeasurable standard of "all deliberate speed" on the part of the defendants certainly sounded like a retreat from the decision in *Brown I,* especially considering the legal truism that a constitutional right is a personal and present right which, if not exercised when desired, is forever lost.

During oral argument the NAACP had recommended that

A Certain Blindness

the Court demand desegregation to begin in autumn 1955 and be completed by autumn 1956. Realizing that some delay might be necessary in some instances, the NAACP lawyers felt that prompt, decisive action was needed to avoid further impairment of the plaintiffs' constitutional rights.

But the Supreme Court believed that the federal district courts, which understood local conditions, and the school boards, which were responsible for solving the problems, would implement the desegregation order promptly, and the whole process would be short-lived. The ruling itself, however, not only denied plaintiffs their constitutional rights, but also invited delay and confusion. Consequently, while the 1954 ruling known as *Brown I* has been described as a "great decision," the 1955 *Brown II* ruling was a "great mistake."[2] The delay occasioned because of *Brown II* occurred for the sole purpose of allowing compliance on terms acceptable to white Southerners.

Actually, some segregated communities, such as Baltimore, St. Louis, and Louisville, desegregated their schools on a voluntary basis after *Brown I*'s decision, and the process went along well. But while the white student body accepted ten Negro students without antagonism to a school in Milford, Delaware, adult pro-segregationists protested and picketed and stirred up a mob outside the school, and only the firm stand on the parts of the mayor and chief of police restored order. When the arguments for *Brown II* opened, lawyers speaking for the defendants in the Delaware cases (*Belton v. Gebhart* and *Bulah v. Gebhart*) referred to the Milford situation and urged the Supreme Court to permit the transition to desegregated schools to occur gradually. When the *Brown II* ruling was announced, the decision directing immediate admission of the Delaware plaintiffs to public schools on a non-discriminatory basis was reaffirmed, but the justices also sent the two cases back to the Delaware Supreme Court "for such further proceedings" as might be needed.

The plaintiffs in Delaware and Kansas could have enjoyed

immediate relief if the school boards would have divided the total school population into geographic districts rather than racial groupings. Not until thirteen years later was such a plain and simple remedy adopted by the Court in *Green v. County School Board of New Kent County, Virginia* (1968).

That there was an entrenched attitude against mixing the Negroes among white schoolchildren especially in the Deep South was well known to the Supreme Court justices, so they set no firm date by which desegregation was to be accomplished, thus actually providing the means for undermining what they had ordered in *Brown I*. In attempting to placate the white citizenry who would be touched by the ruling, the Court appeared to indicate that it was not going to enforce the very thing it demanded. The justices warned that "these constitutional principles cannot be allowed to yield simply because of disagreement with them," but what the Court demanded flew in the face of centuries of government-sanctioned supremacy. And what happened caused the worst fears of the NAACP attorneys to be realized.

Several months after the 1954 decision, the White Citizens Council was formed in Mississippi, and it soon spread across the South. The express purpose of the council was sworn resistance to school integration "by every lawful means." When the *Brown II* ruling was announced, the *New Orleans Times-Picayune* assessed it as "pretty much what Southern attorneys in general had asked for."[3] A Mississippi lawyer declared: "We couldn't ask for anything better. . . . Our local judges know the local situation and it may be 100 years before it is feasible." In Georgia, Lieutenant Governor Ernest Vandiver was pleased with the role assigned their local judges because "they are steeped in the same tradition that I am."[4] Tom Brady, a Yale-educated circuit judge in Mississippi, explicitly advocated breaking the law:

> When a law transgresses the moral and ethical sanctions and standards of the mores, invariably strife, bloodshed and revo-

A Certain Blindness

lution follow in the wake of its attempted enforcement. The loveliest and purest of God's creatures, the nearest thing to an angelic being that tread this terrestrial ball is a well-bred, cultured Southern white woman or her blue-eyed, golden-haired little girl. We say to the Supreme Court and to the northern world, "You shall not make us drink from this cup." . . . We have, through our forefathers, died before for our sacred principles. We can, if necessary, die again.[5]

And of course many did die and many more had to face violent mobs when they tried to exercise newly won rights. Frank Freidel noted in the book *America in the Twentieth Century* that "each September, mob action against integration in a few communities within the South attracted widespread attention throughout the world."[6] But little progress was being made, as Freidel recounted:

By the fall of 1957, of some 3,000 biracial school districts in the South, a total of 684 had begun desegregation. Schools within these districts in large cities in the upper South or the border area, like Washington, Baltimore, Louisville, and St. Louis, opened quietly on an integrated basis. But 2,300 districts, including all those in the Deep South and in Virginia, remained racially separate. Some districts attempted desegregation on a very slow, "token" basis.[7]

The Civil Rights Act passed by Congress in 1957 gave federal protection to Negroes wishing to vote, and black leaders succeeded in getting more Negroes to the polls, an act which brought white anger down upon some of them. Between the two issues of voting and desegregation there was violence. Three lynchings occurred in Mississippi in 1955. Reverend George Lee and Lamar Smith, both NAACP members, were slain for refusing to strike their names from voter registration lists. Emmett Till, a youngster, was kidnapped and murdered by three white men. As the years wore on, the toll of dead and wounded read like a list of war casualties.

Who was responsible for safeguarding the rights granted

under the laws? The solicitor general admitted to the Supreme Court in 1955 that "the responsibility for achieving compliance with the Court's decision in these cases [the *Brown* rulings] does not rest on the judiciary alone. Every officer and agency of government, federal, state and local, is likewise charged with the duty of enforcing the Constitution and rights guaranteed under it."[8]

But it rapidly became clear that the executive branch of the government was not about to conform to its responsibilities. After *Brown I* federal aid was still provided for the construction of segregated schools, about which President Eisenhower commented, "I am sure Americans want to obey the Constitution, but there is a very great practical problem involved, and there are certainly deep-seated emotions." Displeased with the Court's ruling, Eisenhower withheld the moral support of his office as well as the resources available to the executive branch. Begging the question, the president urged citizens to be calm: "If ever there was a time when we must be patient, without being complacent, when we must be understanding of other people's deep emotions, as well as our own, this is it. . . . But I have never yet given up my belief that the American people, faced with a great problem like this, will approach it intelligently and with patience and with understanding and we will get somewhere; and I do deplore any great extreme action on either side."[9]

Undoubtedly Eisenhower's failure to demand compliance abetted attempts to circumvent the law. One example of this was cited by Harry S. Ashmore in his book *An Epitaph for Dixie:*

> [Virginia] governor Thomas B. Stanley's first reaction was the formal announcement that he would convene a meeting of local and state officials to "work toward a plan which shall be acceptable to our citizens and in keeping with the edict of the Court. Views of leaders of both races will be invited. . . ." Six weeks later Stanley was calling his fellow governors into session to plan resistance and announcing that he would use every means at his command to continue segregated schools. Within a year Virginia

had developed the doctrine of interposition and was using the full weight of state government not only to maintain segregation in those districts that desired it, but to prevent any degree of integration in those that appeared willing to accept it.[10]

Not long after the Court proclaimed school segregation to be unconstitutional, Southern legislators came out with their own Declaration of Constitutional Principles, which came to be called the Southern Manifesto. Signed by nineteen senators and eighty-two congressmen, the document reasoned that "the unwarranted decision of the Supreme Court in the public school cases is now bearing the fruit always produced when men substitute naked power for established law." When they said they were determined to resist compliance by "any lawful means," they were deliberately disregarding established law in favor of maintaining a condition judicially declared unlawful. The Southern Manifesto, like so many other inflammatory statements made by men in high places, also contributed to direct defiance of the law and much violence.

Perhaps no reactions were more incendiary than those of James O. Eastland, senior senator from Mississippi, who asserted that racial integration would never come to his state, claiming "there is no basis for compromise." Speaking in Senatobia, Mississippi, the day the *Brown I* ruling was announced, Eastland declared: "The Constitution of the United States was destroyed because the Supreme Court disregarded the law and decided integration was right. . . . You are not required to obey any court which passes out such a ruling. In fact, you are obligated to defy it."[11] From the floor of the U.S. Senate, he proclaimed, "The Negro race is an inferior race," and he warned the nation that the white people of Mississippi would "maintain control of our own elections and . . . protect and maintain white supremacy throughout eternity." He denounced the decision banning racial segregation as "an illegal, immoral and sinful doctrine" and called on Southerners to fight integration "every step of the way." Eastland assured them "that South-

An Absence of Moral Leadership

ern people would not be violating the Constitution or the law when they defied 'this monstrous proposition.' "[12]

Even William Faulkner, the Nobel Prize-winning author whose writings expressed the thoughtful Southerners' views, could not contain his underlying belief that black children should not be mixed with white. Faulkner protested, "If I have to choose between the United States Government and Mississippi, then I'd fight for Mississippi against the United States, even if it meant going out into the street and shooting Negroes."[13] In eight Southern states, the governors or legislatures—or both—publicly proclaimed a firm resolve to maintain racial segregation in public schools.

But there were a courageous few in the South who mounted the platform in favor of equal educational opportunities for blacks. Among them was John B. Orr, Jr., a Florida legislator who, in 1956, stood alone in voting against bills intended to circumvent the Supreme Court's desegregation decision. Orr stated:

> I believe that had we devoted as much energy, time, and talent to discovering means to live under the law instead of in defiance of it, we could have discovered a way. I believe segregation is morally wrong. . . . If we hope to maintain our leadership among free peoples of the world, if we hope to give hope to those subjugated people behind the Iron and Bamboo Curtains, we must demonstrate by our acts as well as our words that our democratic form of government places no artificial barriers on the opportunity to live and work with our fellow men. . . .
>
> For us to set an example of hypocrisy and deceit—of disrespect for our laws—will surely do more harm to our children than will result from their being seated in a classroom next to one whose skin is of a different color.[14]

Aside from the vicious rhetorical attacks and open defiance, the *Brown* decisions have evoked honest debate by constitutional law scholars. While all court cases are open to varying amounts of criticism, major portions of the legal community

A Certain Blindness

joined in unparalleled condemnation of the Court, most of whom, aside from their obvious racial bias, knew better.

For over 150 years, it had been settled constitutional law that the Supreme Court is the ultimate interpreter of the American Constitution. Chief Justice John Marshall, recognized as the nation's greatest jurist, asserted in *Marbury v. Madison* (1803) that "it is emphatically the province and duty of the judicial department to say what the law is." In *United States v. Peters* (1803), applicable more specifically to *Brown,* Marshall maintained, "If the legislatures of the several states may, at will, annul the judgments of the courts of the United States, and destroy the rights acquired under those judgments, the Constitution itself becomes a solemn mockery." This basic constitutional premise, succinctly stated by Charles Evans Hughes, later Supreme Court chief justice, as "We are under a Constitution, but the Constitution is what the judges say it is," has been fully accepted since the time of Marshall.

The Court had actually done nothing that was not in its power to do. Finding school segregation to be unconstitutional was a logical interpretation of the Fourteenth Amendment, according to Charles Black of Yale University Law School. He reasoned: "First, the equal protection clause of the fourteenth amendment should be read as saying that the Negro race, as such, is not to be significantly disadvantaged by the laws of the states. Secondly, segregation is a massive intentional disadvantaging of the Negro race, as such, by state law. No subtlety at all."[15] As Black pointed out, the first contention of the equal protection clause, that Negroes are not to be significantly disadvantaged, was tested and upheld by the Court in the *Slaughterhouse Cases* (1873) and *Strauder v. West Virginia* (1879).

Strauder overturned West Virginia's law that stipulated that only white males were permitted to serve on grand or trial juries. As Black demonstrated, Justice Strong explained the Fourteenth Amendment in his *Strauder* opinion:

An Absence of Moral Leadership

It ordains that no State shall make or enforce any laws which shall abridge the privileges or immunities of citizens of the United States (evidently referring to the newly made citizens, who, being citizens of the United States, are declared to be also citizens of the State in which they reside). It ordains that no State shall deprive any person of life, liberty, or property, without due process of law, or deny to any person within its jurisdiction the equal protection of the laws. What is this but declaring that the law in the States shall be the same for the black as for the white; that all persons, whether colored or white, shall stand equal before the laws of the United States, and, in regard to the colored race, for whose protection the amendment was primarily designed, that no discrimination shall be made against them by law because of their color? The words of the amendment, it is true, are prohibitory, but they contain a necessary implication of a positive immunity, or right, most valuable to the colored race,—the right to exemption from unfriendly legislation against them distinctively as colored,—exemption from legal discriminations, implying inferiority in civil society, lessening the security of their enjoyment of the rights which others enjoy, and discriminations which are steps towards reducing them to a condition of a subject race.[16]

Since the purpose of the Fourteenth Amendment was intended to abolish all racial distinctions and place blacks on a plane of equality with white Americans, the *Strauder* ruling explained, the amendment "makes no attempt to enumerate the rights it designs to protect. It speaks in general terms, and those are as comprehensive as possible." Clearly when the *Strauder* ruling overturned the West Virginia law, the Court reaffirmed the equality of black citizens to white.

The fact that segregation is a massive disadvantaging was not apparent to the Court until *Brown I* in 1954. In fact, the justices in the 1896 *Plessy v. Ferguson* ruling presumed to show that segregation did not really disadvantage the Negro at all and blamed the plaintiff for faulty understanding. The Court contended: "We consider the underlying fallacy of the plaintiff's

A Certain Blindness

argument to consist in the assumption that the enforced separation of the two races stamps the colored race with a badge of inferiority. If this be so, it is not by reason of anything found in the act, but solely because the colored race chooses to put that construction upon it."

In order to reach the conclusion that "separate but equal" facilities were constitutionally valid, "the Court had to indulge in a willful reading of human nature and to abuse case law, common law, and common sense. In dismissing the wound men suffer when forcefully separated from their fellow citizens for no reason beyond the pigmentation of their skin, the Supreme Court was reduced to pretending that the resulting pain was self-inflicted, the result of an overly fragile psychological makeup. It was unfortunate, said the Justices, but that was life."[17]

Where the Court in arriving at its decision in *Plessy* was guided by self-formulated psychology and sociology, the district court in Topeka, Kansas, in *Brown v. Board of Education of Topeka* (1951) based its finding of fact on the testimony of expert witnesses to conclude that "segregation of white and colored children in public schools has a detrimental effect upon the colored children."

In *Plessy,* of course, neither social science data nor expert testimony was cited or relied on by the Court, but legal use of such information was considered valid. In *Muller v. Oregon* (1908) the Court accepted a vast array of sociological data presented in the famous brief of Louis Brandeis, who defended Oregon's law ordering a maximum ten-hour work day for laundresses, both for their health and for the welfare of the public. While agreeing that it contained "little or no discussion of the constitutional question presented to us for determination," the justices nevertheless acknowledged the contribution of the Brandeis brief in reaching their conclusions.

There is a marked similarity between the *Muller* and *Brown* cases and the relationship of social science to the law. In the *Muller* case, data was used to show the state had a reasonable basis for legislation to protect women who worked too many hours. In *Brown,* the expert testimony was used to show reasonable basis that state-sanctioned segregation arbitrarily disadvantaged Negroes.

Stare decisis ("to stand by decided matters") is the legal doctrine which states that, when a court has set forth a principle of law as applicable to a certain set of facts, it will adhere to that principle and apply it to future cases where the facts are substantially the same. Reliance on previously decided cases is normally a sound judicial course. However, it is a rule of policy and not a rule of law. While ordinarily adhered to, it is properly departed from when reasons for it no longer exist, are clearly erroneous, or are manifestly wrong. The question is entirely within the discretion of the court when it is called upon to reconsider a question. Between 1937 and 1949 the Supreme Court overruled earlier decisions in thirty cases; twenty-one of the reversals were on constitutional grounds.

Obviously a vast difference of attitudes toward education occurred between the time the Fourteenth Amendment was adopted in 1868—or even when *Plessy* was decided in 1896—and 1954, when *Brown I* was decided. In the late 1800s education was not universally significant. Public school terms were short and student attendance irregular. But by the 1950s all states required school attendance at least through the age of sixteen, indicating the high priority grass roots Americans had given the education of their young. Regarded as the basis on which to build good citizenship, awaken cultural appreciations, and prepare for later professional training, education was, in fact, too important a function to be left solely under local jurisdiction, and so came under regulation by the state as well. To deny a child a proper education was tantamount to depriving him at least of his ability to adjust to his environment and perhaps even of his ultimate success in life. Considering the weight of testimony showing the separate Negro schools to be decidedly unequal, it can hardly be seen as a departure from sound judicial practice for the Court to demand in 1954's *Brown I* ruling that the practice end.

A Certain Blindness

School segregation, which the plaintiffs in the *Brown* cases maintained was a violation of rights under the Fourteenth Amendment since it supplied inferior education, was of great interest to Justice Felix Frankfurter. A scholarly man who had been a professor at Harvard University Law School, Frankfurter had been concerned for a long time with the intentions and understandings of the Thirty-ninth Congress, which ratified the Fourteenth Amendment in 1866. "For nearly 20 years I was at work on what was to be as complete and as scholarly a book on the Fourteenth Amendment as I could make it," Frankfurter told his colleague Justice Hugo Black in 1947. "How anyone could have gone through the debates in Congress on the subject of the Fourteenth Amendment and have respect for the intellectual clarity of hardly anyone in the debate beats me." Frankfurter himself found the amendment's legislative history "inconclusive."

When the *Brown* case came to the Court in 1952 Frankfurter had his clerk Alexander Bickel compile the legislative history of the amendment. (Bickel later became a leading authority in the field of constitutional law.) The law clerk did not find anything conclusive on the subject of school segregation and told Frankfurter, "It is impossible to conclude that the 39th Congress intended that segregation be abolished; impossible also to conclude that they foresaw it might be, under the language they were adopting." But the history "did not foreclose future generations from acting on the question, either by congressional statute or judicial review."[18]

The other justices brought various backgrounds to the issue as well. Hugo Black, a former Ku Klux Klan member, had been confirmed by the Senate in 1937. At the time, NAACP executive secretary Walter White expressed confidence that Black would measure up to what was expected of a Supreme Court justice, and White was not disappointed. A senior associate justice on the Court in 1952, Black believed the Thirteenth, Fourteenth, and Fifteenth Amendments outlawed school segregation, no matter what else the legislative history on the subject revealed.

An Absence of Moral Leadership

Many years later Black's colleague Justice William O. Douglas was to acknowledge the existence of a kind of moral evolution when he remarked that "notions of what constitutes equal treatment for the purposes of the equal protection clause *do* change."[19] But Black rejected that line of reasoning. "I do not vote to hold segregation in the public schools unconstitutional on any such theory. I thought when *Brown* was written, and I think now, that Justice Harlan was correct in 1896 when he dissented in *Plessy v. Ferguson*." (John Marshall Harlan's had been the *only* dissenting voice in the decision that sanctioned separate but equal facilities for Negroes, and Harlan countered that no matter what the Court said, segregation was a form of servitude.) Hugo Black remarked: "My view was, we had a simple question: Does [school segregation] give the colored people of the nation equal protection of the law? . . . Well, I lived in the South, practically until I came up here. . . . I didn't need any philosophy about changing times to convince me that there was a denial of equal protection of the laws."[20]

For his part Chief Justice Earl Warren felt that the knowledge of the plain meaning of the plain words themselves should be enough to lead anyone to conclude that segregation was wrong. Appointed just in time to hear the arguments in the *Brown* cases, Warren had a salutary and catalytic effect on the Court.

He had extensive experience as a public servant, since being elected district attorney for Alameda County, California, in 1926, and Warren served as California state attorney general from 1939 to 1943 and governor of California for three terms, from 1943 to 1953. Though he had no judicial experience, his "selection seemed like an appropriate one," as Richard Kluger noted in *Simple Justice*. "Earl Warren had always carried himself with exemplary dignity. His private behavior was beyond reproach, and there had never been a whisper of scandal about his conduct of public office."[21]

Warren did have one large blemish on his record, though. Soon after Pearl Harbor he had advocated interning the Nisei,

A Certain Blindness

Americans of Japanese extraction, in refugee camps and detention centers when it seemed possible that they might sabotage America's war efforts, and the Nisei were held until the closing months of World War II. "By then," Kluger wrote, "Warren and many others had begun to regret the massive deprivation of liberty that had been perpetrated without any justifying evidence of disloyalty. [As governor] he called emergency meetings of state officials to ensure that returning Japanese-Americans would be reintegrated into their communities peaceably and with full protection of the law."[22]

The new chief justice had demonstrated throughout his public life that he had "a capacity for broadening his views to fit new offices . . . at each successive stage of his career," as Curtis Skinner wrote in *Contemporary Authors*.[23] And his Supreme Court office was no exception:

> An activist in temperament and background, the chief justice found himself drawn to the Black/Douglas liberal wing of the Court as a broad range of civil and constitutional rights issues arrived on the national agenda in the 1950s and 1960s. Warren later acknowledged that "on the Court I saw things in a different light" than he had as a prosecutor concerned with compromise and constituencies. Rather, as chief justice, he came to understand his principal judicial role as one of protecting and expanding the basic freedoms of all Americans at a time of historical social change.[24]

And protection of basic freedoms was what was at issue in the *Brown* cases. Differing from Hugo Black's approach as to whether segregation was permissible but arriving at the same conclusion, Justic Felix Frankfurter also acknowledged that America of the 1950s had come a long way from the nation that passed the Fourteenth Amendment in 1866. Frankfurter reasoned, "The effects of changes in men's feelings for what is right and just is equally relevant in determining whether a discrimination denies the equal protection of the laws."[25]

An Absence of Moral Leadership

The statements of these jurists reveal their capacities for clear thinking, which is especially significant since most of the attacks and adverse comments on the decision they arrived at in the reasonable exercise of judicial authority have been the result of individual views of race relations without regard to organic law. As Chief Justice John Marshall said over one hundred years before *Brown* came to the Court, "Ours is a Constitution intended to endure for ages to come and consequently to be adapted to the various crises in human affairs." The Constitution, including the Fourteenth Amendment, is concise yet ambiguous and not precise and clear, and it is the duty of the Supreme Court "to say what the law is."

In their unanimous *Brown* rulings the Supreme Court justices had addressed the Constitution to a twentieth-century crisis. A court victory could have produced a social victory, but the judicial branch received no support from the legislative and executive arenas of government. What became apparent so quickly was that "even when it won a legal victory, as in the *Brown* case, black America could not count on the president to implement it. Moral confrontation would have to supplant litigation."[26]

And that is what began to happen. As Richard Kluger noted in *Simple Justice,* "Lawsuits are proceedings too technical and lengthy to form the basis for a mass movement, though they may set that movement in motion. Direct action is required."[27]

On December 1, 1955, several months after the *Brown II* decision was announced requiring school integration to proceed only with "all deliberate speed," Rosa Parks refused to yield her seat on a bus in Montgomery, Alabama. All the seats on the bus were filled, and Parks was in the first row of seats allowed to Negroes under Montgomery's segregation laws. When a white man boarded the bus and had to stand, the bus driver demanded that the Negroes in the row with Parks move to the back. Three moved, but Parks claimed that since she wasn't in the white section she shouldn't have to move. Threatened with arrest,

A Certain Blindness

Parks, burdened with a bag full of groceries, held her ground. The police were summoned and arrested her for violating the race laws.

In his award-winning book *Parting the Waters* Taylor Branch indicated the serious nature of arrest under these circumstances:

> At the station, officers booked, fingerprinted, and incarcerated Rosa Parks. It was not possible for her to think lightly of being arrested. Having crossed the line that in polite society divided Negroes from niggers, she had reason to expect not only stinging disgrace among her own people but the least civilized attentions of the whites. When she was allowed to call home, her mother's first response was to groan and ask, "Did they beat you?" . . . Rosa Parks was in danger every minute she remained in jail. If anything happened to her there, Parks would be utterly without recourse or remedy.[28]

Rosa Parks was a seamstress at a department store in downtown Montgomery, and she was also secretary of the Montgomery NAACP. Her mother called the house of E. D. Nixon, a railroad porter who had served as Alabama branch president of the Negro Brotherhood of Sleeping Car Porters for nearly thirty years and had been the local NAACP chapter president for five years. "He was famous to Montgomery Negroes as the man who knew every white policeman, judge, and government clerk in town, and had always gone to see them about the grievances of any Negro who asked him for help," Branch wrote in *Parting the Waters*. "Nixon seldom got anything close to justice, but he usually got something."[29] When Nixon and his friend, white lawyer Clifford Durr, returned Parks to her family, they recognized that this was possibly the opportunity they were waiting for to challenge the constitutionality of bus segregation. Against the objections of her family and especially of her husband, who feared for Rosa's life, Rosa Parks agreed to participate in a suit, thus precipitating a nationally significant mass movement on the part of the black community in pursuit of equal rights.

Nixon made the case a rallying point to protest segregated bus seating. Some teachers from Alabama State University

An Absence of Moral Leadership

quickly wrote a flyer urging Negroes to stay off the buses on Monday, December 5, the day Rosa Parks's case was scheduled to go to court. The one-day boycott was so successful that the civil rights leaders who banded together to plan a Monday night mass meeting decided to use the ploy as a bargaining tactic.

Among the Negro leaders sat Nixon and ministers such as Ralph Abernathy and Martin Luther King, Jr. Recently installed as pastor at the Dexter Street Baptist Church, King, then twenty-six, was nominated and—when no one else was nominated—was elected president of the newly organized Montgomery Improvement Association.

MIA demands included courteous treatment for Negro riders; seating on a first-come, first-served basis, with blacks filling up the back of the bus and moving forward and whites filling up the front of the bus and moving back; and black drivers for predominantly black routes. During the course of the boycott the MIA modified the last demand to require that the transit company accept applications for Negro drivers and fill positions as openings became available.

The logistics of operating a bus boycott placed a terrific strain on the black citizens of Montgomery. Bus fares were very low, and the MIA leaders hoped to enlist the Negro taxi drivers as a kind of army charging only an emergency ten-cent fare. When the police commissioner hinted he would order the arrest of any drivers charging less than the minimum forty-five-cent fare, the taxicab army idea had to be abandoned. A plea to the wealthier Negroes brought offers of more than 150 cars the first night of the appeal, when MIA leaders anticipated more than twenty thousand riders a day would need transporting. (Later on the figure rose to between thirty and forty thousand.)

A similar bus boycott in Baton Rouge, Louisiana, lasted only two weeks before it fell apart. Through sheer force of will and the mutual support of the MIA leaders and the black population, the Montgomery boycott lasted from December 5, 1955, to December 21, 1956, the first day integrated seating on the buses was finally implemented.

A Certain Blindness

Aside from the daily hardship of managing alternate transportation to work and home again, the boycott exacted other costs as well. There were countless mass meetings to organize and attend, sometimes several on a single night—but these at least inspired everyone to continue their efforts. The negotiating meetings between the MIA and the city commissioners were often stalemated, the white majority claiming any proposals that would entail mixing of the races to be illegal. Police harassment imposed countless traffic violations on the carpool drivers. King himself was arrested on January 26, 1956—on charges of speeding thirty miles per hour in a twenty-five-mile zone—as he dropped off some riders at one of the carpool stops. Then on January 30 King's house was bombed, and two days later, the same day papers were filed in federal court to end segregated bus seating, the front yard of E. D. Nixon's house was bombed. Pressure mounted on all sides to end the boycott, and when MIA negotiations with city commissioners arrived at an impasse, 115 Negroes—including King—were indicted on February 21, 1956, for conspiring to conduct an illegal boycott.

Turning the tables on authorities, however, the indicted leaders began arriving at the courthouse to be arrested, accompanied by throngs of cheering Negroes. On February 22, when King arrived back in Montgomery from an out-of-town conference, he was greeted by television cameras and a contingent of boycotters. Newspapers began covering the mass movement, and King was becoming widely known both at home and abroad. He arrived at the courthouse to turn himself in, accompanied by his father—"Daddy King"—and minister Ralph Abernathy, already out on bond. Only the day after the indictment had been handed down, King became the twenty-fourth minister to be booked.

Until this time the NAACP had not been involved because the MIA had not initially demanded an end to segregated bus seating. When the MIA pressed this issue, however, the NAACP stepped in to defend the indicted ministers. (King, whose case in the illegal boycott trial came up first, was convicted and sentenced to a five hundred dollar fine or a year at hard labor. His attorneys appealed.)

A three-judge panel heard the bus segregation case, cited as *Browder v. Gayle,* and their 2-1 decision to strike down bus segregation was announced June 4, 1956. Judges Richard Rives and Frank Johnson determined that segregated bus seating violated the due process and equal protection laws of the Fourteenth Amendment. They referred to the precedent set in the *Brown* ruling, "that the separate but equal doctrine can no longer be safely followed as a correct statement of law." In fact, the judges ascertained, "we think that *Plessy v. Ferguson* has been impliedly, though not explicitly, overruled."

Five months later, on November 13, 1956, the Supreme Court affirmed the *Browder* ruling. News of the victory came to Martin Luther King, Jr., again in court when Montgomery city lawyers were seeking an injunction against the MIA car pool as an unlicensed municipal transit system. The Supreme Court ruling suddenly made the injunction irrelevant, but the Alabama judge handed it down anyway.

Before any Negro citizens would board the buses, though, five weeks would elapse before the orders to integrate the buses would reach Montgomery. During this time the MIA car pool could not be operating because of the injunction placed upon it—and so Montgomery's Negroes were walking again. They walked until December 21, 1956, when the Montgomery bus boycott ended and King and other MIA leaders jubilantly boarded the city's first integrated buses.

Considering that approximately 75 percent of Montgomery's bus ridership was Negro, the boycott cost the transit company $750,000 in lost revenue. The cost to Montgomery's Negro population is impossible to calculate. In addition to the hardships they imposed on themselves, there were people hostile to the effort: three homes were bombed before the Supreme Court affirmed the outcome of *Browder v. Gayle,* and afterwards the violence intensified. Within a month of *Browder,* five churches and three more houses were bombed, and snipers began shooting at integrated buses. The second time King's house was bombed, seven white men were charged; the first two were acquitted despite signed confessions; the charges were dismissed for the remaining five defendants.

Nevertheless, the Montgomery boycott gave new stimulus to organizations committed to the struggle for civil rights and racial equality. The Congress of Racial Equality (CORE) intensified its efforts, as it had long utilized nonviolent protest to achieve its goals. Various religious, labor, and civic organizations also gave support and aid to those involved in direct action. In 1957 the Southern Christian Leadership Conference (SCLC), a direct outgrowth of the Montgomery boycott, was formed to serve as a coordinating agency for groups employing the technique of nonviolent protest. Martin Luther King, Jr., now internationally famous, was elected president at its organizational meeting.

King's commitment to nonviolence had great impact on the American psyche, and his extraordinary skill and dedication are well known. He was able to express the hopes and aspirations of black Americans—and to communicate these feelings to white Americans—and King thus attracted many Americans to participate in the cause of human dignity.

It is to the enduring credit of those many Americans, both white and black and of various backgrounds and faiths, who came forward to act and in too many cases even to lose their lives in defense of basic freedoms. These civil rights workers understood what King meant when he said that "only when people themselves begin to act are rights on paper given life blood."

Our government officials, however—charged with enforcing the Constitution—were not willing to perform their sworn duties. When the *Brown* case was decided, the judiciary should have received support from the legislative and executive departments. But, despite the sincere efforts of a few members, Congress refused to take any steps to back up the Court decision. The executive branch also refrained from giving any support on

An Absence of Moral Leadership

the subject of desegregation. After the district court decided that bus segregation was unconstitutional, President Eisenhower was asked at a September 15, 1956, news conference to use his "tremendous reservoir of good will among the young people" and advise them on how to conduct themselves in the face of boycotts set up as some schools began integrating. Eisenhower's weak response was: "Well, I can say what I have said so often: it is difficult through law and through force to change a man's heart. . . . We must all . . . help to bring about a change in spirit so that extremists on both sides do not defeat what we know is a reasonable, logical conclusion to this whole affair, which is recognition of equality of men."[30] Apparently Eisenhower viewed as extremists not only those who sought to prevent Negro Americans from exercising their freedom under the law, but also the NAACP lawyers and workers who sought to enforce the constitutional guarantees.

With no support from the White House and practically every Southern congressman professing white supremacy and defiance of *Brown,* Southern public officials used any loophole they could devise to thwart the *Brown* decision. Segregationists even viewed the enforcement provisions in *Brown II* as a victory and believed compliance could be postponed forever. Clearly, when the Court placed the "primary duty" with school authorities for determining how and when schools should be desegregated and allowed district court judges to decide when the authorities were "acting in good faith" and proceeding with all deliberate speed, the Court gave segregationists all the leeway they needed.

Since May 1955, any member of a board of education who failed to use his official status to start to desegregate the schools flouted the Constitution, violating his sworn oath and the criminal law of the United States (Section 251 of Title 18, U.S. Code). That is because each school board member in the approximately three thousand school districts operating racially separate schools in 1955 had taken a solemn oath to support the Constitution of the United States, despite anything in the constitution or laws of his own state to the contrary. The Court's ruling that segregation was unconstitutional was, therefore, binding on each board member without the need of further legal action.

In many instances, school board members were law-abiding and wanted to comply, but powerful groups took great efforts to persuade them that they had no obligation to obey the law, efforts which were compounded by the conduct of some judges and lack of support by the Justice Department. Without support from President Eisenhower, enforcement of *Brown* fell upon the judicial arm of the government. Black citizens, lacking the political power to force school boards to comply with the law, were forced into the courts again to seek those constitutional rights that continued to be denied. Not only did these Negro Americans have to initiate and carry through the judicial process, a long and costly legal action in its own right, but they also had to endure threats of physical violence, threats of discharge from employment, and other forms of intimidation.

Clearly the law gave district court judges ample power to compel boards to desegregate schools, but, for the most part, the law was applied adversely to the claims of the plaintiffs. Judges construed the Supreme Court's rulings narrowly or adopted a "go slow" philosophy as advocated by President Eisenhower. In many instances judges purposefully allowed their orders to be circumvented, and some wrote opinions encouraging segregation.

Throughout the process of enforcing the constitutional rights of Negroes, public officials defied the law and judicial orders, which led directly to numerous acts of violence and, in some instances, to the death of innocent persons. Reckless and irresponsible acts by men in high places create a disrespect for the law among citizens and encourage unlawful conduct. This is especially true of those elected officials who, by their offices, are duty-bound to provide moral leadership.

The manner in which state governors responded to the *Brown* decision and subsequent court orders is well docu-

An Absence of Moral Leadership

mented, but the attitude of President Eisenhower was to have far-reaching consequences, not only in how *Brown* was implemented but also on future race relations.

One of the early cases reflecting open defiance of the court order occurred in Texas. Mansfield, Texas, elementary schools were segregated and, since the only high school in Mansfield was for whites only, Negro high school students were forced to attend school in Fort Worth, approximately twenty miles away, to which they had to provide their own transportation. The Fifth Circuit Court of Appeals found that there were no administrative difficulties as a basis for delay and ordered the immediate admission of Negro students to the Mansfield high school.

After resistance to the admission of the Negro students continued, Governor Allen Shivers ordered the Texas Rangers to remove the students under the pretext of preserving order. He announced, "It is not my intention to permit the use of state officers or troops to shoot down or intimidate Texas citizens who are making orderly protest against a situation instigated and agitated by the National Association for the Advancement of Colored People."[31]

While Governor Shivers boasted of showing the proper way to resolve racial controversies, President Eisenhower characterized the Mansfield situation in a press conference as a local responsibility. The president refused to criticize the governor's action against the students and denied a request for federal assistance. NAACP chief counsel Thurgood Marshall immediately condemned the president's posture as giving "support to many in this country who have sought to confuse the issue by trying to divide responsibility for such situations between lawless mobs and other Americans who seek only their lawful rights in a lawful manner."[32] In the face of the president's acquiescence, mob action was obviously seen as an effective way to avoid complying with federal court orders.

When Autherine Lucy was admitted to the University of Alabama, rioting immediately flared, and she was quickly removed. Lucy was later unjustly expelled from the school, and

A Certain Blindness

again no help was provided by the federal government. Alabama governor George Wallace stood in the schoolhouse door to prevent Lucy's entrance and later stated, "I say segregation now, segregation tomorrow, segregation forever."

It was in Arkansas that President Eisenhower was finally forced to assume the full responsibilities of his office. The Little Rock School Board had devised a plan of "gradual integration" to begin with the high schools in 1957. In the spring, thirty students were initially to be part of the effort, but the number had been gradually reduced to nine. The students were called together by the superintendent and prepared for facing certain behavior, including "name calling and verbal abuse." However, the officials were in no way prepared for the violence that followed.

During the month of August, various ministers and other community leaders waged an intensive campaign in Little Rock attacking the plan of the school board, which was labeled a tool of the NAACP. The highlight of one large rally was the appearance of Marvin Griffin, governor of Georgia, and Roy V. Harris, exccutive director of Georgia's State's Rights Council. Both were guests of Governor Orval E. Faubus at the state's executive mansion. Governor Griffin told the gathering that he would never allow integration in Georgia, and Harris urged the citizens of Arkansas to join Georgia in its resistance. He stated Georgia would use its highway patrol as Governor Shivers had done and suggested Governor Faubus do the same.

Faubus, greatly influenced by the Georgians, also received many messages to the effect that "we don't have to do this when the Governor of Georgia says nobody else has to do it." A few days before schools were scheduled to open, an injunction was issued by the local court temporarily enjoining the school board from proceeding with the desegregation plan. However Judge Ronald Davies of North Dakota, temporarily sitting in the Little Rock Federal District Court, ruled that "the plan of desegregation ordered by the federal court is still in force and effect." Meanwhile, the night before school was to begin, Governor

An Absence of Moral Leadership

Faubus called out the National Guard, as he said, to prevent massive violence. The guards blocked the entrance of the school to the Negro students who were forced back through a large, jeering mob. President Eisenhower, following the events from Washington, mildly commented, "We are going to whip this thing in the long run by Americans being true to themselves and not merely by law."[33]

The school board then appealed to Judge Davies for a delay in light of the governor's action. Davies rejected the petition: "It must never be forgotten that I have a constitutional duty and obligation from which I shall not shrink. In organized society there can be nothing but ultimate confusion and chaos, if the court decrees are flouted, whatever the pretext."[34] The judge also declared that the plan for desegregation would have proceeded without serious public disturbance, except for the governor's intervention, so Davies enjoined Governor Faubus from obstructing or interfering with the court order.

Faubus then removed the National Guard, but a hysterical mob continued to grow to over a thousand persons. Mayor Woodrow Mann, realizing the situation was "out of control," advised a presidential assistant that unless the president sent in federal troops, the police would not be able to contain the mob. Later that day, Mann telegraphed a second message to President Eisenhower: "I am pleading with you as President of the United States in the interest of humanity, law and order, and because of democracy worldwide to provide the necessary federal troops within several hours."[35]

Eisenhower finally issued the order for deployment of troops of the 101st Airborne Division at Central High School. In a national television address, the president noted the adverse propaganda impact abroad and his duty to uphold the order of a federal court. Reversing his laissez-faire approach, Eisenhower now declared: "When an obstruction of justice has been interposed or mob violence is permitted to exist so that it is impracticable to enforce the laws by the ordinary course of judicial proceedings, the obligation of the President under the Constitution and laws is inescapable. He is obliged to use whatever means may be required by the particular situation."[36]

The president did not continue to pursue his obligation, however, as the Department of Justice announced it would not prosecute known violators. On the day Attorney General William P. Rogers announced there would be no federal prosecutions, thirteen white persons arrested during the rioting were released by the Little Rock Municipal Court. The only person convicted was a Negro student; authorities also refused to prosecute all except two NAACP officials.

For Little Rock's Negroes, the legal process had totally broken down—even unruly students at Central High were not disciplined. The black students were spat upon, shoved, their books destroyed, and their lockers broken into. There were bomb threats, fires, and explosions. In one instance a white student was arrested for disorderly conduct after spitting on a Negro girl; the judge released the boy, stating he "just gave way to an emotion he could not control." Two girls were expelled, one white, one black; the white girl was readmitted following a television address sponsored by segregationists; the black girl was expelled permanently for calling one of her tormentors "white trash."

By the end of the year Negro student Carlotta Weeks was on her class honor roll and Ernest Green, who was later to become an assistant secretary of the U.S. Department of Labor, graduated. But, in the case *Cooper v. Aaron* (1958) the school board decided to seek a two-and-a-half-year delay in the desegregation process because of the overall racial climate. District court judge Harry Lemley granted the school board's petition. He wrote:

> It is important to realize . . . that the racial incidents and vandalism which occurred . . . did not stem from mere lawlessness on the part of the white students in the school or on the part of the people of Little Rock. . . . Rather, the source of the trou-

An Absence of Moral Leadership

ble was the deep-seated popular opposition in Little Rock to the principle of integration. . . . To this composition was added the conviction of many of the people of Little Rock, that the Brown decisions do not truly represent the law. . . . It is not denied that . . . the Negro students . . . have a constitutional right not to be excluded from any of the public schools on account of race; but the board has convincingly shown that the time for the enjoyment of that right has not yet come.

In order to secure rights guaranteed in *Brown*, Negro plaintiffs had to appeal the *Cooper v. Aaron* decision, an expensive and laborious process. The Eighth Circuit Court of Appeals held, "We say the time has not yet come in these United States when order of a federal court must be whittled away, watered down, or shamefully withdrawn in the face of violent and unlawful acts of individual citizens in opposition thereto."

On appeal directly to the Supreme Court regarding the stay order, Solicitor General J. Lee Rankin argued a point which President Eisenhower should have recognized much earlier. He stated, "Opposition to the *Brown* decision expressed in violence cannot justify the abandonment or modification of the plan."[37]

When it read its decision in the *Cooper v. Aaron* case, the Supreme Court spoke forcibly and with urgency—tones that were tragically lacking in the *Brown II* ruling—regarding the constitutional rights of the Negro children of Little Rock: "The constitutional rights of respondents are not to be sacrificed or yielded to the violence and disorder which have followed upon the actions of the Governor and legislature. . . . Law and order are not here to be preserved by depriving the Negro children of their constitutional rights." It continued its position in forceful clarification:

> "The federal judiciary," said the Supreme Court, citing the 1803 precedent of *Marbury v. Madison*, "is supreme in the exposition of the law of the Constitution. . . . The interpretation of the Fourteenth Amendment enunciated by this Court in the Brown case is the supreme law of the land. . . . Every state legislator

A Certain Blindness

and executive and judicial officer is solemnly committed by oath . . . to support this Constitution. . . . No state . . . officer can war against the Constitution without violating his undertaking to support it. . . . A governor who asserts a power to nullify a federal court order is similarly restrained."

Justice Felix Frankfurter, who wrote a concurring opinion in the *Cooper v. Aaron* case, more strongly stated that to grant the request for delay would have meant the "law should bow to force. To yield to such a claim would be to enthrone official lawlessness. . . . For those in authority thus to defy the law of the land is profoundly subversive not only of our constitutional system but to the presuppositions of a democratic society."

Even in the face of *Cooper v. Aaron* some state governors continued to see open defiance of the law as an acceptable way of life. Governor Ernest Vandiver of Georgia, elected the year after the upheaval in Little Rock, pledged not to desegregate a single school during his term in office. Reg Murphy and Hal Gulliver reported in *The Southern Strategy*[38] that, upon consulting with his legal advisers, Vandiver concluded that the law could be effectively circumvented through various legal procedures and that compliance could be postponed almost indefinitely. But Vandiver was frustrated in his efforts. Following the admission of honor students Hamilton Holmes and Charlene Hunter to the University of Georgia, an outbreak of violence occurred on the campus, and they were suspended. Judge William A. Bootle immediately ordered their reinstatement according to an order he had issued a few days before. When Vandiver "tried to close the University of Georgia to avoid desegregation, Judge Bootle issued a restraining order even before the Governor could sign the proclamation."[39]

Mississippi governor Ross Barnett went on radio and television to announce his intention to defy a federal court order to admit James Meredith to the University of Mississippi. Meredith, an Air Force veteran, had applied fourteen months before. Barnett overruled the Board of Higher Education, which had agreed to abide by the order, and personally barred Meredith's

An Absence of Moral Leadership

entry to the school. The governor was found guilty of contempt, and Meredith finally became a student—but only after 2 persons were killed and 132 others were injured, including 28 federal marshals, who received gunshot wounds. Twelve thousand troops were called up, and 300 remained on the campus for nearly a year.

In a democratic society, persons in positions of political leadership have a specific moral responsibility to support and uphold the principle of law. In our country, of course, the president holds the highest position in this regard, and as President Franklin D. Roosevelt once stated, "The Presidency is above all a place of moral leadership."

President Eisenhower, however, adopted a different view regarding the *Brown* decision and enforcement of constitutional rights declared therein. Soon after the initial decision the president claimed that a declaration of its support by him would "lower the dignity of government." Eisenhower apparently saw the enforcement of the constitutional rights involved in *Brown* as being different from enforcement of the law generally. In this instance, he later revealed: "Because it is not in man's nature to accept unhesitatingly the dictation of law of his moral conduct, it is necessary that he be shown the course that is just and right. Then he will accept it if understanding and moderation are used by officials of government at every level of enforcement."[40] Eisenhower made little attempt to show that respect for the law and the rights of other citizens were the "just and right" course. He obviously failed to understand that respect for the law first affects conduct and then a change in attitude will follow. E. Frederic Morrow, White House aide during the Eisenhower administration, wrote that Eisenhower "was a great, gentle, and noble man," but, he added, "his background and viewpoint on civil rights was Southern. He was fair and honest in most things, but he couldn't take that single bold step of courageous pronouncement that would have moved the blacks another mile toward freedom. . . . In my many talks with him in this area, I found

A Certain Blindness

him neither intellectually nor emotionally disposed to combat segregation in general."[41]

The contradictory nature of Eisenhower's approach certainly took on racial connotations, because he failed to take an unequivocal stand for racial justice and did not bring the weight of the federal government to bear on the legal enforcement of the constitutional rights of Negro Americans. Once the president criticized a group of spineless congressmen: "They do not seem to realize when there arrives that moment at which soft speaking should be abandoned and a fight to the end undertaken. Any man who hopes to exercise leadership must be ready to meet the requirement face to face when it arises; unless he is ready to fight when necessary, people will finally begin to ignore him."[42] Yet Eisenhower himself ignored flagrant violations of the law and the denial of constitutional rights until there was absolutely no recourse, and he was forced to assume his legal obligation.

Some years after he left office and was comfortably situated in Gettysburg, Eisenhower roundly condemned disrespect for law in language that was highly appropriate and entirely applicable for use during his presidential years. How ironic that he should state, "the United States has become atmosphered, you might say, in a policy of lawlessness. If we like a law, we obey it. If we don't we are told, 'you can disobey it.' "[43]

Beginning with the *Brown* decision itself, the whole process of its implementation has been replete with irony. When the Court allowed recalcitrant school boards and judges to determine when constitutional rights of black citizens should be enjoyed, it effectively nullified its expressed concerns "that it should go without saying that the vitality of these constitutional principles cannot be allowed to yield simply because of disagreement with them." The very purpose of *Brown II* was to allow time for its acceptability, and over these many years all litigation has been geared toward further delay. Constitutional principles have simply been allowed to yield, and thereby gave way to busing, quotas, and *Brown III*.

An Absence of Moral Leadership

If President Eisenhower and his administration had handled the whole matter in accordance with usual law enforcement procedures, I believe there would have been less ill will and less need for continued litigation. When he announced during his second presidential campaign that he would not use troops to enforce federal court desegregation orders, it was clear he was prepared to compromise his responsibilities under the law. Only when he finally acted according to the law and in fulfillment of constitutional duty did the reign of chaos and lawlessness begin to abate.

Countless other officials have totally abdicated their duties to enforce the law as described in the *Brown* decision in 1954. Their reluctance to perform responsibly has compounded existing problems and created many more requiring further litigation. The early argument of the NAACP urging a definite and immediate plan of enforcement was eventually shared in a roundabout way by Arkansas governor Orval E. Faubus. With more than a touch of irony Faubus blamed Eisenhower and his administration for creating the explosive condition that occurred in Little Rock when they failed to enforce the law. Governor Faubus declared: "They would just sit back and fold their hands and let somebody else reap the storm. Well, hell, it was their storm. A bunch of goddamn cowards for not coming in in the beginning and saying, 'This is a federal court order. We're going to have federal authorities here to see to it that it's obeyed and enforced.' Then I wouldn't have been involved."[44]

8
The Lawyer: A High and Noble Calling

When I entered Washburn University of Topeka Law School, the dean met with first-year law students, asking each of us to look to the student on our left and then to the student on our right. The dean made a calm, matter-of-fact statement that one of us would not be present at the time of graduation. We all, of course, looked at each other. I smiled and said to myself, "Now, look, you fellows should get together and work this out because I definitely will be here."

Several Negro students were attending Washburn Law School at the time, including Samuel Jackson and Sherman Parks, who later was elected the first black appellate court judge in Kansas.

I found that both the faculty and students at Washburn were generally cooperative, polite, and hard-working. However, the legal fraternities on campus that controlled the student

The Lawyer: A High and Noble Calling

body and other social activities did not admit Negro students. Although the discriminatory practice was totally incongruous with the mission for which we were preparing, the hard work and stiff competition caused it to be one of my lesser concerns. I was reminded once again of my mother's uncompromising attitude concerning these situations.

While race relations were improving in some instances, too many unjust practices continued. Wilma, the youngest in our family, also encountered racial abuse and humiliation. Upon her graduation from high school, she decided, like our sister Mary, to become a nurse. Although Mary had been denied acceptance at Hurley Hospital School of Nursing in Flint, Michigan, Wilma and my cousin Sharon Wilson Simpson, applying several years later, were accepted as the first black students there. But both instructors and students made life difficult for her. (Resistance to school desegregation, which followed some years later in several Michigan cities, brought to light strong anti-black feelings that the minority segment generally had not previously experienced in their communities. The difference in attitude doubtless stemmed from a great concentration of Southern white job seekers locating there over a period of time.) Wilma complained to Mom that the harassment was so upsetting she could hardly concentrate on her school work and even suggested that she might drop out of nursing school, since it was clear she was not wanted in the school. Wilma was not spared Mom's indignation with dealing in such matters, and Mom's reply was typical of her views on the subject. What she told Wilma I do not think my sister ever forgot, as it was the strongest rebuke she probably would ever hear. "Quitting in anything," Mom declared, "especially in that pertaining to education, is totally unacceptable in our family and it will not be tolerated. You are not there to be 'wanted,' you are there to learn. If the other girls can study and grasp the subjects, you can do it, too, for their brains are no better than yours. Child, God gave you a brain, and don't let anyone keep you from using it!" With that speech ringing

A Certain Blindness

in her ears, Wilma entered wholeheartedly into her anatomy, physics, and chemistry classes. She thereafter refused to be distracted by those who tried to annoy her and consistently received the highest grades and went on to become president of her graduating class.

Mom visited me in Topeka periodically and continued west to California to visit Mary. Mary and Clay had moved to Palo Alto, where Clay worked as a patent attorney for a large corporation.

Once during my junior year in law school my brother Lind contacted me by telephone, saying he had a strong premonition that he should see our aunt Nettie. She had visited us in Michigan for extended periods during our early years but lived in Van Buren, Arkansas, where my uncle Bass lived when originally named a marshal. This was also my father's hometown. "It just came to me that I must see her," Lind confided. I suggested he come to Topeka during Easter break and we would drive down to Van Buren. When we reached Van Buren, we learned Aunt Nettie had been ill, but we had a very pleasant visit with her and also with Aunt Kate, Dad's younger sister. Her daughter, our cousin Mildred, continues to reside in Van Buren. Among the things we talked about was a possible visit to Muskogee, approximately sixty miles to the west. Aunt Nettie wanted me to meet cousin Alice (Uncle Bass's daughter, Alice Spahn) who lived there, and she was certain Alice would give me a gun or some other memento that had belonged to her father.

As we prepared to leave Aunt Nettie, I told her I would be back to visit her as soon as school closed for the summer, and we would drive over to Muskogee. "No, don't say that," she remonstrated, "say you will be down to see me if the Lord is willing!" Within three weeks Aunt Nettie died. My wife, Betty, was hospitalized at the same time, and upon advice from her doctor, I was not able to attend Aunt Nettie's funeral.

Washburn was justifiably proud of its commitment to the education of good legal professionals. It provided me with a

The Lawyer: A High and Noble Calling

range of courses that prepared me in many ways for the problems lawyers face in practicing the law. It could not, however, prepare me to confront the prejudice and racial discrimination that, I was to learn, existed in the legal profession itself and permeated the whole justice system in America. For the moment, however, upon completion of law school, I felt certain that at last, with hard work and dedication, nothing could impede success and happiness in my career and personal life. I recalled that one of our country's earliest leaders, John Adams, defined a republic as a "government of laws and not of men." This had special meaning to me in light of my family's history, because now I was among those instrumental in governing under the law. For Adams and other early adherents of the rule of law, the concept was rooted in a common religious and moral order. The inscription over the entrance of Langdell Hall at Harvard Law School testifies to this common foundation—"Not under man, but under God and the law."

Not having had any close relationship with lawyers or the legal profession, I somehow had formed a naive view that lawyers, like ministers of the Gospel, personally accepted a responsibility beyond profession ethics or an established standard of conduct. I had learned that the rule of law, not being the same as majority rule, is the only principle of order for protecting individual rights and unifying a nation of so many disparate groups. In this perception of government of laws and not men, the men of law are necessarily charged with the high calling of interpreting and guiding American constitutional democracy. Likewise, in our society, which is committed to equal justice under the law, each member of society has every reason to rely upon the legal profession to implement that principle.

To this end, the American Bar Association (ABA) was organized in 1878 with a stated objective to "promote the administration of justice." The ABA has become the largest and one of the most influential professional associations in the world. Attracting presidents, congressmen, cabinet officers, and leaders of business and industry to address its meetings, its influence

A Certain Blindness

not only affects the selection of federal judges but national legislation as well.

In 1905 President Theodore Roosevelt sharply criticized members of the Bar for assisting their clients in evading certain regulatory legislation. After a committee recommended a code of professional ethics, thirty-two canons of professional ethics were adopted by the ABA during its annual meeting in 1908. The preamble to the canons declared in part: "The future of the Republic, to a great extent, depends upon our maintenance of Justice pure and unsullied. It cannot be so maintained unless the conduct and the motives of the members of our profession are such as to merit the approval of all just men."

However, despite its expressed commitment to the administration of justice and its lofty concerns for the honor and dignity of the profession, the ABA adopted a racially exclusionary policy. In 1912 the association mistakenly admitted three black lawyers to membership. Upon being informed of its oversight, the executive committee quickly passed a resolution rescinding the admission "since the settled practice of the Association has been to elect only white men as members." The attorney general of the United States protested, as one of his assistants in the Department of Justice, a Harvard Law School graduate, was one of the contested members. The attorney general was assured by the ABA secretary that the rescission resolution had been adopted only with "a sincere purpose to do what seemed . . . to be right and just."

Blind to the hypocrisy operating between its professional canons and its policy of excluding Negro lawyers, the American Bar Association had a strangely circumscribed understanding of the meaning of justice, which it claimed was a godly quality. The laying of the cornerstone for the Supreme Court building in 1932 was conducted under the auspices of the ABA. Its president, who presided, declared that the building "will be a monument to justice; justice which every human being yearns for and which is the right of all . . . justice in whose service we are sworn; justice that is the final attribute of God himself."[1]

The Lawyer: A High and Noble Calling

William Hastie was appointed federal district court judge for the Virgin Islands in 1937. Following his proposed membership in 1939 there was much disruption in the ABA, and finally, in 1943, a resolution was adopted that "membership in the American Bar Association is not dependent upon race, creed or color." The practice, however, of requiring applicants to designate their race in the ABA application form continued until 1956. A Red Label File, which contained applications from black lawyers, was also maintained by the ABA membership department.

In commemorating the 1978 centennial of the ABA, its journal presented a special section devoted to "the history of the Association and of the law and lawyers in America." At no place in the nine articles, specially written for the memorial by eminent lawyers and scholars about the ABA and its achievements, was there reference to the peculiar role of the black lawyer in the history of the ABA or American law.

Legal historians have noted that, from the nation's earliest years, lawyers have been viewed as a respected class. Alexis de Tocqueville, writing in 1835 on the role of the American lawyer, offered:

> If I were asked where I place the American aristocracy, I should reply, without hesitation, that it is not composed of the rich, who are united together by no common tie, but that it occupies the judicial bench and bar. . . . The special information which lawyers derive from their studies ensures them a separate station in society, and they constitute a sort of privileged body in the scale of intelligence. In America there are no nobles or literary men, and the people are apt to mistrust the wealthy; lawyers consequently form the highest political class and the most cultivated circle of society.[2]

The presence of the Negro lawyer on the American scene presented an irreconcilable conflict in values. A member of "American aristocracy," he was yet deemed inferior because of his color and could be held in perpetual bondage.

A Certain Blindness

The first known black lawyer in America was Marcus B. Allen, admitted to the State Bar of Maine in 1844. During the 1850s John Mercer Langston became a member of the Ohio Bar and Robert Morris was admitted to the Massachusetts Bar. In 1857 Garrison Draper became a member of the Maryland Bar, and Jonathan J. Wright was known to have been a member of the Pennsylvania Bar before the Civil War.

These men enjoyed noteworthy careers. Allen returned to his native South Carolina during Reconstruction and later became an elected judge in Charleston. Langston became first head of the law department of Howard University in 1869; later he served as a congressman from Virginia and as first president of Virginia State College. Wright served as a state senator and later as associate justice of the Supreme Court of South Carolina. Morris practiced law successfully in Massachusetts.

It is indeed remarkable that records of these lawyers exist, no matter how short, and I mention them proudly to show that, in spite of the inhumanity of slavery, the minds, wills, and ambitions of blacks prevailed.

The Reconstruction period provided an encouraging atmosphere for the training of Negro lawyers. It was the time when law school training, instead of sponsorship by other lawyers, became a requisite for the practice of law, and Howard University was founded. Several outstanding Negro lawyers of this period deserve special notice. George Lewis Ruffin received his law degree from Harvard Law School as that school's first black graduate in 1869; an exceptional student, he completed the eighteen-month course in one year. Ruffin served in the state legislature and in 1881 became judge of the Municipal Court of Charlestown, Massachusetts—the first black to hold a judicial position in the North. In 1872 Charlotte E. Ray became the first woman to graduate from Howard Law School, and some hold that she was the first woman to receive training at any law school; she also is reputed to be the first woman to practice before the Supreme Court of the District of Columbia. Josiah T.

The Lawyer: A High and Noble Calling

Settle received his law degree from Howard University and, although admitted to practice in the District of Columbia, he established a law practice in Memphis, Tennessee; in 1885 he was named assistant attorney general of the Criminal Court of Shelby County. He also was one of the moving forces behind the Colored Bar Association of the State of Mississippi, the first bar association organized by "colored lawyers" (the Greenville Movement).

During the brief period of Reconstruction there were many outstanding black men and women who held governmental positions. In South Carolina, for example, reflecting that state's majority Negro population, the three U.S. congressmen were black, including Robert B. Elliott, a lawyer who had been trained in England.

Following Reconstruction, black citizens were denied the usual and ordinary place in the American legal system as well as in the profession. Howard Law School was forced to close its doors. While sixty-two students received their LL.B. degree from Howard between 1871 and 1876, none were graduated for the next four years.

In Georgia, where my grandfather C. R. Wilson lived, the state bar association was organized in 1883. During his lifetime and throughout the period I received my legal training, neither of us could have obtained a legal education or membership in that state's bar association because of our skin color. In celebration of the Georgia Bar Association's first century, the *Georgia State Bar Journal* briefly recounted the state's history through the War of 1812. It continued:

> Later, dissentions among the colonies brought on the War Between the States—followed in Georgia by frustration and poverty of the bitter Reconstruction—enforced by troops.
>
> There had been little opportunity for lawyers of Georgia to devote to organizing themselves to protect the law and the bar and the building of a state and nation, "indivisible, with liberty and justice for all." Even so Georgia had among its individual

A Certain Blindness

lawyers many leaders of the State and the colonies who gave of their talents in establishing law and orderly government in both the United States and in Georgia.

The progress of impoverished Georgia and its neighbors accomplished in this century, the hundred years since Reconstruction, is an inspiration to the present and a challenge to future generations. An epoch when defeat was turned into victory by determined people—with only fertile land and favored climate—working to restore the Southland—a people blessed with faith, faith in themselves and faith in their destiny.[3]

The 1984 statement, while denouncing the "bitter Reconstruction" and citing subsequent progress, failed to consider the interests of black citizens during that most difficult time. Georgia's legal profession stood aside from its acknowledged responsibility by refusing to admit black lawyers to membership until 1962.

Georgia has shared the same general attitudes on racial matters with other states in the South. These attitudes, unfortunately, have resulted all too often in distorted views of the law, the responsibility of lawyers, and the entire system of American justice. Equal justice under the law is hardly attainable when the legal profession is structured to reinforce inequality. The bar's complicity in maintaining unequal justice was clearly shown during the crusade for civil rights in the South. Jerold S. Auerbach wrote: "Few dared to defend advocates of racial equality. Daring was costly: it prompted harassment by courts, legislatures, vigilantes, and fellow professionals (while the American Bar Association shrugged aside the problem as a 'political' issue beyond its purview). In Mississippi, the president of the ABA (along with forty other lawyers) refused to represent a civil rights advocate. One white lawyer in the state, one of a mere handful who demonstrated the courage of his professional convictions, was disbarred. In Mississippi what occurred, therefore, was a complete breakdown in the professional responsibility and obligation of the bar to provide legal representation."[4]

The Lawyer: A High and Noble Calling

William B. Spann, Jr., a prominent Atlanta lawyer and former ABA president, spoke in reference to this problem:

> I have seen examples of this at first hand. In parts of this nation for many years black citizens who wanted no more than their rights under the law—their right to vote, for example— were accused of crimes they did not commit or were charged with crimes far more serious than those they did commit. Once charged, their chance of acquittal before a white judge and white jurors tended to be slim. Some prosecutors felt they had to prosecute to be re-elected. Some lawyers, who might otherwise have ably defended the accused, backed away under pressure from clients.[5]

As late as 1968 only six black lawyers practiced in Mississippi, where the black population was nearly one million. In Alabama, with a higher black population, there were twenty attorneys; and in Georgia, out of fifty-five hundred lawyers, only thirty-four were black, almost half of these being federal government employees.

Black lawyers were often subjected to harassment, insults, and even threats of physical harm. Some of the conditions under which these lawyers practiced in Atlanta are described by Geraldine R. Segal in her book *Blacks in the Law Across the Nation*:

> It was not until the *Brown v. Board of Education* decision in 1954 that the black lawyer in Atlanta had the freedom to function effectively as a professional. Before then, as Atlanta attorney Stanley Foster recounted in a recent article, association with white lawyers was inconceivable, and until 1962 blacks were excluded from membership in both the Atlanta and the Georgia Bar Associations. "The judicial machinery," Foster observed, "mirrored the private practices of the local and state bar associations."
>
> No black faces could be counted among the judges, law enforcement officers, and various other court personnel who constituted the dispensers of justice. Of course, it must be noted that within the physical confines of the court building black practitioners and their clients drank from separate water fountains, used

A Certain Blindness

separate lavatory facilities, and lunched at H. L. Green's or at establishments on Auburn Avenue, because the lunchroom within the courthouse was reserved for "whites only."

Segal also noted, "Another result of the *Brown* decision, which would be realized years later, was increased opportunities for blacks to gain a legal education."[6]

Of course the policy of excluding black men and women from the legal profession begins with the denial of a legal education. Traditionally Southern law schools had been completely closed to black students, only a limited number of whom have been able to enroll in Northern schools. Howard University provided the legal education for the majority of black lawyers in the United States up to the 1960s. When Thurgood Marshall decided to become a lawyer and could not enroll in the University of Maryland in his hometown of Baltimore, he was required to commute to Howard in Washington, D.C.

Marshall, who became one of the outstanding lawyers of our time and the first black man to sit on the U.S. Supreme Court, came under the tutelage of Charles Houston. Later, in collaboration with Houston, Marshall led the legal assault on racial discrimination, especially segregation in public schools. In 1936 Marshall joined Houston, by then general counsel for the NAACP, in successfully gaining court-ordered admission for a Negro student to University of Maryland Law School. After a favorable Supreme Court decision in 1938 in the *Missouri ex. rel. Gaines v. Canada* case, several other victories followed, striking down segregation in public graduate and professional schools. These cases, which challenged the equality of schools under the separate-but-equal principle, culminated with the Supreme Court decision in *Sweatt v. Painter* in 1950. Marshall also received the cooperation of some white legal experts, including Thomas I. Emerson, professor of Yale University Law School, and Louis Pollack, later dean of Yale Law

The Lawyer: A High and Noble Calling

School. These experts formed the Committee of Law Teachers Against Segregation in Legal Education. In regard to Marshall's move against segregation in public schools, Pollack himself remarked, "I would not have had the courage to go after segregation per se—and certainly not at the public school level."[7]

The matter of legal education in Georgia has involved two of my personal friends, both outstanding men of the law. Attorney Donald L. Hollowell represented Horace T. Ward in a 1950 lawsuit against the University of Georgia in the U.S. District Court in Atlanta after Horace had been denied admission to the law school on the basis of his race. Following dismissal of the suit in district court, Horace was forced to seek his education outside his home state. After graduating from Northwestern University Law School in 1959, Horace returned to Georgia and joined the highly esteemed Hollowell in his law practice. In 1961 they subsequently filed suit against the University of Georgia, and this time, after the *Brown* decision, the court directed admission of the first black students to that institution. In 1979 Ward was appointed the first black federal district court judge in Georgia. He was sworn in in the same courtroom where his earlier law suit had been dismissed.

(As a footnote, it should be remembered that at one time the courts of Atlanta had a degrading policy that required separate Bibles for taking oaths from black and white witnesses.)

Another barrier to entering the legal profession has been state bar examinations. In 1971 a committee of the Pennsylvania State Bar Association concluded that black law school graduates were being discriminated against after discovering that their passing rate was 25 percent compared to an overall 81 percent. In 1972 all forty-one black applicants failed the Georgia Bar exam, including graduates from Harvard, Yale, and Columbia universities. In Alabama the passing rate was 20 percent, compared to 70 percent overall. The passing rate in Ohio was 27 to 43 percent, while white applicants ranged from 75 to 88 percent.

A Certain Blindness

In the days before the American Bar Association finally overturned its policy prohibiting Negro membership, there was a great need for a lawyers' group to help achieve racial justice. The National Bar Association was organized in 1925 when twelve black lawyers (eleven men and one woman) from across America met in Des Moines, Iowa. Although not restricted in membership to black lawyers, it has become our chief professional association in helping to further the aspirations of black lawyers and protect the rights of all people. The National Bar Association has had a permanent impact upon our nation, remaining true to its commitment to "protect the civil and political rights of all citizens."

The numbers of black lawyers grew during the 1930s and 1940s, although the attractiveness of the profession was dimmed by their exclusion from bar associations and the mainstream of society. In his 1944 book, *An American Dilemma,* Gunnar Myrdal foresaw great opportunities for black lawyers, "so considerable were the wrongs inflicted upon their people." But before this time a talented group of lawyers had begun to demonstrate professional excellence in the field of "civil rights," even though they continued to be denied their rightful place of prestige and respect within the legal profession. This outstanding group consisted of NAACP lawyers assisted by members of the Howard Law School faculty, and its graduates in private practice served as architects in the revolution of civil rights law. As a result the NAACP has become a model for other groups in effectively litigating concerns for the environment, consumer rights, and many other causes. The cadre of NAACP lawyers controlled almost all major litigation involving Negro rights for several decades and was responsible for charting the course leading to success in *Brown*.

But it was Charles Houston who, through his brilliance and commitment to racial justice, provided the leadership and inspiration for these and so many other black lawyers to excel. Houston graduated magna cum laude and Phi Beta Kappa from Amherst College. Commissioned an officer during World War

The Lawyer: A High and Noble Calling

I, he gave up his rank because of the unfair assignment of black officers and disparaging reports regarding the ability of Negroes to train. Houston was re-trained and became an artillery officer overseas, where he faced violent racism by Red Cross workers and from white enlisted men and officers alike. It was the racial injustice he encountered at home and abroad that caused him to choose a career in the law. Houston earned honors at Harvard, where he served as an editor of the prestigious *Harvard Law Review.* In addition to an LL.B., he received an S.J.D. (Doctor of Judicial Science). One of his professors at Harvard, Felix Frankfurter, was quoted as saying Houston was one of the most "brilliant and able students at Harvard" within his memory.

After a few years in the practice of law, Houston accepted the vice-deanship at Howard Law School and later became the first full-time attorney and general counsel in the Legal Department of the NAACP. Until his death in 1950, Houston worked unceasingly to direct and inspire other lawyers in securing equal justice for all. He felt strongly about equal educational opportunity including, of course, legal training. Continually emphasizing the need for black lawyers, Houston saw the importance of "the service he can render his race as an interpreter and proponent of its rights and aspirations."

The summer following the Supreme Court's decision in *Brown II,* I was preparing to enter my senior year in law school. Betty and I decided to visit several cities in the East and Midwest in order to help us decide where we wanted to eventually locate. It was a trip similar to the one my parents had undertaken some thirty years earlier. Betty and I first went to Washington, D.C., because I was particularly interested in learning what the prospects were for employment in the Department of Justice. With the ruling in *Brown,* I felt there would be increased litigation and a need for attorneys. I met with the appropriate persons at the Department of Justice and several other agencies. The results were most discouraging, and even those who expressed mild interest seemed pessimistic for the future. Further

A Certain Blindness

contact, including more detailed inquiry, proved to be of no avail. Conditions for the practice of law in Washington were not favorable, either. Only recently had racial barriers been removed, allowing Negro attendance to all law schools. Black lawyers were excluded from bar review courses and only after a lawsuit three years earlier were black lawyers allowed to use the law library in the federal courthouse in our nation's capital.

Following the trip and after giving considerable thought to where I would want to locate, I decided Chicago was the place for me to launch my legal career. I believed that Chicago, with its large black population and accompanying political strength, would be in the forefront of making changes that appeared likely throughout America as a result of *Brown*. Chicago at the time had attracted a black population of over nine hundred thousand and had a powerful and influential political base headed by Congressman William Dawson, sometimes referred to as "the most powerful politician in America." I thought the climate was right for a young and unknown but ambitious attorney.

Congressman Dawson's powerful influence in the election of Richard Daley as Chicago's mayor in 1955 has been highly publicized. Elected to Congress in 1942, Dawson took up the fight against the poll tax and the "reactionary and prejudiced clique" in the military for its policy on Negro personnel. As the only Negro in Congress of thirteen million black Americans and a subsequent committee chairman, he undoubtedly used his power and influence to advance the cause of his race. However he and his political allies did not distinguish themselves in the fight for civil rights, fair housing, and equal job opportunities.

Despite the strong Daley-Dawson alliance, Negroes held a disproportionately low number of high-level city or county political positions and judgeships, simply because they were not slated as candidates. This was true of elective and appointed positions alike. The Chicago Urban League in 1965 conducted an analysis of the decision-makers in Cook County with a black population of about 20 percent and Chicago with 28 percent. It revealed that Negroes held only 2 of 156 top city administration posts and only 58 of 1,088 policy-making positions in governmental bodies. In major county institutions Negroes held only 285 policy-making positions out of 1,088. In federal posts, 1 of 31 presidential appointments and 8 of the top 368 civil service positions were held by Negroes. The private sector showed even less representation, and Chicago labor unions showed only 2 to 5 Negroes as top unionists out of 100. If there was anything positive about the low figures of representation, it was reflected in the Chicago Crime Commission's list of syndicate members: only one Negro was reputed to have even minor authority.

The source of Dawson's strength and his primary concern obviously were the rewards to his followers in minor patronage jobs and political favors. His stature and faith in the Democratic party apparently exceeded his commitment to social change.

From its founding by a Negro, Jean Baptiste DuSable in 1790, through sending Oscar DePriest to Congress in 1928 as the first black congressman since the turn of the century, Chicago has been recognized as a political power base for Negroes. But otherwise it has not been unlike other large cities outside the South in practices of racial discrimination.

It can reasonably be said that, at the time I arrived in Chicago, most of the black residents lived in two large enclaves—ghettos, where the housing, schools, stores, and public utility services were generally of a substandard nature. While *Brown* had given tremendous impetus to the struggle against segregation and generated many favorable court decisions, the long established evil of housing segregation persisted.

Betty and I first lived in a newly constructed high-rise apartment building on the near southside near Lake Michigan. We were very close to the Michael-Reese Hospital complex, and both of our children, Paul, Jr., and Laura Kathleen, were born there. Before they were school age, we moved to our own home on the far southside in a quiet residential neighborhood quite close to a good school.

Our early years in Chicago were exciting and full of promise for the future. Since *Brown* and the changes it represented were current subjects, I received many invitations to speak to community groups, churches, and organizations, which helped me to become more well known. I became active in the Chatham-Avalon Neighborhood Organization, the Junior Chamber of Commerce, the area Boy Scouts, and maintained membership in the NAACP and Urban League. We joined the Monumental Baptist Church where Morris H. Tynes was pastor, and I served as a trustee. The director of religious education at Monumental was William H. Robinson, a Republican state legislator. I worked with him in a number of community efforts and came to know him well and respect his commitment to change. Besides being a moving orator, he was a brilliant educator, scholar, and statesman. I do not believe that party affiliation mattered so much to him in view of his overriding concern for unity in the betterment of our people and racial justice.

In time I learned the unfortunate fact that the reasons Chicago appeared so attractive were the same reasons opportunity was so limited. The powerful political system would not allow for change and yet there would be no change without it. Martin Luther King, Jr., was to later share with me a similar hope and subsequent disappointment regarding the Chicago situation. Only after the Daley-Dawson political mold was broken some years later were significant advances made.

My enthusiasm and idealistic approach to living the American dream as an attorney began to wane when I fully realized how severely limited a black professional was. These limitations were due in large measure to the pervasive racially discriminatory legal system composed of bar associations, large law firms, judges, and those in control of governmental agencies. The black lawyer was actually relegated to the "fringe of the profession." Despite the legal brilliance of numerous black lawyers across the country, the black lawyer was not accorded the customary courtesy and recognition or afforded the opportunity to achieve positions of power and influence that were taken for granted by his white counterparts.

During the more than ten years that I was engaged in the

The Lawyer: A High and Noble Calling

practice of law in Chicago, I had the good fortune of being associated with highly competent and successful lawyers. For the most part in association with William C. Starke and Frank A. Anglin, we later joined with several other firms to form one of the first racially integrated law firms on a partnership basis in the country. We continued to be placed at a disadvantage, however, due to the discrimination of large businesses and institutions. There were many interesting sidelights resulting from our association, and they point up that distance between the races often never allows for the truth to be known.

Prior to opening our new firm, we had designated several members of our group to determine the available office space in the downtown area and make a recommendation. After viewing space in a newly constructed office building adjacent to the judicial center, one of the agents for the building casually remarked to an architect that "those niggers can spin their wheels all they want, but they won't get into this building." The agent could not have imagined the architect was a friend of one of our partners and, when a report was made to the owner of the building, a large insurance company, we were able to secure premium space without the slightest problem.

On another occasion, a white partner planned to move into a new home and give up his apartment in a deluxe building on Chicago's south shore. Advised that there were no tenants available, it appeared he was bound by his lease. Since we suspected the building discriminated against Negro tenants, I applied for an apartment specifically requesting his size. I was told there were no apartments available nor would there be in the near future. When management was confronted with the facts and its discriminatory policy exposed, he was allowed to move without breaking the lease and Negro tenants were welcomed thereafter.

We also experienced discrimination in other forms. Early after our firm's formation, we, of course, were very busy seeking additional clients, particularly large businesses, as we faced tremendous expenses. We were quite relieved to learn that a large business organization had agreed to allow our firm to represent it, and only some details remained to be worked out. It came as a terrible blow when it was disclosed we lost the potential client because our partner refused to engage in a homosexual relationship with a high executive in the company. When the matter was discussed at a meeting, there were some very humorous exchanges among the partners, because we desperately needed the lucrative business which was at stake.

The plight of the black lawyer in his attempt to secure justice came under scrutiny in a Department of Labor study in 1963. Labor Department secretary Willard Wirtz declared the legal profession "the worst segregated group in the whole economy or society . . . and the legal profession has got a lot to answer for on this particular score."[8]

There could be no question that in this great country committed to "equal justice under the law," there can be no actual justice when the legal profession, so vital to attaining justice, operates on a basis of racial inequality. Although I soon learned of the racially discriminatory conditions after entering the legal profession, I could not have perceived the extent black Americans were deprived of the basic opportunity to live comfortably and work at decent jobs. Yet the idea persists that one can achieve totally in accordance with his own capacity. The 1956 *Bicentennial Almanac* noted: "The economy is still booming with personal income, production, and business profits all setting record highs. . . . Many Americans credit Eisenhower's administration for the country's happy state of affairs."[9] Although *Brown* had broken the back of legal segregation, Negro Americans could not share in the nation's prosperity, abundance, or "happy state of affairs." A different story of history would have been written had it been seen from the Negro's perspective.

Upon finishing nursing school in Flint, Michigan, my younger sister Wilma remained there for a while and worked in surgery. Having visited Mary in Palo Alto, California, on several occasions, she decided to settle in nearby San Francisco. It

The Lawyer: A High and Noble Calling

was not very long before Mom, who had developed a heart condition, experienced a series of illnesses. While Wilma enjoyed California living, she nonetheless returned to Flint to be helpful to Mom. She subsequently finished Michigan State University, then Wayne University, where she also taught.

Because of Chicago's location, I was able to maintain closer contact with my family, and we visited often. On one occasion, Lind drove alone down to see me as he wanted to discuss something of his future plans. He revealed that, through meditation and prayer, he felt "called to the ministry." We talked many hours, late into the night. Of course I supported him and encouraged him in following what was obviously his strong conviction.

As we had grown older, I was aware of my own tendency toward thinking more logically, but I noted increasingly that Lind gravitated toward the spiritual. This had been apparent in some ways when he served in the army during World War II. Although often serving under fire, Lind never allowed the personal abuse and injustice he encountered as a black serviceman to affect his outlook. He successfully lived out Mom's theme that, in the face of adverse conditions or hostile persons, we should remain steadfast and unyielding in purpose. Lind studied the Bible while in the field and held Bible classes with his soldier friends throughout his stint in the army. While in Florence, Italy, he became closely associated with a church and its pastor, a friendship he maintained for many years. This interest in man's religious nature persisted; pursuing the ministry seemed a natural next step for him.

When Lind returned to Michigan, he immediately pursued part-time studies at a seminary in Pontiac until he completed a degree. As he contemplated a career in the ministry, he was confronted with problems in his own church involving his role as a seminary graduate. Rather than force a confrontation, he withdrew to form another congregation, Grace Emmanuel Baptist Church, with eight members and himself, their pastor. Grace Emmanuel has since built and paid for one church and,

A Certain Blindness

because of its increasing size, has built a second church, which it now occupies.

Not long after his ordination, Lind's experience in performing marriage ceremonies within the family began. Wilma became the first after she had met Henry "Hank" Watts, a native of Buffalo, New York, who was a professor at Wayne. Hank, a Ph.D. and Phi Beta Kappa, teasingly claimed that the family "ganged up" on him, since I gave Wilma away and Lind saw to it the ceremony was most proper. The following year, we returned to Topeka, where Lind officiated at the marriage of our cousin Nancy Todd to Raymond Noches (and my daughter, Laura, participated as the flower girl). During the visit, a chess match was arranged between Lind and Dr. Karl Menninger. The world-famous psychiatrist refers to the game as a chance to express one's aggressiveness, allowing the mind to be "washed." Lind had learned to play chess from the British soldiers he had met overseas and later became amateur champion for the state of Michigan. When he played—and defeated—Dr. Karl, the psychiatrist declared he was pleased "to play a champion."

While Betty and I were able to meet the needs and demands of our respective careers, we apparently were unable to make the necessary commitment for a successful marriage. One of the tragedies of our divorce was that my children were to be deprived of what I wanted most for them—to grow up in a close family with both parents.

The hard fought victories, primarily in the South through the courts following *Brown,* and in the streets, had a profound effect on the enactment of federal civil rights legislation. Thus there was great impetus for change in other parts of the country. For example, in 1963, 220,000 black Chicago school children, about one-half the total enrollment, boycotted the schools to protest de facto segregation and the discriminatory policies of the school system. The following year boycotts were held in New York, Cleveland, Cincinnati, Chicago, and Boston. Some civil rights organizations in the North took on a more militant approach seeking immediate changes in the plight of black citi-

The Lawyer: A High and Noble Calling

zens, whose voices had long been unheard. Equal access to all areas of community life was demanded in many cities throughout the North, causing a hardening of white attitudes. As change and demands for change swept across the North, many civil disturbances and riots erupted, and during 1966 and 1967 the worst racial disturbances in American history occurred. In 1967 over forty riots were recorded and more than one hundred other incidents took place in various cities, including Newark, Detroit, New York City, Cleveland, Washington, and Chicago. The most serious were in Newark, where twenty-six persons died, and in Detroit, the most violent and costly, where forty-three were killed.

On Friday, July 21, 1967, I had driven to Detroit with my children, Paul, age eight, and Laura, seven, to visit my sister Wilma and her family for a few days. We had an early breakfast on Sunday morning, as my children were eager to get started on a promised trip to Canada. On our way I planned to briefly visit an old friend, Gertrude Williams, before spending the remainder of the day in Canada, crossing the Detroit River by bridge one way and by tunnel the other. At about noon, as we were preparing to leave my friend's home, several large columns of black smoke were seen rising high into the sky from the direction in which we were heading. Thinking we might have to reroute our trip, I decided to check the news for any reports that streets were blocked for firefighting purposes. We learned that the police had raided an establishment believed to be selling liquor illegally—leading to rumors of police brutality—resulting in the looting and destruction of property. Within a couple of hours after deciding to delay our trip, we heard the sound of many sirens coming from Dexter Boulevard at the end of the block. Soon we could see smoke rising from Dexter and persons running about, carrying household appliances and furniture. Cars loaded with stolen items sped down the street in front of the house, and it became obvious there was a riot of great proportions taking place. I decided to remain at my friend Gertrude's house, as she was alone except

A Certain Blindness

for her small children. Heavy smoke with its attendant odor, speeding autos—both police and private—and the sound of sirens were to persist for several days. Occasional explosions were intermixed with the sound of gunshots. The following day we learned military troops were being brought in to restore order.

Central High School, at the opposite end of the block from Dexter, was used to house troops and provide an operation base. During the day military vehicles passed back and forth in front of the house, and each evening jeeps with mounted machine guns and trucks carrying troops would proceed toward Dexter. We could hear snipers shooting at the vehicles as well as machine guns firing in return. The children were terrified, and I realized we were caught up in the midst of a war. Before it was over, 43 persons were dead, 2,000 injured, and over 14,000 paratroopers, national guardsmen, and police were involved. Damage was estimated at over $44 million, and there were over 250 fires.

On July 27, 1967, President Lyndon B. Johnson formed a Special Advisory Commission on Civil Disorders in Washington to thoroughly investigate the cause of the disorders across the country and recommend remedial action. He named Governor Otto Kerner of Illinois as chairman and Mayor John Lindsay of New York as vice-chairman. On February 29, 1968, the Kerner Commission reported that the United States was "moving towards two societies, one black, one white, separate and unequal," and stated that the principal cause of the riots of recent years was "white racism."

Following the April 4, 1968, assassination of Martin Luther King, Jr., riots erupted in 125 cities; 68,887 troops were called up to curb the violence that resulted in at least 48 deaths and 3,500 injuries. In Washington, D.C., 7 people were killed, 1,166 were injured, and property damage was estimated at $15 million. Troops numbering 15,000 were required to control the violence.

A federal survey, reported in the June 13, 1968, *Wall Street*

Journal, showed that the nation's major utilities had the worst record of any industry in hiring Negroes. Of the persons employed by the major electric, gas, and combination utilities only 3.7 percent were Negroes, according to the Equal Employment Opportunity Commission (EEOC) report. When confronted with this evidence, the industry was quick to point out that the Federal Power Commission (FPC), which had broad regulatory power over the industry, was itself obviously guilty of practicing racial discrimination for its failure to employ Negroes in professional-level positions. The most glaring example of this discrimination was an absence of black attorneys representing the FPC in cases with various utility companies, so the federal government was in the untenable position of seeking to correct an injustice which it was apparently unwilling to do itself.

The history of blacks in the employment of the federal government parallels that of private industry and other public institutions. This includes attorneys and other professionals. The policy of discrimination in federal employment was probably most firmly established during the administration of President Woodrow Wilson. As a candidate for president in 1912, Wilson openly appealed for the support of black citizens who were moving back into political life for the first time since Reconstruction. He stated at his first inaugural that "the firm basis of government is justice. . . . There can be *no* equality of opportunity, the first essential of justice in the body politic, if men, women and children be not shielded in their lives, their very vitality from consequences of great industrial and social processes which they cannot alter, control, or singly cope with. Justice and only justice shall always be our motto." Many Negroes, who had long been loyal to Republicanism, strongly supported the new freedom offered by Wilson, but unfortunately it was to have no meaning for them.

A number of bills were introduced in Congress within a few months of the new administration directed toward establishing a policy of segregation in government. One was a bill "to effect certain reforms in the Civil Service by segregating clerks

A Certain Blindness

and employees of the white race from those of African blood or descent." While most of these bills were not enacted into law, they indicated the feeling of members of Congress whose importance and influence in the new administration was increasing. Although Wilson did not approve of the demagoguery of his more rabid Southern supporters, he shared their view on race relations. Soon the Post Office Department and Treasury Department instituted segregation in offices, shops, restrooms, and lunchrooms. Within a matter of months, the nation's capitol and offices of the federal government had about as many varied practices of segregation and discrimination as any capitol building in the former Confederate States.

Even with the coming of Franklin D. Roosevelt's New Deal, the door remained closed to professional opportunity for black employees except on very rare occasions. Black lawyers were subjected to the same disappointment in government employment as encountered in the private sector. One black attorney, seeking a position in a government agency, was kept waiting for three hours while every white applicant was interviewed. Finally he was told that the position was reserved for whites only. Angrily he exclaimed, "One is driven to hate either his color or his country."

When the 1968 Equal Employment Opportunity Commission survey results became public, the Johnson administration responded by announcing it was committed to equality. Faced with a highly embarrassing situation over its longstanding policy of unfairness, the Federal Power Commission agreed to employ an experienced black lawyer as a member of its staff of trial attorneys at a reasonably attractive salary. EEOC placement director Joe Rollins suggested strongly that such a lawyer, in addition to being eminently qualified professionally, would have to possess qualities of maturity and temperament necessary to cope with an uncomfortable—if not hostile—work environment. While there are always problems for the "first" hired in an employment situation, there were special ones presented in these circumstances because a black man would receive a higher salary than many of his colleagues. Also, this position was with a very prestigious agency where jobs were historically reserved for the elite of the legal profession. The EEOC was, therefore, particularly concerned that the "right" person be found who would reflect favorably on the newly formed placement section.

For several years after my divorce I had been interested in government service and had been offered several appointments but had turned them down because they were either of an "administrative" nature or were "dead end" from a legal point of view. If I made a change, I definitely wanted to enhance my legal career. This idea of a Negro attorney getting a position with the Federal Power Commission was inconceivable until after the Civil Rights Act of 1964, and I recognized the nature of the opportunity. I knew in that position I could develop an expertise in the lucrative field of public utilities law, which previously had been virtually closed to black lawyers. An appointment was arranged for me to meet David Bardin, the FPC deputy general counsel in charge of hiring the new attorney. He was a highly intelligent and competent lawyer and administrator who expressed a sensitivity to the problem of racial discrimination and, more specifically, to the problems facing a black lawyer coming to work in the Federal Power Commission.

Dave seemed favorably inclined during the course of the interview and was especially interested in my association with the Menninger Foundation. Subsequent to providing copies of briefs I had filed in cases before the Illinois Supreme Court, I was offered the position. The key to my acceptance was the assurance that I would be actively engaged in the trial of cases as a member of the trial staff. I was determined not to be a mere statistic for show purposes on behalf of the FPC and was prepared to pay the price for the substantive benefits that I could accrue as a trial attorney. At the same time, it was made rather clear that the general counsel was not going to be concerned with any special problems that might arise in the course of my work or with other employees.

I spent my first Thanksgiving in Washington as a guest in

A Certain Blindness

Dave Bardin's home. It was a comfortable visit as his wife and children were enjoyable and she was a good cook.

The Federal Power Commission had jurisdiction to regulate the pricing and flow of electricity and natural gas in interstate commerce, and it granted certificates and licenses and established the pricing structure for those companies and municipalities seeking such power from various suppliers. I was assigned to the certificate section of the natural gas division. The assistant general counsel in charge of the section was on leave convalescing from a heart attack, so his assistant was my acting section chief. He was very knowledgeable as well as cooperative and helpful. He never told me but I believe that, if he had had more authority, it would have been better for me.

For my first several cases I was to serve as co-counsel with another lawyer. A native of Ann Arbor, Michigan, he was a bright young attorney who graduated from the University of Michigan Law School, then served as an air force officer. He was very conscientious and gladly shared with me what he knew. I could not have chosen a better person to work with during that period.

A month or so following my arrival, the assistant general counsel returned to work. He had been with the FPC since its inception and was extremely well informed. He did not seem to disapprove of me, but I certainly got the impression there was an indifference to my presence. I continually expected him to explain more fully the certificate section's work and what I was expected to do in fulfilling my tasks under his supervision. No such meetings were ever forthcoming. Several times I purposefully went to his office hoping to have some general discussion about our work, in addition to asking specific questions. Oftentimes I was referred to the acting chief or received some vague response, but always it seemed I was not taken as seriously as I would have liked.

During this time, I enrolled at Georgetown University Law Center for courses in public utilities law and accounting in order to fully master this area of the law. My co-counsel and I

The Lawyer: A High and Noble Calling

were eventually assigned a large and complex case requiring several extended hearings through the spring and continuing until fall after the summer recess. Upon return from a vacation I learned that he was offered an attractive position with another department of government and hurriedly accepted it. The section chief assured me that, because of the nature of the case, two lawyers were required, and he would assign someone to work with me. He never told me that he changed his mind, but I soon realized that he was not going to provide any assistance. This presented quite a dilemma. If I demanded help, I was quite sure that the request would be used to show that I was incapable of handling the required work load. It might in fact provide an excuse for those interested in my removal from the trial staff. On the other hand, if I goofed up, I myself would be providing ample basis for my removal.

After much thought I decided to stick it out and do the best I possibly could. So much of my career was in the balance. Recalling my mother's admonition to my sister Wilma years before, I knew I could not allow this man to interfere with what was so important to me. As a result I was required to work long hours into the evening, often over weekends, and sometimes during holidays in order to conscientiously prepare the case for trial. A member of the engineering staff and sometimes economists or accountants are assigned to assist the attorney as consultants; in the case I was working on, the engineer was originally from Pittsburgh and the son of a former major league baseball player. He understood my situation and provided invaluable assistance and performed well beyond what was ordinarily expected.

It was commission policy that all legal briefs were to be reviewed and initialed by an assistant general counsel before they could be printed. I would always complete my briefs and allow sufficient time for review and revisions before printing. Several times my section chief waited until the last minute to review my briefs, which almost caused me to miss the filing deadlines set by the court. Despite my reminders and urging, he just ceased to review my work. His secretary could not explain

A Certain Blindness

why my briefs remained on his desk day after day; sometimes she would come to my office and ask that I not attempt to see him because of his particular mood that day. I realized that since I was responsible for meeting the deadlines set by the court, I could not abdicate my professional responsibility because of his conduct. (Only after my section chief died suddenly was I able to verify that he resented me working there.) I resorted to setting my own deadline and retrieving my work from his office whether approved or not, in order to allow time for printing. There were several black employees in the printing plant who understood my problem and were most cooperative. I was very grateful to them.

The black employees in the commission were very supportive and took pride in assisting me whenever they could. Many of them were locked into menial dead-end jobs and over the years had suffered many forms of discrimination. After word got around that I was concerned with their problems, my office became somewhat of a legal aid center. It was particularly important to me for them to know that we all shared many problems, regardless of my professional standing.

Some of my white colleagues, as well as other employees, were friendly and helpful, but for the most part my presence seemed to cause uneasiness. In the early days of my FPC employment I joined with a group of lawyers for coffee each morning. I wanted to appear friendly and not to isolate myself or appear withdrawn, but I became increasingly aware that they seemed to expect me to seek their acceptance and be overjoyed at being there with them. There was an unmistaken message that I should continually strive to measure up to some imaginary standards they set and controlled. This came to a head one morning when a bright Harvard Law School graduate and self-professed "liberal" thought to pay me a compliment. I should be very pleased and realize a great measure of self-satisfaction, he told me, in coming all the way from "the ghetto" to becoming a lawyer with the highly prestigious Power Commission.

The Lawyer: A High and Noble Calling

He wanted me to know that he was sensitive to the many problems I had necessarily encountered and the obstacles that I had overcome. He was also aware of how difficult it must be for me to work in daily contact with so many white people. Everyone at the table sat very attentively, pleased that one of their own would have such depth and insight regarding the plight of this lonely black man. They imagined I would be appreciative and be quick to acknowledge a debt of gratitude.

I calmly and clearly explained that I had never lived in a ghetto, as he had presumed, but I was fully aware of the problems of black folk, wherever they lived. In addition I informed them that I had lived in close contact with white people all my life and that it was not I who was uncomfortable or had problems being in the company of the "other" race.

Thereafter I decided to have my coffee at my desk, as I had more than enough work to do, and I simply did not have time to further "educate" these brilliant lawyers. While often sought out for my views on certain racial matters, I was always courteous but did not express an abundance of patience. Sometime later I was discussing the legal aspects of Adam Clayton Powell's expulsion from the U.S. House of Representatives with an attorney. Clearly out of the blue and having nothing to do with the law involved, she stated that she did not like Powell because he was "such a loud mouth" like Muhammad Ali. I did not want to hurt her feelings, but I had to expose her racist view of the matter. I pointed out her need to compare two outspoken black men—not Powell with another congressman or public official, and not Ali with other boxers or professional athletes. She admitted that she had always looked upon black folk in a different light than whites but stated she was unaware of it. She reluctantly agreed that her real problem was resenting all black persons who freely and forcefully expressed themselves, regardless of whether she agreed with them or not.

On a number of occasions people complimented me for not being "bitter." Although the persons involved were well

A Certain Blindness

intentioned, I realized that in most instances an explanation of my feelings would be as much a waste of my time as thinking I could cause the blind to see.

Of course I realized my experiences were far from unique. The January 12, 1969, *New York Times* reported on the status of black Americans: "Some officials believe that statistical advances made by Negroes may have been more than offset by the hardening of attitudes and the polarization of whites and Negroes throughout the nation, as found by the National Advisory Commission on Civil Disorders." In February of 1969 the Kerner Commission released "One Year Later," which concluded, "We are a year closer to two societies—black and white, increasingly separate and scarcely less unequal."

When Richard M. Nixon won the 1968 presidential election, I surmised that Nixon's so-called "Southern strategy" would create changes in FPC top personnel that would not bode well for me. Public opposition to desegregation had played a major role in Nixon's campaign; according to many, Nixon opposed further school desegregation. The approach of this new administration became clear when it brought political pressure to bear in the Mississippi case *Alexander v. Holmes County Board of Education* (1969). The Fifth United States Circuit Court of Appeals ordered thirty-three Mississippi school districts to submit plans for desegregation, which would be put into effect during the forthcoming school year. But upon a motion made by the Department of Justice and a recommendation of the secretary of the Department of Health, Education, and Welfare, the court suspended its order and postponed the date for submission of desegregation plans. This was the first time since *Brown* that the government opposed the plaintiffs' position. The Supreme Court countered, "Under explicit holdings of this Court the obligation of every school district is to terminate dual school systems at once and to operate now and hereafter only unitary schools," thereby reinstating the order to desegregate. Expressing his views on the subject, President Nixon remarked at a press conference that those who wanted "instant integration" were as "extremist" as those who wanted "segregation forever." Nixon's statements made it plain that he was blind to the constitutional rights of black Americans.

More evidence of the new administration's federal racial policies came to light in how it handled EEOC findings. Since the commission had no authority except to recommend, it had urged the Justice Department three times to file a charge of "pattern or practice of discrimination" against the entire motion picture industry. Acknowledgment of the requests had not been made nor had the attorney general found time to discuss civil rights matters with Chairman Clifford Alexander, as the EEOC suggested three months earlier. Senator Everett Dirksen of Illinois resented the commission's investigative activity and declared, "This punitive harassment . . . is going to stop . . . or I'm going to the highest authority in Government to get somebody fired." The very next day the White House announced that EEOC chairman Alexander, the target of Dirksen's wrath, would be replaced.

Dirksen's outburst at a Senate hearing had obscured the facts disclosed in Alexander's testimony that a black college graduate earns $1,040 less than a white person who never attended college. The EEOC also found that the movie industry almost completely excluded black and Mexican Americans from craft jobs by a collusive system. In the aerospace industry, minorities were generally placed at the bottom of the job ladder, though many had education or training superior to whites in higher positions. In three large Southern firms awarded contracts by the Pentagon, one of sixteen whites was an official or manager compared to one out of a thousand blacks. One plant refused to hire a black woman because she had a child out of wedlock, but the company admitted hiring white unwed mothers.

Since I was a direct beneficiary of EEOC efforts in providing equal employment opportunity I was particularly stung by Alexander's firing. I felt quite vulnerable and in a tenuous employment situation, because FPC policies have always reflected the philosophy of whatever administration was in power. Gener-

A Certain Blindness

ally the views of an administration would either favor the interest of the producers of natural gas—the large companies in the Southwest—or the consumers more—in the Northeast. The change in administration also meant the appointment of a new general counsel and deputy general counsel. I never knew the party preferences of most of the lawyers employed by the FPC, but all of a sudden there was a large number of announced Republicans. One lawyer told me how pleased he was "the Jews" were out as now his star would shine (however, when I left the commission, he was still doing the same mundane job).

At the time Gordon Gooch was named as the new general counsel, I was in the middle of an extended trial, but I knew of the scramble among the lawyers to meet him and curry his favor. Shortly after his arrival he arranged to meet with the legal staff, excepting those lawyers engaged in trials whom he would meet individually at a later time. He required that all lawyers submit a brief biographical sketch.

The word was that Gordon Gooch seemed like a decent guy who acted as though he were going to be his own man. All I knew was that he was young, big, walked fast, and was from Texas, where he had been a member of a large Houston law firm. The morning after my trial ended I called Gordon's secretary to arrange to meet him at his convenience. She immediately called back to tell me to come in.

I had decided to be frank as far as my past experiences in the commission were concerned. My preference was to remain at the FPC, but, depending upon his attitude, I was prepared to leave rather than continue as before. Gordon gave me the impression of being a pleasant and decent person with a no-nonsense, hard-driving approach. Having my biographical sketch before him, he asked me some questions about Topeka and my background without disclosing what he knew about the *Brown* case or that he once served as Chief Justice Warren's law clerk. He asked my views of the Power Commission and my working relationship with other staff members. I freely explained my strong feelings of responsibility to the staff as a loyal team member and that in

The Lawyer: A High and Noble Calling

turn the commission had not met its responsibility to me. I also spoke of my professional goals and my desire to have the experience of handling more rate cases. Even though I was unaware of Gordon's thinking, I was pleased that I had gotten so much off my chest and felt I would receive a fair shake. In any event, I was prepared to take whatever came along.

Several days later I was surprised to receive a call from Gordon advising that, upon the closing of my last case, I was to be transferred to the producer rate section for regular assignment of cases. Also, he wanted me to assist in some new projects the commission was planning to undertake. This was not the call I had expected to get from the new general counsel. Having suffered myself on many occasions as a victim of stereotyping, I had been just as ready to stereotype Gordon Gooch. I had been about to pronounce judgment on this man because of his race, his political persuasion, and the region of the country he had come from. Had I done so, I would have lost so much.

After I became more secure in my job and comfortable with the working conditions, I was able to devote more time to outside interests. Beginning as a volunteer in a neighborhood legal services office, I soon became deeply involved in recruiting government lawyers to volunteer legal assistance. This effort proved quite successful, especially since there were so few black lawyers in government at that time and the white lawyers mostly lived outside the District of Columbia. The staff attorneys for the legal service agency were, for the most part, highly dedicated and overworked, though some tended to pick over the cases and choose only those which presented novel questions of law and which they believed might result in landmark decisions. Most of the cases arose under tragic circumstances and had resulted from the legal process being used to victimize those persons who actually were most in need of the protection afforded by the law. On some occasions I thought of reducing the number of cases I was handling, only to find my caseload increased due to the emergencies involved.

While the work of providing legal assistance was generally

A Certain Blindness

distressing, my activities with the Bill of Rights Program of the Federal Bar Association was wholly gratifying. The purpose of the program was to have lawyers in the association volunteer to periodically lecture high school classes on the practical application of the Bill of Rights and discuss leading cases arising under each constitutional amendment. I found myself returning to several schools on my own, welcoming the opportunity to stress the importance of seeking justice through the legal process. I will always believe that my efforts resulted in some students gaining a new and healthy respect for the law and becoming better citizens. There were others, I believe, whose keen interest may have sparked a legal career.

The one thing that was so clearly impressed upon me in the course of my volunteer work was the number of persons who were obviously "trapped" in our society and on the verge of being helpless. I found myself relating many personal experiences to illustrate the importance of maintaining a sense of hope. I believe that "But for the grace of God, there go I," so as a black professional I felt an obligation to provide assistance and support to the poor and oppressed. I could not allow myself to be blinded by the myth that hard work leads to assured success, in view of the forced barriers of racism and oppression faced by all black Americans.

The commendations I have received for volunteer legal work have provided me with a genuine source of pride, and in spite of my out-of-office activities I was able to earn a supervisory position at the Federal Power Commission through the diligent and effective handling of my case assignments.

I came to know and respect Federal Power Commission general counsel Gordon Gooch, whom I found to be a patient listener despite the heavy demands the job placed on his time. I was especially impressed with his strong sense of fairness and equality. I learned that Gordon clerked for Chief Justice Earl Warren after graduating from the University of Texas Law School, where he had distinguished himself as one of the outstanding students in the country. Gordon maintained a close

The Lawyer: A High and Noble Calling

relationship with Warren afterwards, and as a result I was able to meet the former chief justice and talk at length with him about his personal views on the *Brown* case and the issue of racial equality.

Gordon himself was receptive to my idea of actively recruiting black lawyers. We arranged to hire students from Howard University Law School, a predominantly black institution in Washington, to work part time at our offices, in the same manner as we hired law students from other schools in the area. Officials from Howard told me that, based on previous experiences, they had traditionally "written off" the Power Commission as a potential employer for their graduates.

In 1971 I was selected to participate in an important FPC project. The Power Commission was launching a nationwide investigation into the cost and adequacy of the nation's supply of natural gas. FPC department heads and other high officials assembled in the general counsel's office. Aside from Gordon, there were only two other lawyers present, John Williams and myself. John and I were named as the officers to conduct this premier investigation, looking toward the setting of rates for future sales of natural gas by producers throughout the United States.

Work on the project was fascinating as well as challenging. John, who became a personal friend, was a pleasure to work with. A native of Bartlesville, Oklahoma, he had experience in all phases of the oil and gas business, from field hand to attorney with a large oil company to Power Commission staff attorney, and he readily shared his vast knowledge. I have enjoyed many visits with John and his family in their Rockville, Maryland, home.

The FPC investigation required me to meet with top officials of the major oil and gas companies throughout the United States, and I also conducted public hearings in six major cities from New York to Los Angeles. All of this activity accorded me a high level of recognition in the FPC as well as in the private sector. Our final report sparked considerable controversy within

A Certain Blindness

the industry and on Capitol Hill, and at one point there were rumors about my being subpoenaed to appear before a congressional committee to report on our findings. John and I each received the Power Commission's highest efficiency award for our work on this nationwide project.

My contact with industry officials resulted in some attractive offers of employment, particularly one from Michigan Consolidated Gas Company in Detroit. Though I was especially interested in a judgeship by this time, I left the Federal Power Commission in 1972 after receiving an appointment as a hearing examiner with the Department of Health, Education, and Welfare's Bureau of Hearings and Appeals. Temporarily assigned to Detroit, I viewed this as a perfect opportunity to evaluate Michigan Consolidated Gas Company's offer more closely and to observe firsthand the living conditions in the area.

Moving about Detroit, I was struck by the highly visible distance that existed between the races. A local school desegregation case then in United States District Court typified the racial problems affecting Detroit. Eventually Judge Stephen Roth—a native of Flint, Michigan, as I am—decided that the Detroit School Board knowingly created and perpetuated segregation in its schools. In fact the city school board had contracted with a suburban school district to transport Negro high school students to all-Negro or predominantly Negro schools in Detroit, instead of to nearby white schools within the district or to nearby suburban white schools. Realizing that a local remedy would not be effective, Judge Roth ordered the adoption of an inter-district desegregation plan encompassing the entire metropolitan area. School authorities refused to comply with this order and preferred to violate the constitutional rights of black children, a disheartening situation considering that *Brown* had declared segregation unconstitutional nearly twenty years before.

There was no need for me to further consider remaining in Detroit as I received news that I was to be appointed to the newly designated position of administrative judge. The news elated me, though leaving Detroit would mean missing my

The Lawyer: A High and Noble Calling

frequent and enjoyable visits with family, especially Mom and Art, who were both doing so well. But a conversation I had with my hearing assistant surely disturbed me.

A neat, intelligent, and extremely efficient young black woman, my hearing assistant and I were working to close out my cases. She tearfully explained how much she appreciated what I had done for her. I had an excellent working relationship with her and had spoken highly of her, but I never felt I had done so much as to warrant so deep an appreciation. As we talked, she revealed that she thought I had personally chosen her and been responsible for her promotion. She recounted that, when it was learned from Washington that I was black, the woman who previously had the necessary classification and was assigned to work for me refused, saying she would not work for a black man. Rather than forthrightly dealing with the secretary, the decision was made to promote the black woman to a higher classification and pay level.

While I was pleased I had been the means for advancement that might not have occurred otherwise, I also felt that same old sense of powerlessness in the face of white prejudice. The reality was that the white woman assigned to work under my supervision actually wielded more power and control over our work relationship than I, simply because she had white skin. There was simply no way I could have retained any one of my positions had I refused to work with anyone because of their race. In spite of having improved my circumstances and in spite of becoming a member of an esteemed and honored profession, I was abruptly reminded that skin color continued to be a controlling factor in determining my status in our society—with the attendant humiliation and degradation.

About one hundred years before, a white posseman refused to work for my uncle Bass for the same reason. Sanctioning the bigotry now was a governmental agency.

9

On Being a Judge

Appointment as a judge in the court system of the United States represented my highest mark of achievement, both personally and professionally. The recognition and esteem associated with being a member of such a powerful and select group were sources of great pride for me and my family. Vested with the authority to determine the rights of my fellow citizens, I felt called to ensure the constitutional protections of freedom and justice—the same freedom and justice my grandparents were completely denied and my parents found so elusive.

My personal experience over many years had proven that there can be rewards for hard work and perseverance in the absence of political favor or family status. And on a personal level I was acutely aware that I had achieved a position—as federal administrative judge—that no black man had ever attained before; what was possible for me in 1972 had seemed unattainable even as recently as my first years out of law school. I was grateful for the opportunity and realized how fortunate I

On Being a Judge

was, especially in contrast to the tragic experiences of so many I had known.

While there are hardships encountered whenever people strive to change their circumstances, most white Americans cannot perceive the frustration and hopelessness caused by racial barriers to progress that many generations of black Americans have had to face. Without any doubt, the special problem of my skin color has far exceeded all the other difficulties I have encountered in my efforts to advance myself.

America's tremendous growth in population, mobility, economic activity, and high crime rate has resulted in important social, economic, and cultural issues being placed before the judiciary. In addition to the problems of guilt, innocence, property rights, and redress for their infringement, greater emphasis over the years has been placed on personal constitutional protection, such as the principle that "no person shall be deprived of the equal protection of the law." Under this phrase, new and complex legal questions have arisen regarding the rights of the unborn, children, mentally ill, prisoners, as well as those having unpopular political, religious, or social beliefs. New laws and remedies have been required for the protection of these rights, and members of the judiciary have found themselves in the incomparable position in our society to contribute to the common good of all Americans.

Regrettably, however, the fact is that the administration of justice is still affected by considerations of race and color, because the constitutional context of these issues has never been settled. The judge, of course, is the most important single element in our judicial process, and to a great extent the quality of our justice depends on the quality of our judges.

As for myself, I was confident of my own knowledge of the law and, charged with the special responsibility of my new role, I welcomed the opportunity to "do justice." I recalled that the *American Bar Asociation Journal* had published an article, "Ten Commandments for the New Judge," which emphasized: "If we judges could possess but one attribute, it should be a kind

A Certain Blindness

and understanding heart. The bench is no place for cruel or callous people regardless of their other qualities and abilities." I believe this attribute to be an essential one for judges, and I am also mindful of the scriptural passage cautioning that from those to whom much is given, much is required.

Lawyers are motivated to become judges for various reasons, but generally security, status, and power are among the main factors in seeking a judgeship. Although judges are not significantly different from any other group of comparably educated professional persons, it would seem apparent that they should possess additional qualities as well. This is particularly significant in light of the role judges play in making crucial decisions that control the lives, hopes, and aspirations of their fellow citizens. While some judges maintain that humanity and compassion should have no part in legal justice, it is obvious, however, that the quality of justice they render reflects something about their personal traits. In addition to having adequate knowledge of the law, good judges are basically good men and women, and it follows that persons before the bar of justice will be affected by their character, common sense, and experience in living. Though judges are bound by rules of procedure and evidence and make rulings based on the law, their concepts of marriage, family, religion, and social standing can affect a decision, as can their views on racial equality.

History has proved that it is possible for judges to use the law as an instrument to perpetuate injustice and oppression, so therefore the manner of selecting judges should be a matter of grave concern. Professor Anthony Amsterdam of Stanford University maintains, however, that "the problem is not who the judges are and how they are selected from the lawyers," but "who the lawyers are, and how they are self-selected from the people."[1]

By comparison, the ideals of students in medical school are similarly important. Dr. Karl Menninger of Topeka's Menninger Foundation declared that "the value systems, standards, and ideals of the Doctor are very important. To be sure, these are

On Being a Judge

for the most part features of character which become part of the man before he goes to medical school." Moreover, "their effectiveness [is] . . . related in large measure to the stature and breadth of their own personalities."[2] Menninger believed it was the responsibility of a school of psychiatry to select those persons most likely to become good psychiatrists. Certainly, no less a procedure should be undertaken in selection of lawyers. Instead, as Amsterdam has accurately observed, as a group lawyers

> are disproportionately scions of the privileged classes; they are unduly motivated by the desire to do well rather than to do good; they are affected by the timorousness and tunnel vision one might expect from those who select a profession long dedicated to making the rich richer and the poor poorer; and all their worst proclivities in these directions are reinforced by the structure of legal education and the legal profession. No judicial-selection system can touch that problem; and, until it is exposed and cured, we are going to have bad courts, bad judges, bad law and bad lawyers.[3]

The Book of Job has an apt remark about the situation Amsterdam has described: "In the eyes of those who are at ease there is contempt for misfortune."

Although our Constitution and all statutory law are premised on equal justice under the law, justice has not been realized because judges have not adhered to this premise. This is clearly seen in the case law dealing with race and color and leading up to *Brown,* including the decisions in *Dred Scott* and *Plessy.* Ironically many decisions after *Brown* continued to follow a policy of inequality as judges struggled to keep the old order intact.

The quality of justice one receives in our country is still determined by the person's skin color. Donald Dale Jackson, in his fine book entitled *Judges,* reported on an informal interview he conducted with three judges (from Michigan, Colorado, and Tennessee) attending the National Judicial College in Reno, Nevada:

A Certain Blindness

  Despite the range of their political and geographic backgrounds, they had more similarities than differences. All believed, for example, that judicial sternness was important in the face of increasing crime, that "respect for law and order" was declining, that all lawyers secretly yearned to be judges, and that a judge was a fine thing to be.

  "The prestige, the robe, all that means a lot," said Judge Michigan, and "don't believe them if they tell you differently."

  All three were worried about "niggers." "We got a nigger judge in Denver now," Judge Colorado reported.

  "We got a bundle of 'em in Michigan."

  "You know, justice is different in the black part of town," Tennessee said. "These bleeding hearts talk about equal justice. Hell, the black part of town's different, that's all. It's a different world, different standards, so you have to deal with them differently." The other two nodded and sipped their beer.[4]

These particular judges, and most white judges, are hardly qualified to preside over trials involving the rights of black persons, who are totally alien to their backgrounds, experiences, and way of life. Racism permeates our judiciary, and it is nowhere more pronounced than in sentencing. Since judges are not bound or restricted by any set criteria, their personal values and prejudices come to the fore. All too often the key to sentencing lies in the attitudes of the judges and not the facts of a case. Jackson proved this among the judges attending National Judicial College. He disclosed that judges were asked to pass sentence in a hypothetical case with indentical fact sheets. The defendant was identified as black on half the fact sheets and as white on the other half, with no other details changed. When the defendant was white, jail sentences varied from three to ten days; when black, the range was five to thirty days in jail. Jackson also reported that in seven Southern states the average sentence for black defendants convicted of major felonies was 18.8 years; white defendants were sentenced to 12.1 years.[5] These findings were supported by a federal court study that found 48 percent of blacks convicted of interstate theft received

On Being a Judge

prison sentences while only 28 percent of whites convicted of the same crime went to prison.

The matter of a dual standard of justice is confirmed by many unbiased studies. The President's Crime Commission reported in 1967 that racial prejudice permeates the court system. These were the same concerns expressed by the Kerner Commission a year later. Similar conclusions were reached by the U.S. Commission on Civil Rights in its 1970 report. The National Minority Advisory Council on Criminal Justice (NMACCJ) presented its data to the Department of Justice showing that minorities are arrested, indicted, and imprisoned more frequently than whites; the study concluded that the nation's criminal justice system is racist. Its 1982 report, based on studies and public hearings, declared, "glaring disparities in the sentencing of poor and minority defendants, as compared to those convicted of crimes who are affluent and white, lack a principled basis."[6] On April 30, 1989, the *Atlanta Journal-Constitution* reported that in Georgia more blacks than whites were sent to jail for committing the same crime.

Nowhere has the inequitable application of penalties been shown more than in death sentences. In Pennsylvania, for example, over a forty-year period, only 11 percent of the black inmates on death row had their death sentences commuted while 20 percent of the white inmates' sentences were commuted. Yet all had been convicted of first-degree murder.

In 1972 the United States Supreme Court struck down the death penalty, citing, among other reasons, that it discriminated against the poor and minority groups. The *Los Angeles Times* on January 8, 1984, reported that a study conducted in Florida between 1973 and 1977 revealed that 72 white men on death row in early 1978 had all killed other white persons. However, of 111 white persons who had killed black folk in Florida over the period, none received a death sentence. The *Atlanta Constitution* reported on November 9, 1983, on two separate studies conducted in the state of Georgia, one by a University of Iowa law professor and another by a Stanford University researcher.

A Certain Blindness

The editorial stated: "The pattern is clear. Most juries find the killing of a white person more heinous than the killing of a black. That is exactly the sort of arbitrary application of the death penalty that the U.S. Supreme Court sought to avoid when it struck down the old laws in 1972." It would appear that many of the more than one hundred inmates on Georgia's death row are not there because of the crimes they committed but because of their skin color or the skin color of their victims. As of 1977, of the 366 people executed in Georgia since 1930, 298 were black and 68 were white. Of the 299 executions for murder, 234 were of blacks and 65 were of whites. Of the 61 executions for rape, 58 were of blacks and 3 were of whites.

Our nation's juvenile system follows the same pattern. In 1989 Victor Strieb, law professor at Cleveland State University, reported that of the 281 juveniles (those whose crimes were committed while under the age of 18) executed in this country, 69 percent were black. Of the 43 juveniles executed for rape or attempted rape, 42 were black. All of the victims were white.

A white person who lives with a black person will also fare worse at the hands of a racist judge. Bruce M. Wright, now a New York judge, recalls an experience he had when he was a practicing attorney:

> In New York City the lawyer asked the judge to put the defendant on probation to facilitate his rehabilitation. All there were white. Scanning the probation report about the defendant, the judge muttered bitterly three times, "How can he be rehabilitated. He's living with a colored woman." Hearing that, a black lawyer stepped forward to offer some expert testimony on the question of living with a colored woman, but the judge hurried away when the lawyer announced his purpose. Charges were preferred, but the judge was exonerated. Later he became a Supreme Court justice.

In Florida following the divorce of a white couple, the wife was granted custody of their daughter. After three years, during which time she was forced to return to court several times to

On Being a Judge

seek support payments, she married a black man. Her former husband, alleging neglect of his five-year-old daughter, was immediately granted custody without offering evidence of any neglect. A similar case arose in Georgia where a white woman gave birth out of wedlock to a daughter fathered by a black man. Custody of her son by a prior marriage was now granted to her former husband because the judge considered her "unfit." The ruling was based entirely upon the color of the children, because she was permitted to keep her black daughter.

In Michigan, a judge found a man guilty of manslaughter rather than murder in the ax killing of his wife. The judge remarked: "Here's the defendant, for the first time, faced with the horribleness of an infidelity, not only an infidelity—and I do not wish to be called a racist—but we are in a court of law and a spade has to be called a spade—but an infidelity with a Black man."

Historically the U.S. Supreme Court has been reluctant to disturb state criminal sentences. In 1983, the Court, by a five to four decision, set aside a life-without-parole sentence given a South Dakota man who had kited a one-hundred-dollar bad check. He received the stiff sentence under the habitual criminal law because he had seven prior misdemeanor convictions. Yet two years previously a life sentence was allowed to stand for a fairly small offense received under similar circumstances to those of the South Dakotan.

The crucial question is at what point in the eyes of the justices could a cruel perversion of justice become too cruel and cease to square with the Constitution's ban against "cruel and unusual punishment." These justices of the Supreme Court, making up the most powerful court on earth, are also moved by their own perceptions, values, and prejudices. Their respective outlooks necessarily affect the course of American law in carrying out the Court's chief responsibility of defining individual rights and the boundaries between the individual and the state.

Although the federal judiciary is widely held to be independent of influence from other branches of government, selection

A Certain Blindness

of judges and justices of the Supreme Court is all too often made by the president with the belief that their decisions will reflect his own views on society's purpose and direction. This practice was established early on, as members of the first Supreme Court were chosen by George Washington from his Federalist party. This practice has profoundly influenced American law through the Court's interpretation of the Constitution, and generally it has been followed down through the years. President Lincoln made appointments to the Supreme Court that he could count on to insure the constitutionality of his various war measures. President Roosevelt went so far as to attempt a restructuring of the Court with the promise that his appointments would provide a court "willing to enforce the Constitution as written, and unwilling to assert legislative powers by writing in their own political and economic policies." President Nixon spoke of appointing only those persons to the federal judiciary who would be "strict constructionists" of the Constitution. President Reagan declared his appointees would carry out the "original intent" of the framers.

Early in our country's history, Chief Justice John Marshall in *Marbury v. Madison* (1803) established the power of judicial review, that the Supreme Court had the authority to declare an act of Congress or state laws unconstitutional, or no law at all. But afterwards Roger Taney became chief justice. Taney was a member of a slaveholding family who injected his personal views into his decisions in holding that Negroes (slave as well as free) "had no rights which the white man was bound to respect."

Following the Civil War and the enactment of the Reconstruction amendments, American law continued to be primarily concerned with economic and property interests as the system of free enterprise expanded. The property-minded justices of the Supreme Court soon extended the scope of the Fourteenth Amendment to consider corporations as persons entitled to "due process" and "equal protection of the laws," thereby declaring economic regulation of corporations as unconstitutional.

On Being a Judge

(To this day, emphasis on the protection of property rights has been reflected in the traditional courses offered in law schools, such as property, business associations, commercial transactions, and contracts.)

Beginning with President Roosevelt's New Deal programs and his Supreme Court appointments, including Hugo Black and William O. Douglas, a gradual shift began toward individual rights and social change. The trend toward upholding the basic principles of the Bill of Rights and individual liberty against governmental power reached its apex under the Earl Warren Court, beginning with the *Brown* decision. This Court followed with landmark decisions regarding voting rights, criminal justice, and freedom of the press and religion.

In the long history of the Supreme Court, no decision was more harshly condemned as a distortion of the Court's constitutional jurisprudence and viewed as so threatening to our established form of constitutional government than 1954's *Brown v. Board of Education*. On the one hand, the Warren Court had some supporters, such as Yale Law School professor Fred Rodell, who described it as "the most brilliant and able collection of justices who ever graced the high bench together. The superstars of the Court were the champions of judicial restraint, Felix Frankfurter and Robert Jackson, and the archetypes of judicial activism, Hugo Black and William Douglas."[7] A similar tribute was also paid to the chief justice: "After serving only a few months as Chief Justice, Warren brought all elements of the Court together—activists, conservatives, Northerners, Southerners—and lighted a beacon that has pointed the way for champions of human justice ever since."[8]

But what was it that was so different about the *Brown* decision that would precipitate a move to impeach Chief Justice Warren and create such a climate that made it unsafe for Justice Black to travel to his home state of Alabama for twelve years? Certainly, this Court acted no differently than the Marshall Court over one hundred years earlier when Chief Justice Mar-

A Certain Blindness

shall observed that his Court "never sought to enlarge the judicial power beyond its proper bounds, nor feared to carry it to the fullest extent that duty required."

The underlying, though often denied, fact surrounding the rage and fury unleashed with the *Brown* decision was that for the first time in history a branch of government had forthrightly stated without qualification that black Americans under the Fourteenth Amendment were on an equal level with all other Americans.

The ruling in *Brown II*, of course, gave the power and authority to U.S. district court judges to compel boards of education to desegregate schools. Records show that many, if not most, of these judges in the South, where the brunt of the enforcement took place, immediately joined with state legislatures and school boards to use elaborate strategies to circumvent the "law of the land," the law they had sworn to uphold. Some wrote opinions encouraging segregation and prompting delay during the midst of litigation and required more motions, hearings, and appeals, thus bringing truth to the statement "As long as we can legislate, we can segregate."

There was, however, a small group of brave, dedicated judges who, in the face of community hostility and sometimes personal violence, acted to establish equal justice under the law. These few judges, through their wisdom, strength, and humanity, were determined to ensure justice for all Americans. They did great service to themselves, their profession, and our country. We will probably never know why some men possess the moral courage and integrity to stand up and do what is right in the face of crisis when others will fearfully capitulate or remain silent.

Among these unrecognized heroes of the American judiciary were district judges J. Waites Waring, J. Skelly Wright, and Frank Johnson, Jr., and federal appeals court judges Elbert Tuttle, Richard Taylor Rives, John Wisdom, and John R. Brown.

Judge Waring, a native of Charleston, South Carolina, and

son of a Confederate veteran, gained nationwide attention in 1948 when he was sharply critical of South Carolina and Democratic party officials for attempting to circumvent the Fifteenth Amendment. In his ruling in the case *Brown v. Baskin,* Waring told those officials, "It is time to realize that the people of the United States expect you to follow the American way of elections" and that it was time for South Carolina to rejoin the Union. In 1951, he was one of three judges who heard the case of *Briggs v. Elliott* in South Carolina, a companion to *Brown,* before it went before the Supreme Court. Waring dissented from the majority ruling in that case, which held that segregation was constitutional, and for that he was subjected to extreme amounts of abuse, his house was stoned, his wife was slandered, and his life was threatened. Judge Waring, previously a member of Charleston's aristocracy, was forced to retire from the bench and move from his home state.

After Frank M. Johnson, Jr., was appointed a district court judge, he was cordially welcomed to Montgomery, Alabama's legal community, as Montgomery's afternoon daily, the *Alabama Journal,* reported on November 8, 1955:

> It should have been heartwarming to Frank M. Johnson, Jr., our new United States District Judge, to receive the hearty welcome and cordial reception given him yesterday by the Montgomery Bar Association as he took the oath of office.
>
> The Luncheon given subsequently in Judge Johnson's honor by the Montgomery Bar was also a touching occasion at which lawyers, jurists, and court officials welcomed the youthful jurist to Montgomery and pledged their cooperation for carrying out the fine traditions of the federal judiciary in Montgomery.

Just over six months later Johnson joined with Judge Richard Rives and declared in *Browder v. Gayle* that the bus segregation law of Montgomery was unconstitutional, bringing an end to the Montgomery bus boycott. Such action was hardly in keeping with "the fine traditions" of the judiciary in Montgomery and most certainly ended any "cooperation" Johnson was likely to get

A Certain Blindness

from the Montgomery Bar. But Johnson, a native of the proud and independent county of Winston in northern Alabama, was not necessarily one who followed any tradition. During Civil War times the citizens of that county, non-slaveholding farmers, had voted to secede from Alabama when Alabama seceded from the Union, thus becoming the "free state of Winston."

As Jack Bass noted in this book *Unlikely Heroes,* while attending the University of Alabama Law School, Johnson was a classmate and friend of George Wallace, whom he later threatened to jail for contempt. His compassion for those victimized by a system beyond their control and his contempt for irresponsible leadership were demonstrated while he was in the military service. In defense of a sergeant during a court-martial proceeding, who admitted to beating and other acts of cruelty to prisoners, Johnson proved the guard was following orders from higher officers and exposed a general in an attempted cover-up. Also, while serving as a U.S. attorney, he obtained the first conviction of peonage in this century. During the murder investigation of a black man who had been horsewhipped to death, Johnson uncovered a system by which two white men paid fines for blacks convicted of minor offenses, then controlled them as slave laborers.

Following the decision in *Browder,* Alabama state senator Sam Engelhardt, who also served as executive secretary of the Alabama Association of White Citizens Councils, issued a statement urging "the white people of Alabama never to forget the names of Rives and Johnson." He stated, "Nothing they can do would rectify this great wrong that they have done to the good people of this state. Already more hate has been generated on this day than since the days of the Carpetbag legislature."[9] Engelhardt's outburst was considered the acceptable view, since in those days, as historian C. Vann Woodward put it, "a 'moderate' became a man who dared open his mouth, an 'extremist' one who favored eventual compliance with the law, and 'compliance' took on the connotations of treason."[10] Bass recounted in *Unlikely Heroes* that both Rives and Johnson received constant threats, large amounts of hate mail, and abusive telephone calls. One night part of the home of Johnson's mother was destroyed by a bomb; and his only son, who committed suicide while still young, endured extreme harassment as a youngster.

It was about a decade and a half after the *Browder* decision that I met Judge Johnson while we were both presiding judges in the federal courthouse in Montgomery. As I came to know him personally, I could understand fully Martin Luther King, Jr.'s statement that he was a man "who gave the true meaning to the word justice."

As Rives and Johnson were models of justice in the civil rights arena in Alabama, so Judge J. Skelly Wright was their counterpart in the state of Louisiana. It is said that by the end of 1960, he had become "the most hated man in New Orleans."[11] As Bass noted in *Unlikely Heroes,* Wright, a native of New Orleans, was U.S. attorney there prior to his election to the bench. Wright recalled an early incident during which he observed from his office window a Christmas party being given by the Light House for the Blind across the street. He watched as the blind people climbed the steps to the second floor where they were met by someone who led black persons to the rear for a party and whites to a separate party. He realized that the blind could not segregate themselves, and he was made aware of how unjust was the system he had taken for granted.[12]

His deepening sense of humanity caused Wright to break precedent even before the Supreme Court came out with its 1954 *Brown* decision. In two separate cases Judge Wright ordered Louisiana State University to accept two black students to its law school and a black student to its undergraduate program, decisions that were affirmed in light of *Brown*. Wright explained later to Jack Bass that personal sympathies aside, "I [ruled the way I did] because the Supreme Court had [declared segregated schools unconstitutional], and there wasn't any way out except subterfuge. Other judges were using subterfuge to get around the Supreme Court, delays and so on, but I grew up around federal courts and had respect for them, and I tried to carry on tradi-

A Certain Blindness

tion. . . . The key in all of this is doing justice within the law."[13] Wright's ruling in a 1956 school case, *Bush v. Orleans Parish School Board*, indicated his perception of the issue's complexity: "The problem of changing a people's mores, particularly those with an emotional overlay, is not to be taken lightly. It is a problem which will require the utmost patience, understanding, generosity and forbearance and from all of us of whatever race. But the magnitude of the problem may not nullify the principle. And that principle is that we are, all of us, free-born Americans with a right to make our way unfettered by sanctions imposed by man because of the work of God."[14] Attorneys representing black citizens came to rely on him for bold application of the law and to provide instant relief when confronted with circumstances that made delay simply unacceptable.

Judge Elbert Tuttle, former chief judge of the Fifth United States Circuit Court of Appeals, was a quiet and courteous man never known to compromise his principles. When his church in Atlanta voted to bar Negro worshipers, he immediately withdrew his membership. Even after his appointment to the bench, Tuttle continued to serve on the board of trustees of Morehouse College, Martin Luther King's alma mater.[15] His education in constitutional guarantees began in 1931 when, as a National Guard officer, he helped save a black prisoner from an angry mob. The prisoner, accused of raping a white woman, was indicted five days after his arrest. The next day, with two National Guard companies present to preserve order in the courtroom, the prisoner was tried, convicted, and sentenced to death by electrocution. The convicted man eventually received a new trial through the efforts of Tuttle and attorney Austin T. Walden of Atlanta, using a 1915 Supreme Court opinion describing how due process did not exist in an atmosphere of mob violence. (Walden, at that time one of the few black lawyers in the South, contributed much in the area of civil rights during his career.)

The July 16, 1987, *Atlanta Constitution* commemorated Tuttle's thirty-three years on the federal bench on the occasion

On Being a Judge

of his ninetieth birthday that month, noting how the judge "helped to revolutionize Southern life and deliver whites and blacks from the yoke of racial oppression." The paper recalled what Tuttle himself said about those days: "When I came on the bench, a black person and a white person couldn't eat in the same restaurant in the South. There were counties in Georgia where 130 percent of the white population was registered to vote, and not a single black. It doesn't take any heroic action to say that's wrong."

Richard Taylor Rives (surname rhymes with "leaves") was described by his law partner, John Godbold, as a man "whose courtesy and gracious manner . . . covered the strongest steel. . . . When necessary, that steel could flash like a sword in the sunlight."[16] Rives distinguished himself as a trial lawyer and served as president of the Montgomery and Alabama bar associations. His concern for racial justice evolved over a period of time, since early on he admitted to once advising the Montgomery Board of Registrars how to thwart an early voter registration drive by blacks, and Rives also was involved once in a trial seeking the disbarment of one of the few black lawyers in the state for soliciting a client, considered a violation of legal ethics. After his consciousness was raised, he represented the estate of a pregnant woman who was killed in a fall down the shaft of an elevator not protected by a guardrail. The insurance company offered one thousand dollars to settle the case, telling Rives that was all he could get for a Negro's life. Considering the offer ridiculously low, Rives took the case to court. When he won the case, the jury awarded one thousand dollars. Rives found the gross unfairness "shocking."[17]

John Minor Wisdom was a fully accepted member of the most exclusive segments of aristocracy in New Orleans. He attended college at Washington and Lee like his father, whose diploma was signed by Robert E. Lee, then entered Harvard University as a graduate student in English, where he shared top grades with Countee Cullen, a Negro who was to gain renown

A Certain Blindness

as a poet. A year later Wisdom returned home and entered Tulane University Law School, where his grandfather was a member of the first graduating class. Recognized as an authority on the Louisiana Civil Code, Wisdom wrote scholarly legal articles and acquired a deep knowledge of New Orleans and Louisiana history, thereby developing a keen understanding of the background of various racial attitudes. In *Unlikely Heroes* Bass recounted that Wisdom, an unpretentious man, on one occasion took time from a guest in his home to drive an elderly, confused black man to his destination after the man knocked on his door seeking directions; another time he invited several black lawyers to his home after they called him to discuss a legal matter.[18] Wisdom served on the board of the New Orleans Urban League, an issue of concern to the conservative senators on the judiciary selection committee. At his judicial confirmation hearing, Senator Eastland inquired whether the league was interested "in . . . the school integration question." Wisdom answered no and assured him that "it had never gone into court, never had a legislative lobby, never exerted any undue pressure."[19] Yet his views on race and civil rights did not cause Wisdom to eschew membership in exclusive private clubs known to deny entrance to blacks and Jews. Wisdom explained to Bass that he associated with his lifelong friends in these clubs; "they know how I stand on these matters. . . . I certainly wouldn't change their views by getting out of the club."[20]

When an opening on the Supreme Court occurred in 1969, a moderate Republican governor suggested to Attorney General John Mitchell that Wisdom fill the vacancy. With a reputation as a proponent of civil rights like Wisdom's, he was unlikely to merit serious consideration. The *Baltimore Sun* reported that Mitchell exclaimed: "He's a damn left winger. He'd be as bad as Earl Warren."[21]

John R. Brown, prior to his appointment to the bench, was senior partner in a highly successful law firm in Houston, specializing in admiralty law. As Bass recounted in *Unlikely Heroes,* Brown served as a port commander in the Philippines during

On Being a Judge

World War II, during which time he gained administrative experience and ability to become one of the most innovative court administrators in the nation. Growing up in a small town in Nebraska where there was only one Negro who shined shoes in the local barber shop, Brown never learned to be racist. He was gifted with raw intelligence and shared with his colleagues on the court the same seemingly boundless intellectual discipline and capacity for work. Described as a loner who masked over his inner self with an outward flamboyant style, Brown remained an active church member and believed strongly in the concept of brotherhood. Speaking at a high school commencement, Brown remarked: "I think we are our brother's keeper because God meant it that way. . . . I can make no claim upon my brother. The claim on me is that I must do for another."[22] When asked what shaped his attitude on race cases, he explained it was the evidence in voting cases in Mississippi, which showed that whites not able to read were allowed to register and blacks with master degrees were rejected. Judge Brown rejected traditional legal arguments and entered the "political thicket" when political abuses could not be corrected at the polls. He declared, "There can be no relief at the polls for those who cannot register and vote. . . . When legislation oversteps its bounds . . . the courts are the only haven for those citizens in the minority."[23]

In 1978 Mississippi Senator James O. Eastland chose not to run for re-election because he knew he could not muster the support of the nearly two hundred thousand black registered voters. A year later Eastland told Jack Bass the role the Fifth Circuit Court of Appeals played in civil rights: "Ramsey Clark [Lyndon Johnson's last Attorney General] told me that the Fifth Circuit had done something that the Supreme Court couldn't do—that they brought racial integration to the deep South a generation sooner than the Supreme Court could have done it."[24]

Following the Eisenhower era there was a period viewed by many black Americans as the second Reconstruction. Great strides were made in the direction of equality under the adminis-

A Certain Blindness

trations of Kennedy and Johnson supported by civil rights legislation and favorable court decisions. But when Richard Nixon attained the presidency, the road to equality was abruptly detoured. Campaigning on a pledge to "bring us together," Nixon actually appealed to those divisive forces opposing desegregation. Reg Murphy and Hal Gulliver reported in *The Southern Strategy* that Nixon struck a deal with Southern politicians during the spring of 1968. During a meeting in an Atlanta motel room, Nixon agreed in effect to ease up on federal enforcement of desegregation if elected.[25] On taking office, President Nixon's policy more than bore out the fact that such an arrangement occurred.

The visible effort to reverse the progress in school desegregation was first seen in February 1969, one month into the new administration. Robert Finch, secretary of the Department of Health, Education, and Welfare (HEW) who was charged with enforcement of certain aspects of the Civil Rights Act of 1964, granted an unprecedented sixty-day grace period to five Mississippi school districts facing a cutoff of federal funds for failure to desegregate their schools. In an interview reported in the March 10, 1969, issue of *U.S. News and World Report,* Finch explained his understanding and grasp of the problems confronting HEW in the area of school desegregation: "The Court has never really said that segregation itself is unlawful, or at least de facto segregation." The enforcement-minded head of the civil rights office in HEW later resigned under pressure, and the regional director in Atlanta, a career employee who had upheld the law, was transferred. The newly appointed director for the six-state region commented on President Nixon's desegregation policy by stating: "The President is a practical man. He realizes that little or no preparation has been made for desegregation."[26]

Nearly fifteen years had elapsed since school segregation had been declared unconstitutional. If delays were being granted, they were purely for reasons of political expediency, and these reasons are an abuse of the orderly process of law enforcement. Nixon's policy of circumvention did not escape notice. When a Georgia county school superintendent resigned after a protest by white students and parents, the official asserted that the school board's concern had been the education of the children in the county. The October 11, 1969, *Atlanta Constitution* quoted the official's remarks: "We recognize Federal Law and want to abide by it. . . . We do not feel . . . that President Nixon is making any kind of statement at all that helps anybody on this. Now, in his campaign he had the Southern people to believe that something could be eased up on it. . . . I feel very strongly that the Nixon administration is one of our real problems. . . . In fact, this recent thing over in Mississippi makes it most difficult." The "recent thing" referred to was the request Secretary Finch made to federal judges to delay the implementation of desegregation plans in thirty Mississippi school districts. Elaborate plans had previously been worked out with HEW officials.

This dramatic retreat was the subject of a full-page ad in the *New York Times* on September 3, 1969, captioned "On August 25, 1969, the U.S. Government broke its promise to the children of Mississippi. This promise was made in 1954 by the highest court in the land." The ad traced government policy since *Brown* and emphatically deduced that "our government, for the first time . . . has gone to court and asked that school segregation be allowed to continue."

The Southern Regional Council, an independent research organization, reported at the end of Nixon's first year in office: "In 1969 . . . there has seemed to be a deliberate effort at work in the federal administrative machinery to reverse such progress in school desegregation as has already been so dearly won. . . . That effort . . . cynically held out the hope to southern segregationists that the law of the land would not really have to be obeyed."[27] The Center for National Review at Catholic University in Washington also examined the Nixon administration's approach toward enforcement of the law in a report entitled "Justice Delayed and Denied." The report documented cases reviewed by HEW to see if school desegregation guidelines were being met. Reviews numbering 128 had been initiated by HEW in 1968. During President Nixon's first year in office, the

A Certain Blindness

number dropped to 16; in 1970 to 15; in 1971 to 11; in 1972 to 9; in 1973 to 1; and in 1974 to 0.

In spite of America's long history of employment discrimination, the Nixon administration actually thwarted efforts to combat these conditions. The "Philadelphia Plan," initiated by my friend Arthur Fletcher, an assistant secretary of Labor in the administration, was designed so the government could exert pressure through federal contracts to improve minority hiring in the construction industry. The plan survived statutory and constitutional attacks and was upheld by the Third Circuit Court of Appeals before the Nixon administration abolished it.

Equal Employment Opportunity Commission chairman Clifford Alexander received no support from the Nixon administration either, as I discussed in Chapter 8, and was forced to resign when Senator Everett Dirksen of Illinois accused Alexander of "harassing" corporate America. The truth of the matter is that Alexander lost his job for striving to implement the Civil Rights Act of 1964. Alexander's dedicated leadership resulted directly in my opportunity to penetrate a color barrier in federal employment by becoming the first black trial attorney employed by the Federal Power Commission.

The Nixon White House sent out the word that racial matters could benefit from a period of "benign neglect," which lessened the hopes of black Americans that conditions would improve. The facts bear this out. Well into President Nixon's second term, a Civil Service Commission report showed that black employees held only 2 percent of all government jobs paying over $20,000 per year, but they held 25.4 percent of the lower level jobs such as janitors. The Department of Labor reported that of black and white males in the department with the same qualifications after five years, the black male earned almost $4,000 less than his white counterpart. In 1970, the difference in black and white families' incomes was $3,957, which escalated to a difference of $5,402 only four years later. The failure of the Nixon White House to faithfully enforce the laws on behalf of black Americans touched all areas of our society. In

1974 the U.S. Civil Rights Commission reported on federal enforcement of the 1968 Fair Housing Act and concluded, "Present programs often are administered so as to continue rather than reduce racial segregation." The commission found that state and local officials were using highway construction zoning laws and building codes to remove or keep out minorities and that real estate boards and brokers likewise engaged in a wide-ranging practice of racial disccrimination.

Yet the most glaring example of the administration's unwillingness to enforce the rights of black citizens was seen in the field of public education. A lawyer himself, Nixon was fully aware of the legal impact of the *Brown* decision. During his 1968 presidential campaign Nixon attacked the decisions of the Warren Court, beginning with *Brown,* and promised to appoint only "strict constructionists" to the Supreme Court. Although Nixon's use of the phrase became popular, as is the doctrine of "original intent," it is actually devoid of meaning in a legal sense, serving only to reflect a political view of the Constitution's role in our democratic form of government. Those judges who interpret the Constitution more liberally get labeled as "judicial activists," a derogatory term that implies that their judgments overstep the role of the judiciary, perpetuating the myth among many citizens that the courts are somehow constrained by the structure of the Constitution's text. No one can rationally argue that the express words of the Constitution, as the framers knew them, can define the boundaries of our constitutional rights as we know them today. The truth is that the Constitution consists of six thousand words, whose phrases are often broad, general, vague, and ambiguous, that require judicial interpretation (for example, due process, unreasonable search and seizure, cruel and unusual punishment, and equal protection of the laws are phrases that, when interpreted, resulted in what many contemptuously called "judge-made" law).

Perhaps this controversy first began in 1717 when Bishop Benjamin Hoadly told the king of England that, in his opinion, "whoever hath an absolute authority to interpret any written laws is truly the Lawgiver to all intents and purposes, and not the person who first wrote them." Similar language was adopted by Chief Justice Marshall in *Marbury v. Madison* (1803) when he said, "It is emphatically the province and duty of the judicial department to say what the law is." Accordingly when Chief Justice Taney concluded, in his *Dred Scott v. Sanford* (1857) decision, that Negroes could "justly and lawfully be reduced to slavery for the white man's benefit," he claimed his opinion was dictated by the language of the Constitution. The racial implication of this strict construction arose during the argument of *Brown* before the Supreme Court one hundred years later. In *Bolling v. Sharpe* (1954), one of the companion cases heard with *Brown,* the counsel for the District of Columbia Board of Education quoted from Judge Taney's *Dred Scott* decision: "No one, we presume, supposes that any change in public opinion or feeling in relation to this unfortunate race, in the civilized nations of Europe or in this Country, should induce the Court to give the words of the Constitution a more liberal construction in their favor than they were intended to bear when the instrument was framed and adopted." The lawyer then proclaimed the passage was "equally applicable today."

Of course the more recent controversy over constitutional interpretation can be traced to the *Brown* decision and its enforcement following default by state and local officials. Sworn to uphold the Constitution and laws of the United States, judges are duty bound to decide the issues of a case or controversy presented to them. Perhaps there is no clearer example of the meaninglessness of labels than is seen in the decisions of Supreme Court justices Hugo Black and William Douglas. Under constant attack for liberal interpretations of the Constitution within the Warren Court, both were the strictest of constructionists. In case after case, they argued the Constitution's authors meant what they said that we are subject to "no law . . . prohibiting the free exercise of religion, or abridging the freedom of speech, or the press."

But whether they are considered "judicial activists" or are exercising "judicial restraint," judges ultimately arrive at a decision they conclude is based on compelling constitutional reasons. It is also true, as stated by former Supreme Court justice Arthur Goldberg, that "our country has sustained far greater injury from judicial timidity in vindicating citizens' fundamental rights than from judicial courage in protecting them."[28]

In appointing Warren Burger to succeed Earl Warren as chief justice of the Supreme Court in 1969, President Nixon stated, "I happen to believe the Constitution should be strictly interpreted," adding, "Judge Burger is a strict constructionist." One of the first cases Burger was to encounter during the fall term of Court in 1969 was the Mississippi school desegregation case *Alexander v. Holmes County Board of Education*. The new chief justice was to begin his tenure on the Court on an issue over which the Nixon administration was at odds with the law. Associate justice Hugo Black, meanwhile, was said to be completely fed-up with court delays of desegregation plans. He had come to realize that Justice Felix Frankfurter's demand to include the phrase "all deliberate speed" in the 1955 ruling "had been a grievous mistake." For fifteen years it had been used by lawyers to defy the law of the land. "I should never have let Felix get that into the opinion,"[29] Black declared. The associate justice therefore demanded a short, simple order that there be desegregation at once or he would dissent. Burger was not politically naive, and "he was alarmed at Black's memo and his threatened dissent. If the Court's unanimity broke apart on a school case, particularly so early in his tenure, he would be declared an instant failure. He and the Court might never recover. The press would compare him unfavorably to Warren, who had held the Court together for fifteen years on these cases. They would say that the Court had collapsed in the first month of Burger's first term."[30]

When they ruled on *Alexander v. Holmes County Board of Education,* both justices were to accomplish their aims. They unanimously rejected any delay and declared that the expression "all deliberate speed" in regards to desegregation was "no longer constitutionally permissible. Thus, school districts were obligated to terminate dual school systems at once."

Alabama governor George Wallace was prompted to observe that under Burger the Court was "no better than the Warren Court." Burger wrested another unanimous desegregation decision in *Swann v. Charlotte-Mecklinburg Board of Education* (1971), which held that the "objective in school desegregation cases is to eliminate from public schools all vestiges of state-imposed segregation" and that "in default by school authorities of their affirmative obligation to eliminate racial discrimination root and branch, the district courts have broad equitable powers to fashion remedies that will assure unitary school systems." In this landmark case the Court allowed district courts to provide relief in the form of busing as a tool of desegregation. Busing was now seized upon to be the ground issue for further divisions among the people and the law. By 1974 it became obvious that the Court under Chief Justice Burger would not depart from its direction of applying equal justice under the law. However, by this time, President Nixon appointed four members to the Court whose presence would weigh heavily against the constitutional rights of black children.

Milliken v. Bradley (1974) originated when district court judge Stephan Roth ordered cross-district busing to desegregate Detroit's schools. The court of appeals affirmed Judge Roth's ruling, and Michigan authorities appealed to the Supreme Court. In a five-to-four decision the Court, for the first time since *Brown,* reversed an affirmative desegregation order; without stating why, the Court determined the remedies for the constitutional wrongs dealt Detroit's black students must stop at the school district line. (*Brown,* of course, had pointed out that district courts could consider "revision of school districts" to achieve desegregation.) The Burger Court ordered desegregation to be eliminated within district lines, but Judge Roth had previously found that such a plan "would not accomplish desegregation."

On Being a Judge

The four dissenting opinions in this case came from justices Nixon did not appoint, presenting views that black children would not be receiving equal protection of the laws under such a ruling. Justice William O. Douglas candidly declared:

> We have before us today no plan for integration. . . . No new principles of law are presented here. Metropolitan treatment of metropolitan problems is commonplace. If this were a sewage problem or a water problem, or an energy problem, there can be no doubt that Michigan would stay well within federal constitutional bounds if it sought a metropolitan remedy. . . . When we rule against the metropolitan area remedy we take a step that will likely put the problems of the blacks and our society back to the period that antedated the "separate but equal" regime of *Plessy v. Ferguson*.

Justice Byron R. White reasoned that the court of appeals had acted responsibly: "Regrettably, the majority's arbitrary limitation on the equitable power of federal district courts, based on the invisible borders of local school districts, is unrelated to the State's responsibility for remedying the constitutional wrongs visited upon the Negro schoolchildren of Detroit."

Justice Thurgood Marshall also issued a dissenting opinion. Marshall had argued *Brown* before the Supreme Court when he was an NAACP lawyer, and he had recommended *Brown*'s immediate enforcement. In his dissenting opinion in *Milliken v. Bradley,* Marshall reflected: "After 20 years of small, often difficult steps toward that great end, the Court today takes a giant step backwards. Notwithstanding a record showing widespread and pervasive racial segregation in the educational system provided by the State of Michigan for children in Detroit, the Court holds that the District Court was powerless to require the State to remedy its constitutional violation in any meaningful fashion." He concluded his dissent with words that appropriately describe many Supreme Court decisions affecting constitutional rights of Negroes: "Today's holding, I fear, is more a reflection of a perceived public mood that we have gone

A Certain Blindness

far enough in enforcing the Constitution's guarantee of equal justice than it is the product of neutral principles of law."

Apparently President Nixon believed his judicial appointments would mold the law according to his preferences. Judge Robert Bork, President Reagan's choice for the Supreme Court who was unable to get confirmation, is a believer in the doctrine of original intent and judicial restraint, and he is said to validate *Brown* on the "abstract intention" of the framers of the Fourteenth Amendment, which was to do racial justice, according to the December 1, 1987, *American Bar Association Journal*.

While there is no objective proof that the racial views of the Supreme Court justices have informed their decisions, on the whole their decisions have never represented a concerted effort to protect the constitutional rights of black Americans.

The purposes of the Thirteenth, Fourteenth, and Fifteenth Amendments are abundantly clear. Yet the right to vote granted by the Fifteenth Amendment in 1870 was not enforced effectively for almost one hundred years; the Fourteenth Amendment, a general guarantee of life, liberty, and property for all persons, actually provided more protection for American corporations; and civil rights acts based on the amendments were rendered ineffective by the various Supreme Court decisions leading to the "separate but equal" doctrine of *Plessy v. Ferguson*. As a result, unequal treatment was allowed to prevail in many forms. Justice John M. Harlan concluded in his brilliant dissent of the 1896 *Plessy* ruling that

> the substance and spirit of the recent amendments of the Constitution have been sacrificed by a subtle and ingenious verbal criticism. . . . Constitutional provisions, adopted in the interests of liberty, and for the purpose of securing, through national legislation, if need be, rights inherent in a state of freedom, and belonging to American citizenship, have been so construed as to defeat the ends the people desired to accomplish, which they attempted to accomplish, and which they supposed they had accomplished by changes in their fundamental law. . . . The court has departed from the familiar rule requiring, in the interpretation of constitu-

tional provisions, that full effect be given to the intent with which they were adopted.

The nation thereupon embarked on a course in constitutional law, as accurately stated by Justice Harlan, "when the rights of freedom and American citizenship cannot receive from the Nation that efficient protection which heretofore was unhesitatingly accorded to slavery and the rights of the master."

The constitutional amendments have been so narrowly interpreted and enforced that they hardly serve the cause of justice and human dignity. When my great-uncle Bass Reeves risked his life to help bring law to a lawless land, he looked forward to the protections of a legal and orderly society offered by statehood. Instead he was subjected to an oppressive, unjust system of law distorted by the recently announced *Plessy* doctrine. Fifty years later the Court ruled that my cousin Nancy Todd's constitutional rights had been violated, but the Court provided her no remedy for the wrong. And twenty years after that, in spite of finding constitutional violations of the highest order, the Supreme Court left the black children of Detroit without a remedy for the wrongs they suffered.

Throughout history, however, black Americans placed hope in our justice system. This country has witnessed what happens when hope is lost, when oppressed people lose faith in receiving justice and feel the law is no longer relevant to them. Crime and social disorder have followed.

The National Advisory Commission on Civil Disorders noted some years ago: "Some of our courts, moreover, have lost the confidence of the poor; the belief is pervasive among ghetto residents that lower courts in our urban communities dispense an assembly line justice; that from arrest to sentencing, the poor uneducated are denied equal justice with the affluent and that procedures such as bail and fines have been perverted to perpetuate class inequities."[31]

In order to maintain a just society, a legal system that provides the equal, prompt, and fair application of the law is a

A Certain Blindness

necessity. But racism, as a part of every facet of American life, is a characteristic of our legal process. Discrimination in the selection of judges, law enforcement officers, and other court personnel has had the effect of depriving minority citizens of the constitutional guarantee of equal protection of the laws.

Undoubtedly the presence of black judges would help their white colleagues to be more conscious of prevailing racism. Black law enforcement officers could help end the practice of some police officers in conducting illegal and humiliating public searches and other practices under the guise of alleged minor offenses. African-American prosecutors and other court personnel could provide more equitable bail and other procedures, resulting in less abuse and illegal imprisonment.

The judiciary, the heart of our justice system, continues as a racially discriminatory body in America as a result of concerted efforts to exclude blacks and other minorities from the process of interpreting and administering the law. Since Robert Morris became a magistrate in Massachusetts in 1852, Negroes have made little progress in gaining representation on the bench. During Reconstruction, black judges served on courts in Arkansas, Florida, and South Carolina, and Jonathan J. Wright was also elected to the South Carolina Supreme Court for a six-year term in 1870. With the restoration of white supremacy, these judges were forced out. It was not until 1924 that a black judge was elected in the North. Albert B. George of Chicago became a member of the municipal court. On rare occasions, black judges followed in New York in 1930, California in 1940, Ohio in 1943, Michigan in 1954, and Pennsylvania in 1956. On the federal level, William Hastie was appointed to the Virgin Islands Federal District Court in 1937. Although two black customs court judges were named, there were no black district court judges named until 1961—James Parsons in Chicago and Wade McCree in Detroit. Aside from my appointment in 1972, there were no other black members of the federal judiciary to serve the South until Robert Collins was appointed to the District Court in New Orleans in 1978. There are presently fewer federal judges in the South, which is a woefully small number in proportion to the black population. At the time of my appointment, the Negro population was 11.1 percent of the national total, but only 1.9 percent of all judges were black. A study also showed that, if representation were in proportion to the black population in the South, there would be twenty-five black judges between Maryland and Texas.

No one is in a more unique position to expose the racist nature of our judicial process and assume a responsibility for improving the quality of justice for all people than a black jurist. It was with this background that the judicial council of the National Bar Association (NBA) was formed in 1972. Its first chairman, George W. Crockett, Jr., then a judge in Detroit and now a U.S. congressman, expressed the hope that the council would "provide the means by which its members could exchange information, encourage each other, and prod their profession to rid the legal system of racism and classism." (The NBA itself was founded in 1925 because the American Bar Association excluded Negroes from its membership. But the NBA never viewed itself as separate from the overall legal community, but rather as a safe harbor, since the legal profession at large refused to embrace all its members. As William Hastie remarked, "It is not a contradiction to say that we band together as blacks in order to speed the day that this will not be necessary.")

As an active member of the NBA's judicial council, I have found the various programs and projects extremely enlightening and have thought more than once that members of the entire judiciary ought to have the benefit of sharing the experiences and insights of our black jurists from around the country. Black jurists become aware of injustices that might otherwise not become known, such as what a chief judge of the juvenile court of a major city discovered. He learned of the practice in which white youth offenders were tried as juveniles, but black offenders of the same age were tried as adults. As a visiting judge, I have personally observed various notations, either in chambers or on the bench, references to the races of parties in cases, such

A Certain Blindness

as "black S.O.B.," "black," or "white." Even in preliminary hearings, suggestions have been indicated for sentences before a full hearing. The presence of blacks on the bench has also provoked varying degrees of negative reactions. In one city an investigation, which was totally without cause, was launched into the judicial activities of its black judges. In another city an investigator for the prosecutor's office testified under oath that he had been ordered to "get a black judge."

In a less hostile sense but more a reflection of blind prejudice, lawyers have often requested black judges to disqualify themselves from deciding matters involving white people. Former U.S. Solicitor General Wade McCree recalled an incident when he was a circuit court judge in Detroit:

> The case involved a black man who had signed over a deed to some property as conditional collateral on a loan from a white man. When the loan was repaid, the white man had refused to return the deed, and the white man was sued.
>
> "The lawyer said that it was no reflection on my impartiality," McCree now recalls, "but since his client was white, and the man suing him was black, his client was convinced that no matter how impartial I tried to be, I would subconsciously make any close rulings in favor of the black man."
>
> McCree said he understood the client's position, and the lawyer was pleased. But McCree then pointed out to the lawyer that a white judge would present the same problem since he would subconsciously make close rulings in favor of the white man.
>
> "I told the lawyer that the only person who could fairly try the case was a mulatto," McCree intones, "and that if he wanted to canvass my white colleagues on the bench to see if one of them was a mulatto, and would take the case, then I would excuse myself. Otherwise, I told him, I would try the case."

While white attorneys have seemingly been more reluctant to go to trial and have opted for settlements when the judge and

On Being a Judge

one party are black, the experience of U.S. Appeals Court judge A. Leon Higginbotham, Jr., focuses more clearly on this matter. When he was a district court judge Higginbotham was petitioned to disqualify himself from hearing a case in which a union was accused of racial discrimination. The following are excepts from his ruling on the petition:

> Thus a threshold question which might be inferred from defendants' petition is: Since blacks (like most other thoughtful Americans) are aware of the "sordid chapter in American history" of racial injustice, shouldn't black judges be disqualified per se from adjudicating cases involving claims of racial discrimination? Defendants do not go so far as to precisely assert that black judges should per se be disqualified from hearing cases which involve racial issues, but, as will be demonstrated hereinafter, the absolute consequence and thrust of their rationale would amount to, in practice, double standard within the federal judiciary. By that standard, white judges will be permitted to keep the latitude they have enjoyed for centuries in discussing matters of intellectual substances, even issues of human rights, and because they are white, still be permitted to later decide rights which they have discussed previously in a generalized fashion. But for black judges, defendants insist on a far more rigid standard, which would preclude black judges from ever discussing race relations even in the generalized fashion that other justices and judges have discussed issues of human rights. Under defendants' standards, if a black judge discusses race relations, he should thereafter be precluded from adjudicating matters involving specific claims of racial discrimination.
>
> If defendants' arguments are asserted in good faith and sincerity, they nevertheless represent an almost subconscious expression of the deportment of blacks and, more specifically, of black judges. If America is going to have a total rendezvous with justice so that there can be full equality for blacks, other minorities, and women, it is essential that the "instinct" for double standard be completely exposed and hopefully, through analysis, those elements of irrationality can be ultimately eradicated.[32]

A Certain Blindness

Even black judges seeking to do justice pose a special threat to America's established legal order.

Charles Warren, who won a Pulitzer Prize for his work *The History of the Supreme Court,* indicated that most Supreme Court decisions relating to Negro rights during the latter part of the nineteenth century were made with an eye toward placating those white Americans who oppose racial equality.[33] Certainly this has been true in light of the oppressive and restrictive doctrine established by the Court in *Plessy* and the vague prohibitory relief and limited enforcement of *Brown I.* Justice Thurgood Marshall described the Court's restriction of constitutional rights in *Milliken* as a bowing to a "perceived public mood." The Court's strict constructionist majority was apparently unwilling to consider the basic purpose and meaning of the Fourteenth Amendment. To Marshall's lasting credit, as our nation's highest black jurist he has not hesitated to speak forcefully in stating the true concept of the Constitution's amendment.

In more recent decisions involving employment rights, so crucial to equality, the Court has overlooked a "jurisprudence of original intent" and has fashioned many distinctions far short of the absolute equality envisioned by the framers of the amendment. Seldom in the history of the Fourteenth Amendment has it been interpreted by the Supreme Court according to its intent. And when so interpreted, as in *Brown,* its enforcement has not been carried out. Ironically the experience of *Brown* has led to the often heard argument that the Court is not a fit vehicle for social reform. But if full meaning is ever to be realized from the intent of the Fourteenth Amendment as well as the Declaration of Independence, such reform will necessarily have to follow in America.

10
Unequal Justice

Justice has been a major concern of Western civilization. The Old Testament prophet Micah asked, "What doth the Lord require of thee, but to do justly, and to love mercy, and to walk humbly with thy God?" Philosophers spoke on the subject of basic fairness in the conduct of human affairs, including the early Christian leader Augustine, who reasoned, "Justice being taken away, then, what are kingdoms but great robberies. . . ." Nearly fifteen hundred years later James Madison took up the theme during the constitutional era when he declared: "Justice is the end of government. It is the end of civil society." Adam Smith, father of America's economic system, saw in "justice the prime virtue of a society," stating, "Society may subsist, though not in the most comfortable state, without beneficence; but the prevalence of injustice must utterly destroy it."[1]

The Preamble to our Constitution declares the intention to establish justice, but the framers of the Constitution permitted the property interests of the slaveholders to prevail, since Geor-

A Certain Blindness

gia and South Carolina would not come into the Union if they could not have slaves. By not explicitly outlawing slavery in the Constitution (and, in fact, by implicitly protecting it), the framers established instead a double standard—even Madison insisted it "would be wrong to admit in the Constitution the idea that there could be property in man."[2] And since law has a role in shaping racial attitudes, favoring the property rights of the slaveholder over the human rights of the slave led naturally to the *Dred Scott* decision—that even free Negroes "had no rights which the white man was bound to respect"—a morally bankrupt position that the Supreme Court approved in 1857.

What became of the justice the Constitution intended to establish? The Fourteenth Amendment, which was intended to overrule the *Dred Scott* decision, gave both lawyers and judges a special responsibility to uphold its provisions, including the phrase that "no person shall be denied the equal protection of the laws." Although our profession is not directly responsible for social injustice, we are responsible for injustices that the law perpetuates or exacerbates. It must, therefore, be recognized that a fair and reasonable application of the equal protection clause over the years would not have led to the Kerner Commission's finding that "our nation is moving toward two societies, one black, one white—separate and unequal." The conclusion of the Kerner Commission reflected the vestiges of *Dred Scott* and a type of continuing duality of citizenship. The Commission, however, only stated publicly what black Americans have known as fact for many generations.

America's failure to follow its principles stated in the Declaration of Independence and the resulting injustices have provoked bitter protests by black Americans since the nation's beginning. In 1829 David Walker, a free black man, published "An Appeal to the Colored Citizens of the World," a series of articles that produced a militant antislavery crusade and fear in the hearts of slave owners. Based on the Declaration of Independence itself, Walker argued emphatically "that all men are created equal, and endowed by their Creator with certain inalienable rights" and "that whenever any Form of Government becomes destructive of those ends, it is the Right of the people to alter or to abolish it, and to institute new Government." Walker asserted:

> If any people were ever justified in throwing off the yoke of their tyrants, the slaves are that people. It is not we, but our guilty countrymen, who put arguments into the mouths, and swords into the hands of the slaves. Every sentence that they write—every word that they speak—every resistance that they make, against foreign oppression, is a call upon their slaves to destroy them. Every Fourth of July celebration must embitter and inflame the minds of the slaves.[3]

In 1852 Frederick Douglass also used the moral force of the Declaration when he spoke of Independence Day from a slave's point of view:

> Your denunciation of tyrants, [are] brass fronted impudence; your shouts of liberty and equality, hollow mockery; your prayers and hymns, your sermons and thanksgivings, with all your religious parade and solemnity, are to Him, mere bombast, fraud, deception, impiety, and *hypocrisy*—a thin veil to cover up crimes which would disgrace a nation of savages. There is not a nation on the earth guilty of practices more shocking and bloody than are the people of the United States, at this very hour.[4]

In an attempt to mute rather than confront the evil of slavery and subsequent racial injustice, America has continually blinded itself to the oppression and suffering it has wrought. The experience of black citizens living in our society has been so glossed over and distorted that it is rarely seen in its proper light, even by those possessing a sense of equal justice. Certainly we have suffered the truth of George Santayana's prophesy that "those who cannot remember the past are condemned to repeat it."

The task faced by the Constitutional Convention to resolve the question of representation was a momentous one and resulted in great debates and compromises on the basis of state size. The

A Certain Blindness

"father" of the Constitution, James Madison, revealed the truth underlying the debates, though, when he commented at the time that "it seemed now to be pretty well understood that the real difference of interest lay, not between the large and small but between the Northern and Southern states. The institution of slavery and its consequences formed the line of discrimination."[5]

After full rights of citizenship had been granted to black men and women, history fails to accurately record the concerted efforts to denigrate their status. Traditional accounts of the Reconstruction period are characterized by imposition of an "abusive government with suppression of the South's legitimate interest—a dark and sordid time in our history." Although Reconstruction was a deeply troubled period, the citizenship of black Americans was not in question, and they were provided the freedom to fully participate in the democratic process. But the white South's perceptions were adopted and recorded.

While the facts surrounding Reconstruction have not changed, famous historian Henry Steele Commager revealed that "historians are coming increasingly to emphasize not the sufferings of Southern whites but the betrayal of Southern Negroes as perhaps the most significant feature of the Reconstruction era."[6] This was the very point first recognized by W. E. B. Du Bois in *Black Reconstruction,* where he maintained: "The whole history of Reconstruction has with few exceptions been written by passionate believers in the inferiority of the Negro. The whole body of facts concerning what the Negro actually said and did, how he worked, what he wanted, for whom he voted, is masked in such a cloud of charges, exaggeration and biased testimony, that most students have given up all attempt at new material or new evaluation of the old.[7]

Francis Simkins, considered a leading authority on Southern culture, typified the biased belief in Negro inferiority when he argued that the "crime of crimes was to encourage Negroes in voting, officeholding, and other functions of social equality. . . . Thus, attempts to make the Reconstruction governments reputable and honest have been treated with scorn, and the efforts of Negroes to approach the white man's standards of civilization are adjudged more reprehensible than the behavior of the more ignorant and corrupt."[8] Although the South acknowledged defeat in the war, Commager concluded that it was not prepared to admit such defeat should have unpleasant consequences. Things were expected "to go on as they had in the past." And "because most Northerners were far too eager to return to normalcy to persist in the effort to impose an unpopular policy upon the South, Northern opinion and Government acquiesced in the southern view of the Negro and, finally, of the war itself."[9]

The extent to which our history has been distorted on the question of race was vividly demonstrated during a debate between the presidential candidates in 1980. Ronald Reagan, in debate with then-President Carter, candidly related that when he was young "this country didn't even know it had a racial problem." At first I refused to believe a presidential candidate of a major political party could seriously make such an assertion, but I quickly realized his statement simply reflected his limited knowledge and experience of the matter. Indeed if this decent and honorable man could draw such a conclusion, how would men of less education, experience, and moral stature view my family's experiences? Nevertheless a forum of experts on presidential leadership, meeting at Harvard University, commended President Reagan for having a "clear vision for the country and the ability to communicate it to the voters." Even after several years in office the president did not fully grasp the "race problem." To paraphrase Santayana, if the president was without knowledge of the racial problem of the past, how could he have an accurate vision of the country's future for all its citizens?

Reflecting on President Reagan's lack of awareness, I thought of my elementary school teachers and their understanding of the "race problem," since they were comparable in age with the president. I speculated about their knowledge of the black man's history in this country. They told us inspiring stories about Horatio Alger and about the "rail splitter" becoming

A Certain Blindness

president, but they told us nothing about the role African Americans had played, so completely had my forefathers been excluded from the histories available to us. I doubt it ever occurred to them that my forefathers were excluded as well from sharing in even basic opportunities, or that my brothers and sisters and I would have far fewer basic opportunities to complete and achieve in our society. From my experience over the years, I must conclude that they did not think of us at all—as though we were of no consequence and simply did not count. There could be no miracles of rags-to-riches for us. Our fate was tied to that of our father and the long line of other black men since their first arrival to this land before the *Mayflower*. The "race problem" continued in our time, and we were precluded from sharing the good fortunes Michigan was to offer the likes of DeLorean and Iacocca, both the proud sons of foreign immigrants.

My parents frequently discussed the problem of racial injustice with each other, but they didn't dwell on such matters with us; their primary concern was to help us know about our family's background and to understand the hardships and sacrifices endured by black people. Even though my father was deeply hurt by racially restricted jobs in the factories, I never heard him complain; in fact, I believe he took pride in his work as well as in everything else he did. Despite the adversity he had known, Dad was undaunted in his devotion to our family. I felt his impact in this regard at an early age. During grade school years, when I was asked what my father did, I proudly announced that he worked in the "main office" at Chevrolet. Although I knew he was a janitor, there was no way I could have thought more of him or what he did if he were president of all General Motors.

As we grew older we were taught the importance of always doing our best even in the face of racial barriers and of conducting ourselves with dignity and self-respect. I recall how upset Mom was when Eleanor Roosevelt said Negroes ought not to do too much demanding; although she admired Mrs. Roosevelt, Mom was firm in her resolve that there could be no compromise with demands for equal rights and respect for personal dignity.

Mom's strict demands for respectful conduct and dignified behavior were at odds with what we were to experience as we left our home environment. The first major conflict occurred while Lind and I served in our nation's fight for freedom. Our home training, obviously wholesome upbringing for good citizenship by ordinary American standards, left us unprepared to deal with the ill-treatment accorded black men and women in military service during the World War II era. Taught to conduct ourselves as first-class citizens, we fully expected to be treated in the same manner. The service, however, provided us with many painful yet unconvincing lessons that, because of our color, we should be satisfied with much less.

Although I had known some servicemen who were killed in the war, I knew countless more whose lives were destroyed back home in the States. Black veterans, including those decorated for heroism, disabled, and former prisoners of war, returned home only to find continued denial of job and educational opportunities. Even basic constitutional rights such as voting were denied, and in many instances lives were lost in the attempted exercise thereof.

Many believe that following World War II marked changes of improvement began for black Americans. But the disappointment at unchanged conditions faced by those returning from war produced a most negative atmosphere. This devastating experience caused many veterans of World War II to adopt an attitude of hopelessness that affected their families and in turn all of society. I believe that the war's aftermath marked the end of the long-held blind hope and promise that had somehow sustained black men and their families over many generations.

During the twenty years after World War II many dramatic changes had occurred, and in fighting our last war in Vietnam America proved to be more than an "equal opportunity employer." At one stage of the war over 60 percent of the men in the front lines were black. They accounted for 23 percent of the

A Certain Blindness

war's deaths at a time when 10 percent of the nation's population was black. By the war's end, however, these heroes were unemployed at a rate several times more than that of their white counterparts. Performing on the battlefields as equals in killing and dying was not equalized in peacetime America.

I personally experienced the frustration facing the returning black World War II veterans, and I felt outraged that such shameful conditions persisted for the returning black Vietnam veterans. The black man was still being kept out of the mainstream of competition to insure his limited status in society. Yet this period, so distinctively void of positive change for so many black Americans, was paradoxically in sharp contrast to the fundamental changes that occurred in my personal life. By the time the Vietnam War ended, I was comfortably settled in Atlanta. I found the lakes, streams, and beautiful pine trees of the area extremely appealing, and although at first I was not certain how long I would live in Atlanta, I could not resist buying a house with a small fishing lake. To own my own "fishing hole" seemed like a true success story. I recalled the countless hours of joy I had known as a barefoot boy fishing with a tree branch on the shores of Thread Lake.

By this time my children, Paul and Laura, had moved to East Lansing, Michigan, where their mother Betty taught at Michigan State University. During their holidays and summer vacations they visited with me, and Paul's dog and Laura's cat enjoyed romping with my own two dogs and cat. My children both loved the outdoors, and I was pleased that Paul had developed into a fine fisherman, while Laura enjoyed playing her flute, practicing ballet, and other activities.

I developed a fine working relationship with my fellow judges and the other office personnel. The judges had not known each other before, as ours was a new office, but there was a fine spirit of cooperation and good will. They were of Southern backgrounds and, during many frank discussions on racial matters, I sometimes felt I was speaking a foreign tongue. Jim Burroughs, a colleague and one of my earliest friends in Atlanta, repeatedly inquired if I had met the popular Xernona Clayton, hostess of her own TV show in Atlanta. She was the first black person in the South to have a TV show, and she was highly respected for her involvement in community and race relations. I had casually met Xernona and thought her to be a busy, public-oriented woman. I knew she was the widow of Ed Clayton, a former journalist who had been the first editor of *Jet* magazine for Johnson Publications in Chicago. At the insistence of a mutual fiend, we both agreed to meet for dinner, when I was pleased to learn that, in spite of her high visibility, she was a very private person. I was also astounded to find out that Xernona came originally from the small town of Muskogee, Oklahoma, my great-uncle Bass's home. Although her mother had been fond of fishing, "Zern" had never fished, nor had she any experience with pets. Her enthusiasm for fishing impressed me, and I was struck with how my dogs and cat had taken to her.

We had a large wedding in 1974 with many relatives and friends from across the country attending, including my old friend Leroy Day, by then a businessman in California. Paul, Jr., was my best man; Reverend Martin Luther King, Sr., officiated, and Lind and Reverend Howard Creecy of Atlanta participated. (Our wedding marked the last public appearance of Mrs. King, Sr., before her tragic murder a week later.)

Zern had developed a fond relationship with my family, and I was pleased with her influence over my children. I became close to her immediate family, including her twin sister, Xenobia ("Little"), as well as Little's husband, Tony, and son, Bradford, and with Zern and Little's brother, James, and his wife, Thelma.

My mother visited us often, particularly in the winter when we could take her to Florida. We also visited Paul at Tuskegee University in Alabama, and Mom enjoyed walking the grounds where Booker T. Washington accomplished so much and Dr. George Washington Carver performed his great scientific works. As we drove through Alabama, this was the

A Certain Blindness

first time Mom had ever seen cotton growing; she seemed fascinated and walked in a field where she took a few branches, as if gathering a rare bunch of blossoming flowers.

After Mom's retirement from the Hurley Hospital School of Nursing, she reduced her activities to mostly church and Blue Star Mothers, serving at one time as Michigan state chapter vice-president. She and Art lived comfortably in the family home, and she came to rely more and more on Art to handle all their affairs. In addition to working, Art enjoyed hunting, fishing, and visiting his many friends. Some came by who had been buddies from his early childhood, including one who was chief of the uniform division of the Michigan State Highway Patrol.

When Mom's health declined, requiring more medical supervision, Mary insisted Mom live with her family in New Jersey. Mary's older sons, Clay Jr., Mark, and Bryan, had grown up and moved out; Dannette lived on campus at her school; and only the youngest daughter, Erica, was at home. Since Mary served as director of public health nurses in the West Orange area and her husband Clay's law practice required him to spend much of his time in Washington, D.C., we hired a practical nurse to attend Mom. Erica was great company for her and acted as a personal "nurse" during her after-school hours.

Our family remained close over the years and visited with Mom often. Lind, living in Flint, served as our spiritual anchor and was always there, with his wife, Peggy, and his children, Linda and Steve. My sister Wilma and her family had moved to Buffalo, where her husband, Hank, was a department head at the university; Wilma was an associate professor of nursing and also headed a large project directed toward recruitment and training of minority nurses. Their two children are Susan and Michael.

On a visit to Flint many years ago it was very gratifying to hear Mom proudly confide to some of her friends that "my children are good to me" and she didn't "want for anything." One summer after she had moved to Mary's, we decided to treat Mary to a vacation. Lind and I agreed to share the expenses, and Wilma cared for Mom during Mary's absence. When Mom learned of our plans, she insisted that Wilma promise to tell each of her grandchildren what their parents had done because they cared so much for each other and their mother. During her final hospital stay in 1984 Mom succeeded in even impressing her doctor with unflagging optimism, and after she passed, the doctor contacted Mary to learn more about "such a remarkable lady."

Thoughts of my mother provide an instant reminder of how her strong influence and guidance have been such a blessing for me. That transitional period following my return from the navy immediately comes to mind. Not yet twenty-one years of age, I found my experiences cruel and devastating and in total contradiction of all I had been taught as the "American Way." Efforts to advance myself by the virtues of hard work and determination proved no more beneficial for me than they had for my father and grandfather. Unable to enroll at General Motors Institute, because of my race, and bumped off my job in the engine service department at the Chesapeake and Ohio Railroad, because of my race, I felt bitter and completely demoralized. I have no doubt that, without Mom's strong sense of high purpose and example of discipline and sacrifice, I would have given up any further attempts to advance in life.

Although Negro workers were pioneers in the railroad industry, the four largest railway unions maintained a policy of white-only membership, so that Negroes were denied employment even during the manpower shortage of World War II, in defiance of presidential directives. The union's policy was in effect at the time the terms of my employment on the railroad were revoked. John DeLorean, by then a former General Motors executive, disclosed that the discriminatory admission policy of General Motors Institute continued in effect for many years after my admission was denied. But most disheartening was the U.S. Navy itself declaring that I had "no chance" for opportunity to advance, after my inducement to enlist and serve.

A Certain Blindness

There is, of course, no better criterion for determining the nation's commitment to its stated purpose than the treatment accorded those who serve as its defenders in time of war. But the returning Vietnam veterans joined other black citizens in not being able to realize the "inalienable" right to their own "pursuit of happiness." A 1977 study revealed that of the veterans serving during the Vietnam War period, 28 percent of the black veterans were unemployed compared to 3 percent of white veterans, who also averaged $81 more per week in earnings.[10] These men, serving in highly disproportionate numbers, included those who were drafted because of their inability to receive deferments and their underrepresentation on local draft boards, facts acknowledged by the Department of Defense.

Willing to fight and die in Vietnam, these veterans eagerly sought training and gainful employment with their white comrades in arms. But, as Whitney Young, then executive director of the Urban League, reported in his book *Beyond Racism:* "One young man sought a job in finance. A disbursing chief in the Army, he handled a monthly payroll of $250,000, but the only work he could find was a job weighing bags of coins and stacking them. Another young man, a Navy radar specialist who studied electronics at three service schools, said: 'I went to several electronics plants back home and they tried to stick a broom in my hand.' "[11] This was five years after passage of the Comprehensive Civil Rights Act of 1964 prohibiting discrimination in employment as well as education. But studies showed black male college graduates earned less than white workers who completed only high school. And the black college graduate's lifetime income would be less than the white worker who finished the eighth grade. Even after finishing college, the black graduate needed more graduate education to obtain a comparable job that paid less than his white classmate.

Whether having served in the cause of his country or not, the free Negro's right to earn according to his capacity has always been considerably diminished. As early as 1846 the *Maryland*

Colonization Journal noted: "Whenever the avenues of employment are crowded—whenever the price of labour is brought low by competition—whenever it is a favour to be employed . . . then the colored man will know that time . . . is at hand. In the struggle for bread the colored man will go to the wall."[12] One hundred years later the Kerner Commission observed that "powerful forces of social and political inertia are moving the country steadily along the course of existing policy toward a divided country . . . [that] can only relegate Negroes to a permanently inferior economic status."

Whitney Young recounted in his book *Beyond Racism:*

> When boatloads of European immigrants were being settled on fertile lands in the expanding West, the black man was tied to the Southern soil in a state of peonage. Legally free, he was in fact as enslaved as ever. Those in the cities saw the few jobs open to them disappear as white employers preferred whites. Even before the Civil War, Frederick Douglass was moved to write of free Negroes in the North: "Every hour sees us elbowed out of some employment, to make room perhaps for some newly arrived immigrants, whose hunger and color are thought to give them a title to especial favor."[13]

Black Americans came to find out that the inspiring "bootstrap" theory, commonly viewed as a means to success for foreign immigrants, was not to relate to the black experience in America.

Adam Smith's principles of free market capitalism held that the public interest is served by the pursuit of personal economic gain and that competition provides the only regulator of an individual's opportunity and freedom in the marketplace. In defiance of our country's basic economic principles, the black labor force was historically excluded from the economic mainstream. My grandfather, C. R. Wilson, for example, who had staked his future on winning a larger share of the economic pie for black workers, was forced to give up his Knights of Labor

A Certain Blindness

union work in the face of terroristic threats and violence. "At the close of the Civil War, five out of every six artisans in the South were Negroes, but by the turn of the century skilled Negro workers probably numbered no more than five percent of the total."[14] There were some rare exceptions when economic justice was served, as in the case of Uncle Bass. No one could compete with his superior knowledge and skill, which simply was beyond the ability of his would-be white competitors. Besides, not too many men would serve where their very lives were continually at such a high risk.

So the basic principle of free market competition gave way to a system of job designation by race. With neither opportunity to compete nor reward for merit, Negroes were summarily rejected as inferiors and incompetents in the labor force. This was the system that prevailed during my father's working life and that relegated him and other Negro workers to janitorial or hot, dirty jobs in the factories of the North. An undeserving white man had no fear of competitive risk from a diligent and hard working Negro. Foundry work, pick and shovel employees, waiters, and janitors were their lot. In an employment situation with white men, the black man could work in a ditch but not supervise from the bank; he could ride on the back of a truck but rarely in the cab, and he certainly could never drive. To work as a craftsman in industry was virtually out of the question. This policy of exclusion remained through our entry into World War II, and during my early adult years no free competition existed for Negro labor in the marketplace. This terrible blight on the American sense of fair play was even more oppressive as it held the victims to the same measure of success and achievement as white citizens.

The Negro laborer, without opportunity to demonstrate his worthiness or ability, was robbed of personal dignity and self-respect as head of his household. Without hope of substantial change or advancement, he was continually haunted by his limited means to provide food, clothing, housing, health care, and education for his children.

Unequal Justice

In 1946 Eli Ginzberg, a professor at Columbia University, took note of the problem and pointed out:

> Most Negro parents have had to work hard most of their lives at jobs which command little esteem, are often extremely unpleasant, and provide no more than a subsistence wage. Many Negroes are likely to feel embittered or resigned about their work, and these attitudes will eventually carry over to their children. The Negro child, moreover, is also likely to respond to the attitudes of the dominant white population toward the work role of his race. Seeing his elders holding down poor jobs and sensing that the white community takes this for granted, the Negro child is not likely to develop high aspirations for himself.[15]

Our government, as other institutions in society, has repeatedly created myths to excuse itself from seeing how the promotion of economic gain for white Americans is made at the expense of black people. No better way is this accomplished than by blaming the victims. One prime example of this approach is the 1965 Department of Labor report entitled *The Negro Family: The Case for National Action*. The report attributed the prime source of the Negroes' problems to instability of the Negro family, the one basic unit in our society that has suffered the most and yet has proven itself unmatched in strength and ability to endure. This government document obviously shifted the focus of white attention away from any inference of racism to blame the Negro himself. With obvious reference to what it perceived to be legitimate concerns, the White House issued a memorandum five years later that "the time may have come when the issue of race could benefit from a period of benign neglect. The subject has been too much talked about. The forum has been too much taken by hysterics, paranoids and boodlers." This recommendation was made a year after a U.S. Senate report disclosed that white high school graduates earned an average of $1,140 per year more than black college educated men. It was also a time when black factory workers earned one-third less than white workers and truck

A Certain Blindness

drivers earned 42 percent less. The employment picture was worsening; with increased technology and overt discrimination in hiring, black workers continued to be locked into marginal, low-wage jobs.

For many decades, the American economy absorbed the mass of unskilled labor, including European immigrants. But these immigrants, through family and friends, were able to enter labor unions and move into skilled crafts. This lack of higher income skilled jobs largely accounted for black workers having a median family income of 58 percent of white income in 1966. Besides the policies and attitudes of management, many labor unions joined in the practice of denying black workers access to the skilled job market. Rather than providing an avenue for opportunity and achievement, these unions placed roadblocks in the black workers' path in the same way my grandfather had known.

Exclusion from craft union membership had been so pervasive that the 1960 census reported only 79 black electrical apprentices in the entire nation. There were 2,191 black Americans in all trades throughout the country, 1 more than 1950. This condition existed in spite of a 1955 pledge by the AFL-CIO at its formation for "all workers to share equally in the benefits of union organization," regardless of color. Although the Brotherhood of Railway and Steamship Clerks abolished "white" and "colored" job classifications, "white" men were placed in "colored" jobs, resulting in "colored" workers becoming jobless.[16] The Civil Rights Commission found that in Detroit less than 2 percent of all craft apprentices were black. In Atlanta the construction industry had 20 black apprentices out of 700, with all the black apprentices employed in the trowel trades—brick laying, cement finishing, and plastering.

While America could announce and carry out a plan to place a man on the moon during that period of time, "the Department of Labor was unable to enforce section 703(d) of the 1964 Act which forbids discrimination in apprentice programs."[17] In Philadelphia "not one of the important craft unions in the building

258

trades has a program that meets the legal regulations of the Bureau of Apprenticeship and Training." The "Philadelphia Plan" was devised to ameliorate this condition, but it was scrapped for political expediency. By the end of 1979, when the Vietnam veterans had returned, 7.6 percent of the nation's work force was out of work; the figure for black workers was 14.3 percent.

In spite of the system that kept them from competing freely in the workplace, black men and women have been able to make authentic contributions in many areas of our society, including American culture and the performing arts. Beginning with the master-servant relation during slavery, slaves who entertained their fellow bondsmen were also required to entertain their masters. My great-grandmother Pearlalee was held in favor by her owners for her beautiful singing. Although primarily the object of amusement and ridicule, many slaves possessed a unique talent in music, song, and dance, which had profound impact on the nation's folklore. Black-faced white minstrels mimicked their songs and dances to become popular on the professional stage, and white musicians borrowed their music to popularize Dixieland bands.

Although imitated and exploited, the Negro's participation in the world of entertainment was generally seen as a form of servility. The freedom to express his talent and ability was not considered to be a real form of competition, so it was acceptable because it was less threatening to the cherished myth of white superiority. However, when the Negro artist performed in a manner that dispelled the myth of his inferiority, threatened white artists found ways to discredit him. This has been true from the time of Frederick Ira Aldridge, the first great Negro actor, demonstrated by the treatment accorded the highly talented and much maligned Paul Robeson. Aldridge, decorated by the king of Prussia and the czar of Russia, and knighted by the king of Sweden, was by 1857 "commonly regarded as one of the two or three greatest actors in the world."[18] Not welcomed on the American stage, he performed in Europe where he found an unbiased outlet for his talent and ability.

A Certain Blindness

Over the years some black personalities gained considerable success on stage, in radio, and in film playing servile roles totally lacking in dignity and subject to unabashed white ridicule. Except for some recent success of several black artists, the same stereotyping generally continues in television. Unfortunately the programming has tended to reflect a false image of black Americans, and black writers, broadcasters, and producers have generally been excluded. This pattern is likewise followed by the nation's press in its reporting, and employment of journalists, editors, and publishers. While the Kerner Commission urged employment of "more Negroes as journalists," 56 percent of our nation's newspapers had no black journalists. There were only two editors of major metropolitan newspapers in 1987, 3.6 percent of all daily newspaper journalists. The characters and roles of those in the world of entertainment and information are highly restricted along racial lines, yet these areas are often viewed as among the most democratic in our society.

A classic example of assignment of roles by race in the field of entertainment is seen in professional sports. This point is perhaps best illustrated by the part played in sports history by Negro jockeys. Just as my great-uncle Bass had developed skill in handling horses while working in his master's stable, a tradition began during slavery that produced expert black trainers and riders. The first Kentucky Derby at Churchill Downs in 1875 was won by a black jockey, and thirteen of the fourteen horses in the race had black riders. Ike Murphy, "the greatest jockey of the 19th century," was black, as were other jockeys who won major races, and William Sims was the first American jockey to ride in England. Murphy won forty-nine of fifty-one races at Saratoga in 1882 and was the first jockey to win the Kentucky Derby three times. When he won the Derby in 1884 on "Buchanan," the trainer William Bird was also black. William Loren Katz in *The Black West* aptly describes the fate of black jockeys in America: "In 1901 and 1902 Jimmie Winkfield was the last black jockey to win the Kentucky Derby. By then most black boys who wished to follow in his footsteps found their path blocked. As horse racing became big business the whites who controlled the purse strings also insisted that only other whites control the reins of the horses. A proud black tradition of several centuries had ended."[19]

Today the dearth of black jockeys is of no moment to horse racing enthusiasts, but if it were, it would undoubtedly be attributed to a shortcoming on the part of black horse riders, since it is traditional to blame the black victim.

It was in the context of such thinking that Al Campanis, vice-president of the Los Angeles Dodgers and director of Dodger player personnel, stated on nationwide television that he did not believe prejudice was the reason for the lack of black field managers and general managers in baseball. He went on to say, "I truly believe that they may not have the necessities" to fill these positions. In support of his belief, he questioned, "How many quarterbacks do you have? How many pitchers do you have? And, why are black people not good swimmers? Because they don't have the buoyancy." Attempting to justify the situation as not unique to the sports field, Campanis asked the interviewer, "How many executives do you have on a higher echelon in your business in TV, I mean. . . ." The blatant and totally unfounded remarks by the sports executive, whether consciously racist or not, were actually perceived by many as authoritatively spoken, which is how the myth is perpetuated. Campanis was fired, but some people were quick to caution against "race-conscious hiring," saying "baseball doesn't need affirmative action."

Jackie Robinson, Jesse Owens, and Joe Louis were able to become national sports heroes by transcending race, and these were gratifying experiences, but their sacrifices and contributions to the cause of fair play, decency, and self-respect were hardly perceptible to most Americans. I was inspired by Jackie's personal victories and success but I could also understand his ultimate despair.

When interviewed in 1969, twenty years after his entry into the major leagues, Jackie said he had hoped by then that no color lines would be drawn in any areas of the game. He was

A Certain Blindness

particularly frustrated by the comments of some executives who believed black players did not possess the skills required for managerial or front office positions. The general manager of the New York Yankees was quoted as saying, "It is very difficult to find qualified Negroes with the right educational background for the front office job." This executive later explained to Jackie that there were "many black players active in baseball who were qualified and that as these players finished their active careers, he felt sure many of them would stay in baseball in nonplaying positions."[20] Jackie protested until the end of his life baseball's lack of interest in further breaking the color barrier and condemned the "hypocrisy of club owners who try to cover up their bigotry." Ten years after Jackie Robinson's death his deep concerns were verified. A 1982 survey of all but two major league clubs (who refused to cooperate) revealed that of 913 white-collar baseball jobs including secretaries, 32 were held by black employees. There were only 15 black scouts out of 568, 1 executive, and 1 third-base coach.

By the time Jackie died in 1972 studies had begun to establish as fact the extent of racism in sports. The August 1972 *Civil Rights Digest,* published by the U.S. Commission on Civil Rights, contained the article "Black Americans in Sports: Unequal Opportunity for Equal Ability," which pointed out that, "since 1947, when Jackie Robinson broke the color line in the 'national game' of baseball, the idea that organized sport has escaped the pervasive effects of racism has become one of the most cherished myths in American life." According to a number of social scientists, journalists, and athletes, "the existence of racism in collegiate and professional sports is especially insidious because the promoters of and commentators on athletics have made sports sacred by projecting an image of it as the single institution in America relatively immune from racism." Studies "found that in 1968 one out of five white major leaguers who had signed since before 1959 had accepted bonuses in excess of $20,000. None of the black players playing in 1968 who had signed in the 1950's had received this inducement. By 1964 the proportion of whites receiving bonuses remained twice as high as that for blacks." It was found "among experienced ballplayers, blacks, on the average, earn less than whites of equal ability." Further, "the Negro ballplayer may have to be better qualified than a white player to win the same position," because from 1956 to 1965 black batters averaged approximately twenty points higher than the white players. Not only did the black player have to be better than a white player to reach the major leagues, he also had to out perform to remain there. Almost 70 percent of black non-pitchers in the majors are everyday starters.

Racially discriminatory practices in sports are not limited to baseball. Football and basketball have similarly failed to utilize black managers, coaches, and front office personnel. Like baseball, football has shown a color line on certain positions. Black players are traditionally running backs, defensive backs, and wide receivers. White positions have been quarterback, center, and offensive guard, considered central players and positions of longevity.

White players continue to prevail over black players of comparable ability, and a recent study showed that black players actually received less pay than a statistically poorer white player. Al Campanis had played shortstop when Jackie Robinson played second base. Campanis did not explain what outstanding qualities he and other white ex–ball players possessed that Jackie and former black baseball men did not possess, but skin color appeared to be the only difference. Yet when Campanis was fired, the Dodger president said Campanis's comments were "so removed, so distant" from what the organization believes that it was impossible for him to continue. Although it had been forty years since Robinson joined the organization, the organization still had not hired a black manager or front office executive. It is difficult to understand how Campanis, with the Dodgers for forty years, did not know the organization's views nor they his. It is also difficult to conceive how his views did not reflect baseball's mainstream views.

Club owners have had a significant role in determining

A Certain Blindness

who would play the game. Black players participated in the National League following its organization in 1876, but by the turn of the century they were totally excluded from play, due to the efforts of league officials. The other club owners roundly condemned Branch Rickey when he broke the color line by signing Jackie Robinson. Immediately after the signing, however, several owners maintained that black players "have always had a chance to prove themselves in the minors" and that "colored players have never been discriminated against in the major leagues."[21] As a result of subsequent efforts to integrate baseball, a joint National and American League committee discussed the "race question" and charged individuals advocating integration as being "political and social-minded drum beaters"[22] and protested that those who believe that "racial discrimination is the basic reason for the failure of the major leagues to give employment to negroes—are talking through their collective hats." Unbelievably the report claimed that "every American boy . . . should have a chance in baseball, but signing a few players under the circumstances would only be a 'gesture,' not contributing to the solution of the real problem."[23]

Then when a black man does succeed in being hired in the majors, his skill is minimized, inferring that he was hired only as a favor. *Sporting News,* the "Baseball Bible," contended Robinson was "reported to possess baseball abilities which, were he white, would make him eligible for a trial with, let us say, the Brooklyn Dodger Class C farm at Newport News, if he were six years younger." Star pitcher Bob Feller of the Cleveland Indians offered the opinion that "if he (Robinson) were a white man, I doubt if they would consider him big league material."[24] But in fact Robinson's performance completely exploded any notion of racial inferiority. In his first game with Montreal of the International League, Jackie Robinson had four hits out of five at bats, including a home run. He scored four times, drove in three runs, and stole two bases. When he joined the Dodgers in 1947 he was named 1947 rookie of the year and most valuable player in 1949, leading to his entry in baseball's Hall of Fame. In nine of eleven years after 1949, Negro players won most valuable player awards in the National League. Many records have fallen to these stars, led by Hank Aaron's surpassing Babe Ruth's home-run record, "long a symbol of unattainable standards."

But upon conclusion of their careers, the overall experience of many black stars has been summed up by Robinson and Aaron. Jackie pointed out, "there is one irrefutable fact of my life which has determined much of what happened to me: I was a black man in a white world."[25] Hank acknowledged that "baseball has done a lot for me," but added, "it has taught me that regardless of who you are and regardless of how much money you make, you are still a Negro."[26]

The problem of acceptance and respect encountered by these black sports heroes has been shared by most of us in other fields as well. This has certainly been an on-going experience for me and is illustrated by an occurrence here in Atlanta in 1986. I learned from a white minister friend that I had been the topic of a conversation at my local health club. He related that several members were discussing my absence one Saturday morning, as we were accustomed to seeing each other. They spoke of missing me and proceeded to compliment my character and intelligence when one executive, otherwise in agreement, commented, "That's all well and good but he is still a nigger."

Twenty years since Jackie Robinson exposed the hypocrisy of baseball's club owners, prominent *New York Times* sports writer Leonard Koppett wrote, "For sheer hypocrisy, the baseball hierarchy's reaction to the discrimination-in-management issue is hard to beat."[27] Koppett pointed out that, while at one time baseball was well ahead of our society in desegregation, it has failed to carry out its original thrust. He observed that the obvious dearth of black decision-makers did not just spring up and has been no secret to all involved, including the commissioner's office and the media. Koppett compared the situation of black ball players to that of black broadcasters, columnists, and reporters, noting the absence of black editors, publishers, and decision-makers in TV and radio news.

A Certain Blindness

Baseball mirrors the rest of society regarding the limits within which black persons have been permitted to participate. While there have been many intelligent black baseball players and knowledgeable baseball businessmen before and after Jackie Robinson, there simply have not been enough Branch Rickeys, in and out of baseball. When Rickey signed the first black major leaguer, he was adamant: "This is supposed to be the all-American game but it is closed to one-tenth of our citizens. I refuse to perpetuate the lie."[28]

In 1989, two years after Al Campanis was fired for making racist statements, major league teams have gone through thirty-six changes at the general manager and field manager levels, yet despite a considerable pool of former players worthy of a chance, only one vacancy has been filled by a black man. For one managerial position, the black candidate was scheduled for his interview four days after a manager was named to fill the vacancy. In another instance, of the five finalists interviewed for a manager's position, only the black candidate was not introduced to the team president. The record of all-white professional football coaches remained intact until the 1989 season.

While success in the sports world generally depends on one's physical ability, intelligence, and leadership, mental achievement is most often cited as the means to ensure success in society at large. Education has always been viewed as the sure way of transforming one from destitution to money and status, so as in other fields strong forces have persisted to deny black men and women opportunities for educational achievement. Such exclusion from the mainstream of American life began with the enactment of slave laws that prohibited teaching slaves to read or write. Originally intended to perpetuate the myth of inferiority in support of the proslavery argument, opposition to education for Negroes continued after the Civil War and during the time my grandfather was in school, effectively thwarting this means of gaining equality. Mastery of even the basic skills of reading, writing, and arithmetic was discouraged. In many instances, up through the pre-*Brown* years, necessary facilities and equipment were denied black schools. This is reflected in the amount seventeen Southern states and the District of Columbia spent per student in 1946, $102.66 per white pupil in average daily attendance and only $57.57 per Negro pupil.[29]

Fifteen years after *Brown,* the Kerner Commission revealed that "schools have failed to provide the educational experience which could help overcome the effects of discrimination and deprivation." While the report stressed the need for additional resources, such as better facilities and teaching materials, many school systems have failed to understand the effects of racism and have ignored cultural differences in black and white children. As a result black students often suffer from testing, classroom ability grouping, and negative teacher attitudes.

The vast distance and misunderstanding that exist between the races in public schools across the country to a great extent have been caused by the education process itself. Though it touched briefly on the disastrous effects of racism and noted inadequate ghetto schools, the Kerner report did not recognize that all our children have been miseducated by distorting their view of the black race and its history. Children's education begins at home, and any fears, prejudices, and motives about race are consciously or unconsciously taught by parents to their children. Unenlightened or fearful parents do not teach their children to respect the inherent dignity of all peoples. The formal educational experience therefore begins filled with all the underlying fears, prejudices, and motives the parent had known. "Such an education, rather than preparing white children to recognize, understand, and deal with the racial contradiction in our society glosses over it as though it did not exist or was not of major importance. Children are brought up to accept America's racism and yet to 'believe in' freedom, justice, and equality for all."[30]

In the state of Georgia, for instance, in defiance of the *Brown* decision the legislature changed the state flag to include the Confederate flag. All efforts by black legislators to amelio-

A Certain Blindness

rate the situation have been stifled, and this racist act prevails unabated.

Formal education in the hands of prejudiced or uninformed teachers and reinforced by stereotyped textbooks perpetuates racism in our educational system. A study of American history textbooks in 1949 and 1961 showed that the position of the Negro in history had not changed; "he remained invisible."[31] A 1964 survey of texts used in the California public schools revealed the implicit denial of "the obvious deprivations suffered by Negroes. In several places they go further, implying approval for repression of Negroes or patronizing them as being unqualified for life in a free society." A study by the American Federation of Teachers in 1967 of junior and senior high texts showed that textbook authors tended to "minimize" individual and institutional racism and to treat black people as immigrants, suggesting that as they become "Americanized," they would enter the mainstream as immigrants did. These authors did not ever acknowledge the barriers placed between black people and full participation in American society.[32] A comparative study of U.S. history books released in 1983 showed that there had been an attempt at more balance in the portrayal of black Americans over the years, but it also indicated "a reluctance among writers to draw a distinction between the experiences of black and white Americans" and to "depict institutionalized racism" or outline present discriminatory practices.[33] All of these studies report that the textbook authors steadfastly remain clear of any discussion or topics that may offend or cause disagreement among whites and also present an overly optimistic view of social harmony.

The fact is that without this information, there can be no understanding of the extent of difficulties black Americans face daily. Without this understanding, white students can persist naively in believing that everyone is benefiting from the American system. Several years ago, while attending an anniversary of the *Brown* decision, I heard a law school professor describe an incident in which a second-year law student at a prestigious Ivy

League school utterly refused to believe the facts of a case under review in a criminal procedure class. The case involved a black man accused of a crime whose basic legal rights were completely disregarded. The law student could not conceive that such a thing could possibly occur under our system of justice. Nothing in his total life experience prepared him to accept as true the type of experience commonly known to black Americans.

Although increased education for black men and women has proven to be disappointing with regard to anticipated reward, by 1976, the two hundredth birthday of the Declaration of Independence, it at least appeared they had gained a fair representation in institutions of higher learning. On a level comparable to the country's general population, black students represented 11 percent of the student population on U.S. campuses. By 1986, however, this slow but definite progress in the direction of racial equality came to a halt. At that time black college students made up only 8.8 percent of the college student population. For example, at the University of Chicago black student enrollment was halved to 2.5 percent, and at the University of Michigan it was 5.2 percent, down from 7.7 percent in 1976. This decline in enrollment signals deep underlying consequences in the various fields, such as the ratio of black physicians to black people, which is half that of white people (and there are those who speak of a surplus of physicians in America). During a time when there exists a crucial need for black teachers in our public schools, there has been a drop in teachers from 7.8 percent in 1981 to 6.9 percent in 1986 (a corresponding drop was seen in black faculty members in predominately white institutions of higher learning by 11.3 percent from 1977 to 1983). Our society becomes increasingly more technological, yet Massachusetts Institute of Technology, a leading school in this area, experienced a reduction in minority students from 5 percent to 3.5 percent.

Various explanations have been given for the decline in the black student population, but no one can attribute it to any one cause. College costs have skyrocketed and budget cuts and re-

A Certain Blindness

duced government student aid programs have taken their toll. In addition, perceived White House hostility has discouraged many of the poor from even considering college, and a federal study appears to support the thesis that family income is now the best indicator of educational opportunity.

For the black Americans who do pursue college, racism continues as a highly visible and pronounced factor. All students, exercising their educational ambition and desiring to advance themselves, have every reason to expect a pleasant learning environment enriched by quality teaching from dedicated instructors. From my own experience of nearly forty years ago, I know the feeling they have when they cannot participate in all campus activities or share fully in academic life. In spring 1984 the *Atlanta Constitution* reported on the campus life of the thirteen hundred black students at the University of Georgia. The reporter was unable to elicit one positive statement about the university from the black students he interviewed, yet he heard many expressions of isolation and not belonging. The students even said they would discourage their friends from enrolling.[34] These experiences are by no means restricted to the South. Black alumni of MIT, responding to a special survey, said relationships with professors were often characterized by poor or inadequate support and occasionally blatant discriminatory behavior. Forty-four percent of those responding actually believed they were impeded by racism during their years at the school. While this school apparently undertook to improve its racial climate, other schools were not so attentive to the problem, as outbreaks of racial hostility toward black students occurred on college campuses in 1986. There were episodes on campuses from Massachusetts to California, and Michigan to Alabama. Many administrators conceded that they were too slow to react to these bold and brazen acts, that too often they passed them off as isolated or insignificant. One wonders how truly committed to full and equal access to education of its young people a nation actually is to allow its citizens to feel free to express racial hostility on such a large scale. If university administrators and professors are unable to see, grasp, and firmly deal with such problems, then how can we expect other areas of society to show vision, concern, and understanding?

In his 1987 book, *The Closing of the American Mind*,[35] Allan Bloom, a professor, discussed how higher education has failed democracy and impoverished the souls of today's students. He believes there has been a failure to grasp basic philosophical truths about human nature and to transmit these truths in an orderly study program. Although Bloom sees universities as true melting pots with no regard to ethnicity, he recognizes the gulf that exists between white and black students, but he maintains that white students are without fault and attributes the racial problems on university campuses to the attitudes of black students and to affirmative action.

On the other hand Pennsylvania State University president Bryce Jordan called some 1989 incidents at Penn State "a frightening series of events." The *Atlanta Constitution* on February 22, 1989, reported: " 'I think it's a national problem,' he said, citing incidents at other universities. 'It's a tragic regression. . . . We're undergoing a downhill slide in terms of combating racism in this country.' "

While universities have a responsibility to show others how to deal with morality and justice, they likewise have an obligation to do justice themselves. "There's a national tolerance of racism created by the Reagan administration and that tolerance is being reflected on the nation's college campuses," declared Charles Moody, vice-provost for minority affairs at the University of Michigan, as the December 1988 *Ebony* magazine reported. Moody remarked: "We can't close our eyes to it and pretend it will go away. It won't. Institutions have a responsibility to all students to admit it is there and take whatever steps are necessary to change it." The president of the University of Michigan, James J. Duderstat, determined to eliminate racism on campus with what he calls the Michigan Mandate. "We have to reinvent what the university is supposed to be," Duderstat asserted, and the university "must

A Certain Blindness

take affirmative action to overcome the inequities imposed by our society" on minorities.[36]

Whether as a factory worker in my father's time or the holder of an M.B.A. climbing the corporate ladder in today's business world, one's advancement continues to be governed by the color of one's skin. Just as black employees have traditionally been relegated to service and support jobs, rather than in production, those who reach mid- or higher lever positions also tend to be placed in staff jobs that provide administrative support rather than positions of corporate responsibility. There are exceptions, but black officials typically serve in public and community relations, personnel, or special markets. Many complain of being underused and barred from senior executive positions; as noted by the *Wall Street Journal*, "they now constitute 3.9 percent of all managers, [but] you'd have a hard time counting a dozen who are head of divisions or subsidiaries of all Fortune 500 companies. Minority managers are concentrated in staff jobs . . . positions that unlike line jobs don't usually lead to the inner sanctum."[37] In the event of layoffs, these positions tend to be eliminated before the line jobs. Levi Jackson, former Yale University football star and the highest ranking black employee in Ford Motor Company history (serving in urban affairs), wondered upon his retirement: "What would it have been like if I was white and came here from Yale? How far could I have gone?"[38]

The American Jewish Committee Institute of Human Relations studied management ranks of America's largest corporations. The subjects of the study were 1965, 1970, 1975, or 1980 M.B.A. graduates of Harvard Business School, including men, women, black, white, Jewish, and non-Jewish, who were or had been employed in *Fortune* magazine's annual list of America's largest corporations. The study revealed that more women than black graduates "made it into the managerial ranks, and that they progressed to higher levels within the corporate structure."[39] It also indicated that, during the Reagan administration, there had been reduced governmental pressure for affirmative action, resulting in diminished corporate leadership toward overcoming discrimination. Twenty-six percent of those interviewed believed that black employees were promoted less rapidly than white employees. Many, both black and white, attributed this to racial stereotyping and perceptions of black inferiority:

> There was widespread agreement, among both Blacks and whites, that under the Reagan Administration there has been almost no pressure to comply with EEO guidelines, and correspondingly less commitment on the part of most companies to hire Blacks. As one white male said: "The changes have been tremendous for women; they're now doing jobs no one conceived they'd be doing ten to 20 years ago. For Blacks, however, it's harder now than it was a few years ago. Affirmative action has waned, and there's more emphasis on women than Blacks."[40]

Another white male pointed out that, under his company's affirmative action program, he believed that if a white male had "two comparable candidates in terms of ability, one black male and one white woman, either consciously or subconsciously he'd pick the white woman."

The American Jewish Committee study exposed a widespread view that black employees lagged behind women in the corporate world. Several explanations were offered, two of which seem most plausible to me. A black male observed: "From a white perspective, all you have to deal with is attitudes about women, perhaps that they belong in the home, or they are too emotional. You probably can relate to that woman, for you have a broader perspective that you share in terms of how you perceive things in general. With Blacks you have to deal not only with stereotypes but also with legitimate cultural differences. You don't share that general experience." A white female explained that women have an "easier time" because "white males at the top have daughters, so they can see a personal relationship with young women. Even if their wives didn't work, even if they don't have daughters who want to go into business, they still know young white women personally, and they can respond to their career goals. But a lot of white males don't know any Blacks personally, and so they're less comfortable, and less able to respond personally to them."[41]

The American Jewish Committee study of Harvard graduates confirms that even at the highest level of our free enterprise system and among the best educated, racial barriers exist in the employment marketplace. The survey also shows that corporate America recognizes a preference for white women in its hiring and promotion policies over black people.

Women, both black and white, have traditionally been subjected to discrimination and deprivation, a condition that obviously demands rectification. But white women, unlike black people, have maintained close and influential relationships with those most responsible for racial discrimination, their fathers, brothers, husbands, and friends. As a consequence of this relationship, white women have been, and are, accepted for positions that were totally out of the question for black men and women. Such was the case when President Franklin D. Roosevelt appointed the wife of Paul C. Wilson, Frances Perkins, to serve in his cabinet as secretary of labor; Perkins held that post from 1933 to 1945. Since then no black man or woman has ever been considered seriously for that position. In 1960, prior to enactment of civil rights legislation, a study of the social and political attitudes of state supreme court justices revealed that they endorsed women's rights but were less committed to racial justice.[42]

Paul Seabury explained in a *Commentary* article the circumstances under which women were included in the Civil Rights Bill of 1964:

> Old Howard Smith, Virginia swamp fox of the House Rules Committee, was a clever tactical fighter. When Dixiecrats in 1964 unsuccessfully tried to obstruct passage of the Civil Rights bill, Smith in a fit of inspired raillery devised a perverse stratagem. He proposed an amendment to the bill, to include women as an object of federal protection in employment, by adding sex to the other criteria of race, color, national origin, and religion as illegitimate grounds for discrimination in hiring. This

tactical maneuver had far-reaching effects; calculated to rouse at least some Northern masculine ire against the whole bill, it backfired by eliciting a chivalrous rather than (as we now call it) sexist response: the amendment actually passed!

Smith, however, had greater things in mind for women's rights. As a fall-back strategy, they would distract federal bureaucrats from the principal object of the bill, namely, to rectify employment inequities for Negroes.[43]

The "strategy" has undoubtedly proven to be a success for women, though racism continues to be an overriding factor. An example of the perpetuation of this racism occurred in 1989 involving my wife, Xernona. As a corporate executive with Turner Broadcasting Company here in Atlanta, she was invited to be the main speaker at an annual banquet of a business and professional women's group in a nearby city. When the organization learned that this highly placed executive is black, Xernona was "disinvited." These women, of vast influence in their community concerning employment, education, and human welfare, saw race as an overriding concern, exceeding their common cause and mutual interest.

For most black Americans the promise of success continues to be illusionary even when they acquire extensive educations. In my own case I am acutely aware that the ordinary methods of determining one's competency for a job were not the only factors that enabled me to become a government attorney at the Federal Power Commission. After many years of study, determined effort, and God's grace, I, like a few fortunate others, have been able to slip through many racial barriers to a select position of employment. The tragic death of Martin Luther King, Jr., and the riots that followed focused attention on racial inequities. It was only in the wake of these crises that, with the dedicated concerns of EEOC, particularly about the government's dismal employment record, I was able to enter government service. This opportunity in turn allowed me to exhibit qualities that eventually earned me a professional achievement award, providing the background for my judicial appointment.

A Certain Blindness

Black lawyers, like other black professionals seeking employment, generally continue to face racial barriers. By its very nature law is a profession that should be a model of opportunity for all. Yet the American Bar Association (ABA) reported that only 1.5 percent of the lawyers in ninety-two of the country's one hundred largest law firms were black.[44] Earlier a *National Law Journal* survey revealed the total number of black lawyers to be near 3 percent and two-thirds of the largest firms had no black partners while one in six employed no black lawyers.[45] In 1984 the ABA created a committee on minorities in the legal profession, which conducted two days of hearings focused on such problems as employment opportunities and career development. One of the goals recommended by the panel and adopted by the association was "to promote full and equal participation in the profession by minorities and women." Grades, the most popular explanation for racial imbalance in law firms, were found not to be the decisive factor they were thought to be, because even when compared with white students of comparable class rank, black students had a harder time finding jobs. Noteworthy is the fact that more than four hundred members of the National Association of Legal Placement were invited to participate in the task force, yet representatives of only two big law firms appeared. The placement organization, which assists students in finding employment, found in 1988 that among the thirty-five largest law firms in Chicago, only 1.8 percent of the lawyers were black.

In Atlanta, where black lawyers represent approximately 10 percent of the total bar, a 1984 survey showed that in the city's eight largest firms there were 8 black partners out of 452 partners, and 20 black associates out of 502 associates. These conditions exist in a city where there is a solid black economic base, a black mayor and numerous black elected officials, and a black population of approximately 67 percent.[46]

Studies continue to show that the black-white income gap in America is as wide today as it was in 1960. John W. Wight, author of *The American Almanac of Jobs and Salaries,* which lists

Unequal Justice

job descriptions and salaries for thousands of positions, stated that the most important influence on one's income is race. The present median income for a white male is $25,931, compared with $17,971 for a black male. Median family income for a white family is $29,152, while it is $16,786 for a black family.[47]

A glimpse at the employment picture in my home state of Michigan shows how crucial the problem is. Five days after race riots had torn Detroit asunder in July 1967, President Johnson established the Kerner Commission. One of the commission's conclusions was that white racism was essentially responsible for the racial violence that occurred that summer. Among the elements of that racism was discrimination in employment. Obviously the urgency of the situation has not been a priority concern of those most able to control it. On the twentieth anniversary of the disorders that swept Michigan, a report, "The State of Black Michigan," was released. Its findings disclosed that in 1986 the unemployment rate for black men and women was 22.3 percent, compared to a white rate of 7.1 percent. The black unemployment rate had remained more than three times the rate of white persons. Even worse was the unemployment situation for black teenagers at the rate of 51.2 percent, compared to the white teenager rate of 17 percent.[48]

The Kerner Commission reported that on January 1, 1968, black unemployment was 7.4 percent and white unemployment was 3.6 percent. Twenty years later black unemployment was 12.2 percent and white unemployment was 5.0 percent. The Kerner Commission stated that a "compassionate, massive, sustained government effort was necessary to reverse the trend of polarization and inequity." But the persistence of racism has endured and the truth of Dr. Kenneth Clark's concerns before the commission has come to pass. Referring to American race riots in 1919, 1935, 1943, and 1966 he said, "I must again in candor say to you members of this commission: It is a kind of Alice in Wonderland, with the same moving picture reshown over and over again, the same analysis, the same recommendations, and the same inaction."

A Certain Blindness

America cannot tolerate dual standards of separate and unequal for its people. Racism, excused in appropriately created myths, defies the concept of equal justice; the myths serve to exonerate white society from fault or responsibility. Currently under the banner of equality of opportunity, there is the myth that such equality actually exists. In reality, equality of opportunity does not transcend race.

11

The Past as Prologue

The sign in front of the National Archives in Washington warns that "The Past Is Prologue, Learn From the Past." This warning has gone unheeded by white America because it refuses to see what it has wrought. In spite of distorted history and myth, the truth reveals that freedom, equality, and the protection of laws have always been less for African Americans. It is as if our rights do not fully count in the equation of justice.

In the early period following enactment of the Fugitive Slave Laws, their effect ensured a diminished legal status for free black persons. Their basic constitutional rights were not protected under this pernicious legislation, which allowed for seizure by enterprising slavers and perpetual bondage. A statement by a group of Free People of Colour in 1826 described their plight with sentiments that have remained true to the present: "We reside among you and yet are strangers; natives, and yet not citizens; surrounded by the freest people and most republican institutions in the world, and yet enjoying none of the immunities of freedom. . . . Though we are not slaves, we are not free."[1]

The laws' much heralded concern for property rights under the aegis of the Constitution was likewise withheld. After the slaves were freed, all black Americans were limited in their participation in the economic mainstream. Economic exploitation continued, and they were denied benefit of laws that allowed opportunity to share proportionally in income and wealth. Settler claims blacks filed under the Homestead Act of 1862 were blocked by intimidation and lack of protection by local authorities. Black settlers were faced with the same problem in the Oklahoma Land Rush, where later discovery of oil and gas produced billions of dollars for white property owners.

By the 1920s racial discrimination in public awards was established government policy. Affected were such laws as the Mineral Leasing Act, granting public land for mineral exploration (coal, oil, and gas); the Federal Air Commerce Act, granting commercial air routes (most pilots having been trained in the highly segregated World War I Army Air Corps); and the Federal Radio Act, which awarded radio station franchises to private citizens. Radio broadcast licenses remain almost exclusively in white hands. No licenses for television broadcast stations were issued to black applicants by the Federal Communication Commission until the late 1970s. Presently, all major franchises are white owned.

In the awarding of government contracts, racial discrimination became official policy at the beginning of World War II. With few exceptions, these contract awards remain with white-owned firms. Following World War II, businessmen and many industries were aided or subsidized by government action, including those in banking, real estate, farming, and manufacturing. Highly successful white business executives preached the Horatio Alger "bootstrap" concept, and yet they had actually profited most from the subjugation of black people. While touting the free market principles of Adam Smith, they refused to recognize that the fundamental rules of free competition and merit have had little application to black Americans.

The failure of African Americans to be assimilated, which began with their exclusion from the white Christian church, forged the impression that black people were unworthy, and the idea of "blame the victim" was born. Restrictive access to education, employment, housing, and public accommodations became the American way. For my grandparents, who had been slaves, emancipation seemed like a fulfillment of the dream to live in a free and just society. Knowing their expectations for themselves and their children to come, I must conclude that America's will, even under the cherished rule of law, has been to deny those dreams.

Lincoln's Emancipation Proclamation, largely political and symbolical, of course, freed no slaves. And his recognition of "250 years of unrequited toil" resulted in no compensation. A similar fate came to Congressman Thaddeus Stevens's impassioned appeal for confiscation of large plantations and "forty acres and a mule" for the freedmen; the movement he inspired ended "like the baseless fabric of a vision." Blatant racial discrimination continued in spite of the post–Civil War amendments and subsequent civil rights acts. After *Brown* and the ensuing civil rights movement, there was national focus on the oppressive life conditions of black Americans. With a professed passion for fairness, America seemed finally moved to act against a policy whereby one's destiny was determined by one's color. Civil rights acts of 1957, 1960, 1964, 1965, and 1968 were intended to remove all racial barriers in the crucial areas of voting, employment, housing, and education. But the fact that there was the need for a series of acts, similar to those intended to carry out the post–Civil War amendments, signaled the continuing ambiguity, confusion, and reluctance to ensure racial justice under the law.

In the crucial area of voting rights, ensured by both the Fourteenth and Fifteenth Amendments, terrorist acts actually superseded governmental enforcement. The head of the Ku Klux

A Certain Blindness

Klan in Oglethorpe County, Georgia, candidly admitted that "the Reconstruction acts and fifteenth amendment put the Southern negroes in politics. The Klan organized to put them out, and it succeeded."[2] Before the turn of the century, South Carolina senator Benjamin R. Tillman admitted in the *Congressional Record* that these private acts of violence continued. Through the ensuing years, many, many persons in high public office, sworn to uphold the Constitution, joined others in its subversion.

In Mississippi, for example, the law required a prospective voter to be able to either read and understand the Constitution or offer a reasonable interpretation of it. From Washington, D.C., Mississippi senator Theodore Bilbo instructed election officials by letter: "who[ever] cannot think up questions enough to disqualify undesirables then write Senator Bilbo or any other good lawyer, and there are a hundred good questions which can be furnished."[3] During the period I was in military service, Senator Bilbo actually encouraged violence against those seeking to participate in the democratic process. He stated: "You know and I know what's the best way to keep the nigger from voting. You do it the night before the election. I don't have to tell you any more than that. Redblooded men know what I mean."[4]

The Civil Rights Act of 1957, like the Fourteenth and Fifteenth Amendments, was intended to assure black citizens the right to vote. It failed to achieve its aim, and the acts of 1960 and 1964 both further addressed the problem, yet discriminatory practices in registration and voting continued. The Voting Rights Act of 1965 was passed to accomplish what was intended one hundred years earlier.

The role and conduct of government itself in matters of racial justice remain far below an acceptable standard for our form of government and national purpose. Even the more recent history of *Brown* and other legal acts intended to achieve racial justice have ended in marked retreat. The initial meanings and purposes have been blurred by lax enforcement, misinterpretation, and delay grounded in racial bias.

The Past as Prologue

Discrimination in housing has long been a mechanism for maintaining black people in a status of second-class citizenship. Housing not only serves the basic human need for shelter, but is also the primary element of an individual's environment. Its character and location will greatly determine his growth, learning ability, and the nature of his social and cultural life. Yet the Federal Housing Administration, from its inception in 1934, favored segregated housing. The FHA itself often refused mortgage insurance for integrated housing. Government policy, therefore, buttressed the loan practices and standards of private lending institutions, setting up a highly racist market structure. This resulted in black families accounting for only 2 percent of $120 billion worth of new housing financed through the FHA and VA. Fortunately my family was among that small percentage, which meant I was able to live in a community unrestrained in my early education and social activity by race.

In 1948 the Supreme Court, in *Shelley v. Kraemer,* struck down the enforceability of restrictive covenants in the sale of real estate. In that case, brought by Negro attorneys, the attorney general also filed a brief that noted the disastrous effects of enforced segregation in housing. The attorney general declared:

> The combination of inadequate housing with racial segregation has most unfortunate economic, social and psychological effects.... The incidence of crime and juvenile delinquency is much greater, and the occurrence of death and disease among Negroes is substantially increased. And to the corrosion which such congested and inadequate living conditions work upon any poorly-housed individual's mental health, as a citizen and a human being, there must be added the peculiar disintegrating acid which enforced segregation distills to harm not only the victim alone, but the whole fabric of American life.

But because the Federal Housing Administration encouraged segregation, the practice continued. In its underwriting manual, the FHA warned that "if a neighborhood is to retain stability, it is necessary that properties shall continue to be

A Certain Blindness

occupied by the same social and racial group." It even advised appraisers to lower their valuation of properties in mixed neighborhoods. With the reinforcement of federal policies, private individuals and groups were free to discriminate in forcing segregated housing patterns. The "block buster," by creating fear, would turn over blocks of homes from white to Negro occupancy for a high profit. In addition home builders and mortgage and real estate interests played major roles. Testimony before the commissioners of the District of Columbia by the Mortgage Bankers Association showed "applications from minority groups are not generally considered in areas that are not recognized as being racially mixed." The Chicago Commission on Human Relations confirmed that the same policy is followed by most of the lending institutions in that city.[5]

While the practice that prevailed in Chicago is perhaps representative across the country, its history is also not unique. As late as 1915 Negroes lived in almost every section of Chicago. But in 1919 a devastating race riot occurred in Chicago as well as twenty-five other cities. One of the principal factors was the outburst of tensions around the matter of housing. The Chicago Real Estate Board had adopted a policy in 1917 that stated, "It is desired in the interest of all that each block shall be filled solidly (with Negroes) and that further expansion shall be confined to contiguous blocks."[6]

The great migration of Negroes to large cities of the North gradually resulted in definite lines being drawn, beyond which there was to be no further expansion without violence by whites. Ninety thousand Negroes lived in a square mile area in Chicago, while whites in "crowded" neighboring apartments numbered twenty thousand to the square mile. In Harlem 3,871 non-white persons populated one city block, which an architectural firm "estimated at a comparable rate of concentration, the entire United States could be housed in half of New York City."

Soon after taking office as mayor in 1956, Richard Daley unbelievably claimed that there was no racial segregation in

The Past as Prologue

Chicago. But within the year, Edwin Berry, the newly appointed executive director of the Chicago Urban League, observed that "Chicago was the most residentially segregated city in the U.S." No one would charge that Mayor Daley was naive about conditions in Chicago. A native Chicagoan and master politician, Daley had no false vision of what the city was and what he saw for its future. He was aware that Governor Adlai Stevenson had had to call out the National Guard in 1952 to protect a black family who had moved into the Chicago suburb of Cicero. A similar riot occurred later when a black family moved into the Trumball Park section of Chicago.

In his book *Boss: Richard J. Daley of Chicago*, journalist Mike Royko documented what went on in the Chicago of Mayor Daley:

> Police were brutal in a casual, offhand way. A black might be picked up as a suspect on a Friday night, tossed in a cell, and kept around for two, three, or four days, while the detective decided whether to charge him with something. If it turned out he wasn't the right man, they'd charge him with disorderly conduct so he could be let out on bond, if he had it. If not he might spend a few more days waiting to go to court. Suspects were beaten into confessions, but white courts and a white news media were indifferent.

Daley would publicly state in 1963 that "there are no ghettos in Chicago," yet within the year, when two black college students rented an apartment near his home in the community of Bridgeport, they were met by angry crowds throwing rocks and bottles and shouting hate-filled messages. Pleas seeking improved living conditions in the Negro neighborhoods, including enforcement of housing codes, fell on deaf ears in city hall. Mike Royko reported that, "to Daley, the blacks were merely going through the same onward and upward process of all other ethnic groups, huddling together and waiting for their chance to move up the American ladder. The Irish had done it and so had the other European groups. They put in their time in rickety neighborhoods then moved on. Daley was a firm believer in the bootstrap theory."

Royko recounted a meeting the mayor had at the request of an Irish nun who wanted to tell him about deplorable living conditions in the ghettoes, including

> black children who were dying of lead poisoning because they ate flaking plaster in the crumbling slums. . . .
>
> She thought that because she was a nun he might pay more attention to her than he did to the black activists who were distrusted by City Hall. But she barely began to speak her piece when he cut in.
>
> "Sister, you and I come from the same background . . . grandparents came here with nothing . . . look at Bridgeport . . . houses as old as on the West Side but the people took care of them, worked hard, kept the neighborhood clean, looked after their children . . . let me tell you something about those people . . . should lift themselves up by their bootstraps like our grandparents did . . . take care of their children . . . work hard . . . take care of their houses."
>
> The nun tried to explain some of the differences between being an Irish immigrant, some of whom went on the police force the same week they got to Chicago, and being a black man, some of whom were thrown into a cell the same day they got to Chicago. She tried to get into the matter of trade unions. His own father had been in the sheet-metal-workers' union forty years earlier, but blacks were still kept out. She barely got a word in. Every time she tried, he came back with more of the bootstrap theory. She gave up and left.

Although Daley, like so many white Americans, was caught up in the myth of "bootstraps," Royko pointed out the fact of big city politics across the North: "Besides bootstraps and fear, it was politically wise to keep the black where he was. Concentrated, the black vote was easily controlled. But if open housing became a reality, the black vote bloc would be lost, and the white voter would be outraged by the presence of the black, and the Machine would collapse."[7]

The Past as Prologue

Ironically, achievement of the powerful black vote in Chicago did not produce social or economic changes in the lives of black citizens. Not only were housing and employment conditions deplorable, but health care facilities were also poor. Although the Chicago City Council passed an ordinance in 1956 to prevent racial discrimination in hospitals, the Civil Rights Commission found seven years later "the situation is especially acute in Chicago." Only Cook County Hospital, serving both indigent and those able to pay, provided sufficient facilities to Negroes out of sixty-nine other hospitals. There were three predominantly Negro hospitals having a total of 329 beds, but 73 percent were termed "unsuitable."[8]

A major part of the 1968 Civil Rights Act dealt with racial discrimination in housing. In 1977 the U.S. Commission on Civil Rights found that the federal government continued to encourage racial division in housing. It maintained that agencies such as the Department of Housing and Urban Development (HUD) failed to use their programs to ensure fair housing. Eleven years after passage of the 1968 Civil Rights Act, HUD itself found that 75 percent of all black persons seeking rental property and 62 percent endeavoring to purchase homes experienced racial discrimination. Again in 1983, in testimony before the Civil Rights Commission, the federal government was accused of engaging in an effort to dismantle the legal foundation of fair housing and of reducing its activities to enforce further fair housing. A survey of thirty-four fair housing centers across the country, seventeen years after passage of federal fair housing laws, showed 97 percent found racial bias to be a severe problem. In 1985 a housing expert and consultant to HUD said the federal government "was deeply involved in the creation of the ghetto system, and it has never committed itself to any remedial action." The effects of housing segregation continue to be felt throughout the fabric of American life; it "cuts off access to jobs" and "it cuts off access to education."[9] Under President Reagan's administration, HUD has slashed the size of its fair housing staff and reduced its investigations. In 1984 five cases

A Certain Blindness

were referred to federal prosecutors—a 90 percent drop from the administration's first year.

In 1987 the largest developer of the Georgia mountain resort area was not prosecuted, although the Justice Department stated it was in violation of federal law. Black persons were denied the right to purchase property or were refused real estate financing offered white customers in two counties, resulting in low black population in both counties. The 1980 census showed 22 black residents out of 11,100 in one county and 276 black residents out of 11,652 in the other county.[10]

A recent series of articles (May 1, 1988) in the *Atlanta Constitution* further illustrated that laws already in place are not enforced. An analysis of $6.2 billion lent by major Atlanta lending institutions over a six-year period concluded that white customers received five times as many loans as black customers with the same income. Careful research and consideration of credit-worthiness and income left color as the only explanation for the disparity. The report noted that the courts have found similar practices to be in violation of the Fair Housing Act, the Equal Credit Opportunity Act, the Community Reinvestment Act, and other federal laws. A study by the Federal Reserve Board, reported in the July 17, 1988, *Atlanta Journal-Constitution*, revealed that racial inequities in bank lending existed across the country. The January 22, 1989, *Atlanta Journal-Constitution* revealed that four federal agencies that regulate banking acknowledged laxity in enforcement of the law; this situation "may have grown worse in the 1980's as federal regulators decreased enforcement of fair-lending laws."

Aside from the apparent illegality of the banking practices, the gross injustice deprives black citizens of the basic opportunity to buy and maintain homes. The *Atlanta Constitution* uncovered the story of a fifty-six-year-old retired railway worker who needed a $5,000 loan to fix the roof of his home, which he owned. He applied for a loan to a major bank where he had done business for over ten years. The bank refused to consider him for a loan or even to allow him to complete an application form. A mortgage company eventually loaned him the money, but the homeowner's $5,000 loan saddled him with requirements to pay back a total of $30,722.30. The size of his debt was only discovered two years after he obtained the loan.[11] In another case, the chairman of the Fulton County Commission in Atlanta who was also a college professor had his loan application turned down by two banks, one of which he had banked at for twenty-five years.

The Comprehensive Act of 1964 contained the mechanism for combating discrimination in education as well as employment. Over many years, public school systems freely disobeyed the *Brown* decision because local officials were not disposed to enforce the law. Congress noticeably took no steps to insure enforcement. The 1964 act was intended to prompt compliance through cut-off of federal funds to non-complying state colleges and school districts. In 1965 the U.S. Commission on Civil Rights reported that:

1. There continues to be widespread segregation or exclusion of Negroes in federally assisted programs at the state and local level.
2. The Department of Health, Education, and Welfare, after drafting and issuing the regulations and formal documents required thereunder, has failed to take steps necessary to achieve compliance.
3. The failure to adopt adequate review and compliance procedures has made it impossible for the Department of HEW to know whether discrimination is actually being eliminated.
4. The Department of HEW has not provided state and local directors and administrators of federally assisted programs with the information, support, and leadership necessary to facilitate compliance under Title 6 of the Civil Rights Act of 1964.[12]

President Nixon's Southern strategy approach, as previously noted, led to delay, evasion, and defiance of these measures with impunity. A prime example of noncompliance and ineffectual enforcement occurred in Georgia, where a lawsuit

A Certain Blindness

was filed in 1970 alleging discrimination in its public college system. Finally in 1979 Georgia was ordered to meet certain goals of black student enrollment by 1983. The schools were urged to act more aggressively, but a university planner regarded such warning as "premature" and stated, "remember we don't have to achieve our goals until 1983." In 1983 the court predictably found that Georgia had failed to desegregate its system and threatened it with loss of federal aid. The *Atlanta Constitution* noted at the time: "Perhaps this will be the shock it takes to prod state officials into vigorous, goal-oriented action—though 'shock' is hardly the word for an ultimatum that has been staring them in the face since at least 1970."[13]

Declaring that the court-ordered goals were achievable, the highest black administrator of the university contended that students and professors are available and it is a matter of "how badly we want them." He reported that the school had appointed a white woman to direct its minority advising program and a white man to the position of affirmative action officer.[14]

In August 1987 the NAACP Legal Defense and Education Fund charged that Georgia was in serious violation of the Civil Rights Act and blamed both the state and the U.S. Department of Education with insufficient enforcement. Its report noted lower average financial aid for black students than white, decline in enrollment, and a lower percentage of employment in professional, secretarial, and skilled craft positions than in 1978–79. The Legal Defense Fund report was confirmed by a congressional committee finding that federal officials were refusing to impose sanctions on states that were in violation of civil rights laws.[15]

In December 1987, this case, originally filed in 1970, was dismissed by the same judge who had entered the previous orders. The judge ruled he was without jurisdiction to proceed in light of the government's failure to seek compliance.[16] As a result of official government inaction, school administrators and teachers were effective in violating the law—exactly their

The Past as Prologue

intention—and black Americans moved no closer to educational parity.

Early in 1988 the U.S. Justice Department moved to dismiss seventeen Georgia school districts from the lawsuit. This was part of a plan to dismiss as many as three hundred such suits nationwide. This action, taken by the Justice Department under President Reagan, comes at a time when many American schools are undergoing a process of resegregation. Some school boards, which for a few years have implemented desegregation plans, now seek to dismantle them and thus return to segregated schools. For example, in August 1988 a panel of three federal judges ruled that Louisiana had allowed "unlawful" segregation to continue despite a 1981 decree which ordered the end of such practice. The judges noted that in some instances there was more segregation than before the decree was entered.

Ernest Boyer, president of the Carnegie Foundation for Advancement of Teaching who served us U.S. commissioner of education, maintains that presently there exists a "double level of segregation" in many school systems; "one is the resegregation that is based upon school and district lines" and "another resegregation within the school based upon class and program possibilities." The move to dismiss these lawsuits is hardly in keeping with the goal of providing quality education and full opportunity for all students. Data obtained under the Freedom of Information Act by the *Atlanta Journal-Constitution* showed that between 1980 and 1984 the number of schools that became segregated (more than 90 percent minority) had doubled.

In 1985, over thirty years after *Brown,* criticism of the decision was revived. The book *The Burden of Brown: Thirty Years of School Desegregation* supported the original critics of the Warren Court. It followed the theme of those who maintained that the justices "read their own idea of proper social policy into the Constitution," ignoring established constitutional construction and usurping the power to amend it. Author Raymond Wolters stated that "the attempt to integrate the nation's schools has been a tragic failure" and that the decision has resulted in

A Certain Blindness

damage to the Constitution as well as public education. In condemning the Supreme Court, Wolters asserted, "The justices actually clothed in constitutional attire the social values of impatient men who happened to occupy seats on the Court."[17] Wolters also placed heavy blame for undesirable educational developments on black Americans and black school children. The American Bar Association awarded Wolters its Silver Gavel Award, but the book was panned in *Reviews in American History:*

> In short, this book suffers fatally from a multiplicity of some of the most serious failings that a purported work of scholarship can offer. Wolters's political opinions and other biases are easily visible to the reader and they are offered with such self-righteous vigor that one suspects that the author will eagerly revel in the denunciations that he justifiably anticipates from political opponents. If forthright political differences were the only issue, this volume could be taken at face value as a biased ideological brief, its rhetorical excesses and shortcomings weighed, and its lack of scholarly status would never be at issue. When such biases and political agendas are clothed in the garb of careful scholarship, however, it is necessary to highlight those fatal shortcomings that completely vitiate any affirmative scholarly values that such a book might pretend to possess.[18]

Regardless of personal biases, misperceptions, lingering debate, and renewed criticism, *Brown* became the law of the land. Despite the law, public officials who were not disposed to enforce it and those who freely disobeyed the law prevented my cousin Nancy Todd and her friends from enrolling in a desegregated school even after their constitutional rights had been vindicated by the Supreme Court. Constitutional rights, which had previously been defined by the Court as "personal and present," were actually sacrificed, and instead a vague promise was made to some black students that sometime in the future their constitutional rights would be recognized. Thirty-two years after Nancy and the other plaintiffs' constitutional rights were held abrogated, black parents in Topeka were back in the district court seeking the same relief. Added support for the parents' cause

The Past as Prologue

came from the state of Kansas itself, which pointed out that there had been a lack of progress in public school desegregation.

In 1955, the district court noted that full desegregation had not been accomplished but reluctantly approved a plan which indicated a "good faith effort toward full compliance with the mandate of the Supreme Court." Jurisdiction of the case was, therefore, retained "until such time as the court feels there has been full compliance with the mandate."

In the case, dubbed *Brown III,* the court noted that at no time during the intervening years had the Topeka school system established that it was in compliance with the original Supreme Court mandate. The court, nonetheless, held that the plaintiffs had the burden of proving illegal segregation. Accordingly, the case was dismissed by the district court because disparity in the schools was not shown to be the product of "intentional segregative conduct."

The United States Court of Appeals on June 2, 1989, held, however, that the district court erred in placing the burden on plaintiffs to prove intentional discriminatory conduct rather than according them "the presumption that current disparities are causally related to past intentional conduct." The appeals court then stated, "we are convinced that defendants failed to meet their burden of proving that the effects of this past intentional discrimination have been dissipated."

The court added that thirty years of desegregation law has made clear "the Constitution requires more than ceasing to promote segregation," that "[b]y no stretch of the imagination can the school districts' conduct be characterized as acting "with all deliberate speed" so that "racial discrimination would be eliminated root and branch." Topeka did not "actively strive to dismantle the system" but for the most part the district "exercised a form of benign neglect."

There was a lot of opposition to the Comprehensive Act of 1964, designed to correct discrimination in education and employment, but the act passed anyway. By the early 1970s the government spoke often and loudly about the importance and

A Certain Blindness

requirements of equal opportunity employment and placing black people in top policy-making roles. The administration under President Nixon boasted of the great strides it had taken in this direction. However, of the 530 people on the White House staff payroll, only 1 special assistant was black. On Capitol Hill only 17 senators' offices had any black staffers. There were 12 legislative assistants and 4 black special assistants, with no black committee counsels or administrative assistants. In the House only 27 of the 435 congressmen had any black staff members, including 2 administrative assistants and 4 legislative assistants. There were no black professionals on house committees except those previously chaired by Adam Powell and William Dawson, both black. Ten years later the Congressional Placement Office showed that 80 percent of 150 job requisitions stated racial requirements. Nineteen congressmen and one senator made skin color a condition of employment in their offices. By the mid-1970s the employment picture at the Supreme Court revealed no progress: "The twenty-one laborers employed at the Court—primarily maintenance and heavy cleaning men—were all black, whereas the nineteen skilled craftsmen—carpenters, painters, electricians, plumbers, and stonemasons—were all white. Without exception, the twenty-two charwomen were black, yet all but one of the secretaries to the Justices were white. All of the Justices' messengers were black."[19]

The racial bias of high government officials shows up in the racial make-up of employees in our lawmaking bodies as well as in the character of our laws and national policy. Despite laws on the books, Congress and appropriate federal agencies have not acted forcefully to eliminate discrimination in the area of employment. The racial employment requirements of the Office of Federal Contract Compliance have been openly defied; the office itself actually failed to enforce its own rules. The Civil Rights Commission and the Equal Employment Opportunity Commission remain essentially investigative and advisory; they have none of the power of other administrative bodies to adjudicate matters before them and to issue orders to compel

The Past as Prologue

compliance with their mandates. This official and unofficial policy permeates all aspects of governmental affairs.

During my tenure in Washington with the Federal Power Commission a national focus was directed toward environmental matters, which required licensees of hydro-electric projects and utilities engaged in other construction to file environmental impact statements. Several of us presented a feasible plan to include the employment policies of these companies, a plan that was summarily rejected. Despite the dismal employment records of these companies, the FPC did not want to associate compliance with environmental concerns with any "unpopular" causes such as development of human potential.

The president of the United States, more than all others, creates the racial climate that will prevail across the nation. When Woodrow Wilson ran for president in 1912, he had the support of W. E. B. Du Bois and the NAACP, who believed Wilson to be a cultured gentleman and a scholar who would be inclined toward a measure of fairness for black citizens. Wilson had said he wished to see "justice done to the colored people in every matter"; he also declared, "I want to assure them that should I become president of the U.S., they may count on me for absolute fair dealing, for everything by which I could assist in advancing their race in the U.S."[20] After Wilson's election, he selected half his cabinet and many government officials from the South, sending a clear message to Negroes about their race. As Lawrence Friedman documented in *The White Savage,* "An unidentified associate of the new Chief Executive warned that since the South ran the nation, Negroes should expect to be treated as a servile race."[21] Indicative of policy having been formed by the new administration, "Postmaster Burleson predicted in December of 1912, a Negro might be a doorman or a messenger under the new administration, but nonmenial federal jobs were out of the question."[22] Within a year of his election, Wilson issued an executive order that segregated most Negro employees working in federal departments and agencies. The NAACP objected strenuously: "This mistaken action of the Federal Government will be cited as the warrant for new racial outrages that cry out to high Heaven for redress. Who shall say where discrimination once begun shall cease?"[23]

President Roosevelt's New Deal, with its objectives of relief, recovery, and reform, appeared beneficial for the Negro worker. However, the Public Works Administration (PWA) permitted construction project contractors to deny employment to either skilled or unskilled black workers. The Tennessee Valley Authority (TVA) openly admitted that no Negroes would be allowed to live in the model towns created for construction workers in electrical power projects. Enforcement of the minimum and maximum wage process of the National Recovery Act (NRA) actually forced many black workers out of the labor market because they were unemployed. The effect of the highly regarded Agricultural Adjustment Administration (AAA) was to force many black farm workers into poverty by driving them off the land.

Responding to the 1941 threat of a planned march on Washington of one hundred thousand Negroes, President Roosevelt established the Fair Employment Practices Commission ordering the defense industries to hire black workers. The FEPC only lasted five years before it was terminated, but it issued a final report, which found that "of the several war centers studied by FEPC during reconversion, all but Chicago showed a heavier loss of jobs by Negro than by white workers and a necessity on the part of Negro workers to accept the lowest paid jobs. . . . Whereas during the war many blacks had risen into the skilled, professional, and managerial categories, by 1946 these openings for them had dwindled to a scant few."[24] The few gains made during wartime were reversed to accommodate the favored white worker.

Both presidents Truman and Eisenhower established committees for government contractual employment, but they were hardly effective. The executive branch under John Kennedy aggressively attacked racial discrimination and provided federal power in support of civil rights. He created the President's Com-

The Past as Prologue

mittee on Equal Opportunity (the forerunner of the Equal Employment Opportunity Commission) and the Federal Contract Compliance Program to combat discriminatory practices in firms holding government contracts.

Perhaps no president possessed the courage to move to correct racial injustice as did Lyndon Johnson. He served vigorously as chairman of the Committee on Equal Employment Opportunity while vice-president, and as chief executive Johnson was highly instrumental in gaining passage of the Comprehensive Act of 1964. Johnson also knew the problems associated with unequal application of the laws. In 1965 at Howard University he declared: "Freedom is not enough. . . . You do not take a person who, for years, has been hobbled by chains and liberate him, bring him up to the starting line of a race and then say, 'you are free to compete with all the others,' and still justly believe that you have been completely fair. Thus it is not enough just to open the gates of opportunity."

The administration under President Nixon established the Philadelphia Plan, an affirmative plan for equitable hiring in the construction industry, but it was abandoned for political expediency in the face of union opposition. When Ronald Reagan campaigned for president, he spoke before the National Urban League, promising that nothing in his administration would be done to abridge the cause of civil rights. As the January 14, 1982, *Atlanta Journal-Constitution* noted, Reagan further indicated his dedication to the civil rights cause by stating, "I am for affirmative action." Soon after Reagan took office, however, some civil rights groups leveled accusations that the "dismantling of civil rights enforcement mechanisms" was actually taking place. In September 1982 the chairmen of thirty-three state agencies affiliated with the U.S. Commission on Civil Rights declared Reagan was responsible for a "dangerous deterioration in the Federal enforcement of Civil Rights." The president countered during his re-election campaign in 1984, "I don't believe there's been any violation of either the letter or the spirit of the civil-rights laws, nor would I stand for such a thing." Yet during the Reagan administration the U.S. Justice Department itself systematically moved to undermine civil rights laws. Terrel Bell, secretary of education from 1981 to 1984, stated in an interview published in the October 17, 1987, edition of *U.S.A. Today* that "the Justice Department was determined to weaken civil rights enforcement."

This was verified by a report of the House Judiciary Committee's Sub-Committee on Civil and Constitutional Rights. On January 30, 1984, the committee stated, "This report substantiates the claims of civil rights advocates that individuals and frequently entire communities are being denied the protections very clearly provided by the Revenue Sharing Act." In Georgia, for example, a civil rights case was closed even though investigators and attorneys for the Department of Justice agreed that a significant disparity existed in fire protection provided to black and white communities.

The Reagan administration was apparently of the view that affirmative action to ensure civil rights for all citizens is more of a threat to society than the racial inequality and injustice that has also been so pervasive in our land.

In Birmingham, Alabama, for instance, following many confrontations by demonstrators and Police Chief Eugene "Bull" Connor in 1963, Martin Luther King, Jr., reached an agreement with a citizens committee for desegregation including hiring practices of the city. It was not until 1966, however, that the first black policeman was hired and 1968 that the first black fireman was hired. In 1974 suits were filed against Birmingham charging discrimination in hiring and promotion of employees. These cases were settled in 1981 with the Justice Department signing decrees with the city requiring that "the city hire and promote qualified blacks and women, where possible, in numbers reflecting their percentages in the city's civilian labor force." Three years later the Justice Department went back to court, but this time it had switched sides and now sought reversal of the action taken by the city under the decrees.

A similar situation also occurred with the state of Ala-

The Past as Prologue

educational entities which 'exert a pervasive influence on the entire educational process.' . . . Racially discriminatory educational institutions cannot be viewed as conferring a public benefit within the 'charitable' concept discussed earlier, or within the Congressional intent."[25] What black Americans know Reagan was completely unaware of. Reagan claimed: "I didn't know there were any [segregated schools]. Maybe I should have, but I didn't. I was under the impression that the problem of segregated schools had been settled."[26]

The essence of the *Brown* decision and the foundation of school desegregation law was challenged early in the Reagan administration, however, when the assistant attorney general for civil rights publicly stated that under him "no white student would be involuntarily assigned to a school to promote racial integration." Such an assertion is an obvious first step toward free choice, which will lead to a return of separate and unequal.

In addition, only 2 black judges were appointed to the federal judiciary out of Reagan's first 184 nominees, representing further proof of the retreat phase currently active in race relations.

There can be no doubt of the increased opportunities for black Americans during the past twenty-five years, but these gains have been shrouded in myth and misperception. On January 18, 1983, Purdue University released a report on the rosy image of black progress held by the majority of white Americans. They disagreed with a statement that there were any limits to black economic advancement, and 53 percent of those surveyed believed black opportunity was better than average due to "reverse discrimination." The researchers claimed that no research supported the premise that black opportunity had been or was equal to that of white people and concluded that these unrealistic beliefs were formed early in life and were not likely to change. Most Americans consider their own opportunity as plentiful and see no reason why it should be different for anyone else.

This myopic concept has even permeated our judicial sys-

A Certain Blindness

tem, causing the Supreme Court justices to declare, in 1883, that some sections of the Civil Rights Act of 1875 were unconstitutional (this act forbid discrimination in inns, public conveyances, and places of public amusement). The majority of the Court declared, "When a man has emerged from slavery, and by the aid of beneficent legislation has shaken off the inseparable concomitants of that state, there must be some stage in the progress of his elevation when he takes the rank of a mere citizen, and ceases to be the special favorite of the laws, and when his rights as a citizen, or a man, are to be protected in the ordinary modes by which other men's rights are protected."

However, Justice Harlan, who later dissented in *Plessy,* was singularly clear on the issue:

> It is, I submit, scarcely just to say that the colored race has been the special favorite of the laws. What the nation, through congress, has sought to accomplish in reference to that race is, what had already been done in every state in the Union for the white race, to secure and protect rights belonging to them as freemen and citizens; nothing more. The one underlying purpose of congressional legislation has been to enable the black race to take the rank of mere citizens. The difficulty has been to compel a recognition of their legal right to take that rank, and to secure the enjoyment of privileges belonging, under the law, to them as a component part of the people for whose welfare and happiness government is ordained.[27]

Richard Cain, a black congressman from North Carolina, said it so adroitly when the 1875 Civil Rights Act was debated in the House: "We do not want any discriminations. I do not ask for any legislation for the colored people of this country that is not applied to the white people. All that we ask is equal laws." Other, similar views were expressed during congressional debates on more recent civil rights legislation, but the idea of equality has never been accepted. What America has not learned from the past troubles it still.

Justice Oliver Wendell Holmes asserted that law is more than logic—it is experience; but the history of civil rights law

The Past as Prologue

contradicts Holmes's assertion. There has been very little progress in this matter; *Brown* and ensuing civil rights acts have been little enforced, and thus history repeats itself. These events, symbolic of progress in racial justice, faced the same fate as the post–Civil War amendments and the civil rights legislation of that day.

The purpose of the amendments is beyond doubt. Yet many distinctions continue to be made between the races, and our courts spend more than a reasonable time deciding questions of discrimination and equality. Inscribed in the marble edifice over the entry to the Supreme Court Building in Washington, D.C., are the words "Equal Justice Under Law." It is equal justice that continues to be elusive for black citizens. While there is much debate in and out of the Supreme Court about various judicial philosophies and constitutional interpretations, the matter of equal justice under the law has not appeared to be the underlying concern.

Even in the absence of malicious intent or ill will, equal justice has not been a reality for most black Americans. We are seen as being less worthy and our rights of less value than white citizens, and sadly our legal system reflects this view. In an extensive study over a twenty-year period, the RAND Corporation's Institute for Civil Justice in the mid-1980s found that before juries "blacks lost more often than whites, both as plaintiffs and defendants, and black plaintiffs received smaller (damage) awards." Our criminal justice system functions in a similar manner. In the face of statistical evidence that discrimination exists in the application of the death sentence, the Supreme Court said in *McClesky v. Kemp* (1987): "Apparent disparities in sentencing are an inevitable part of our Criminal-Justice system. . . . Where the discretion that is fundamental to our criminal process is involved, we decline to assure that what is unexplained is invidious." From the evidence presented, racism emerged as the only possible explanation for what is "invidious."

Using the Court's line of reasoning, capital punishment could result from the inherent unfairness of systematic racism,

A Certain Blindness

yet be dismissed as a tolerable disparity. According to available evidence, whether under our civil or criminal process, basic injustice prevails, rights go unprotected, and a system of white supremacy is staying its course.

12

A Higher Law

Racial justice will prevail across our land when Americans adhere to the "higher law" governing human relationships. This concept of higher law has occurred to the ethical thinkers of every civilized people. Aristotle reasoned that "to invest the law then with authority is, it seems, to invest God and reason only; to invest a man is to introduce a beast, as desire is something bestial, and even the best of men in authority are liable to be corrupted by passion. We may conclude then that the law is reason without passion and is therefore preferable to any individual."[1] Other men, such as Cicero, Thomas Aquinas, Locke, and Blackstone, considered the nature of law in human affairs, and "all insisted that laws by which men live can and should be the 'embodiment of essential unchanging justice.' " In fact, Cicero observed that "there is no one thing so like or so equal to one another as in every instance man is to man. . . . Therefore, whatever definition we give to man will be applicable to the entire human race."[2] The use of the law to establish and maintain man's superiority over man was untenable to the Roman philosopher.

England's Magna Carta contained the concept that the law was binding even on a monarch's supreme authority, for, as Henry Bracton, a medieval jurist, pointed out, "the King himself ought not be subject to man, but subject to God and the law, for the law makes the King."

The premise of a higher law was adopted in the Mayflower Compact, the first "civil body politick" in the New World. The colonists stated their cause was undertaken for the glory of God and promised to frame and obey "just and equal laws."

With fully 75 percent of the people who declared their independence in 1776 of Puritan background, there was strong recognition that governments, constitutions, and laws were instituted to restrain man's sin and, therefore, must be truly of God. Accordingly in 1775 the committee that drafted the Declaration of the Causes and Necessities of Taking Up Arms expressed great concern with man's equality and the government's purpose in this regard, stating an abhorrence of men "who exercise their reason to believe that the Divine author of our existence intended a part of the human race to hold an absolute power in, and an unbounded power over others . . . as the objects of a legal domination never rightfully resistible, however severe and oppressive." They believed that "the great Creator['s] principles of humanity, and the dictates of common sense, must convince all those who reflect upon the subject, that government was instituted to promote the welfare of mankind, and ought to be administered for the attainment of that end." Aristotle's sentiments regarding the rule of the law were later condensed into phrases such as "a government of laws and not of men," which found its way into the Declaration of Independence. These early Americans recognized that "all men are created equal, that they are endowed by their Creator with certain inalienable Rights" as provided under "the Laws of Nature and of Nature's God."

Revolutionary Americans became vividly aware of liberty

A Higher Law

and the fundamental equality of all men. They viewed slavery as a gross inconsistence, since the right to liberty was God's gift to all mankind. The Supreme Court of Massachusetts established legal precedence in this matter when called upon to determine the status of slavery in the commonwealth. The court held in 1783 that the institution of slavery could not survive under a constitution that proclaimed equality and promised liberty. But when the Constitution of the United States was finalized, a government was formed with full knowledge that it permitted slavery. Supposedly grounded in a deeply religious and moral order, this system was in total contradiction of existing legal and religious institutions. Higher law demands the "embodiment of essential and unchanging justice," for, as the Bible says, "we know the law is good, if a man use it lawfully." Our constitutional experience demonstrates the truth of Aristotle's assertion that the rule of law is preferable to the rule of individuals; most certainly "even the best of men in authority" have proved to be "corrupted by passion."

George Washington failed to lend his leadership on the issue of slavery. After the Revolutionary War, he expressed a desire to see slavery abolished and vowed to never buy another slave, but in 1786 he took a slave in payment for a debt. The next year Washington asked one Henry Lee to buy a bricklayer slave for him, stipulating that the purchase should disrupt no family. In his farewell address Washington spoke of the nation's need for the "indispensable supports" of religion and morality; this moral and virtuous man, father of our country, fathered 13 children into the throes of slavery. At his death, he owned 277 slaves.

Slaveholder Thomas Jefferson made many antislavery pronouncements and expressed strong convictions that all human beings possessed God-given rights that did not permit enslavement one by another. Deeply troubled about slavery, Jefferson asked: "Can the liberties of a nation be thought secure when we have removed their only firm basis, a conviction in the minds of the people that those liberties are the gift of God? That they are

A Certain Blindness

not to be violated but with his wrath."[3] Jefferson declared: "Indeed I tremble for my country when I reflect that God is just: that his justice cannot sleep forever.... The Almighty has no attribute which can take side with us in such a contest."[4] Though he condemned King George III for waging a "cruel war against human nature itself," he and other colonists remained equally guilty. He even acknowledged that "nothing is more certainly written in the book of fate than that these people are to be free," but he was not moved to change the status of his own slaves.

Patrick Henry, fiery patriot and slaveholder, exclaimed: "Would any one believe that I am master of Slaves of my own purchase! I am drawn along by ye general Inconvenience of living without them; I will not, I cannot justify it."[5] He lamely predicted that the "time will come when an opportunity will be offered to abolish this lamentable evil."

The evil of this gross immorality triumphed over the integrity of the rule of law and fundamental religious values. From our nation's beginning, the Christian church, wielding enormous influence, has been the one institution one would have expected to set the moral standards for society; instead it has reflected the moral state of its adherents. In 1838 John Quincy Adams noted: "There is in the clergy of all the Christian denominations a time-serving, cringing, subservient morality, as wide from the spirit of the gospel as it is from the intrepid assertion and vindication of truth. The counterfeit character of a very large portion of the Christian ministry in this country is disclosed in the dissensus growing up in all the protestant Churches in the South on slavery."[6]

The role of the Christian ministry to affirm local mores is seen for example in the Baptist denomination. In 1785 the Baptist General Committee of Virginia acknowledged that hereditary slavery "was contrary to the word of God and resolved to use every legal measure to extirpate this horrid evil from the land"; eventually, however, this group consented "to relegate the slavery question to the civil authorities."[7] When the South-

A Higher Law

ern Baptist Convention was formed in 1844 it actually announced that the denomination was free "to promote slavery." The convention president declared the group was not organized to promote "any form of human policy, or civil rights, but God's glory. . . . We will not interfere with what is Caesar's."[8] These Christians amazingly reasoned that to oppose slavery would be to interfere in civil affairs and that promoting slavery would be no such interference.

The issue of slavery became the cause of a division in the Baptist church (and splits occurred in other major denominations as well, such as the Methodist and Presbyterian). After formation of the Southern Baptist Convention the *Charleston Mercury* succinctly reported, "how little is to be expected from any other Union, if the union of Christians fails."

In his book *Confederate Moral and Church Propaganda* James W. Silver bluntly stated that Southern clergymen, as no other group, "were responsible for a state of mind which made secession possible, and as no other group they sustained the people in their long, costly, and futile War for Southern Independence." *Broken Churches, Broken Nation* author C. C. Goen contended that "Silver's book marshals so much evidence for the Southern Churches' uncompromising support of the Lost Cause that one wonders whether secession and the resort to arms could have existed at all without them."[9]

From that early period in our history when deep moral contradictions were being established, a strange phenomenon occurred—African slaves adopted the religion of their masters. While both prayed to the same God, one believed he was more worthy and deserving; and the other, though lowly and despised, believed he was equal before the God of all mankind. Slaves adopted monotheistic Christianity because as Africans they had always believed in one supreme God as the giver and sustainer of life. C. Eric Lincoln, professor of religion and culture at Duke University, noted that from the third through the fifth centuries, when the Christian church established its basic theological formulations, nine of the eighteen or twenty most

A Certain Blindness

prominent leaders were African, notably Cyprian and Augustine, "who were the great intellectuals who worked out the basic political and theological doctrines of the Western Church. How ironic it is that so much light should come from an allegedly 'dark continent,' and that it would eventuate in a civilization called the Christian West. Or that in time the Christian West, goaded by an insatiable economic self-interest, would turn again to Africa, not to bless her, but to suck her blood."[10]

The cleft that developed in the American Christian church was not only over the matter of slavery but was more basically rooted in color. Lincoln reported that "long before Crispus Attucks ran away from slavery to become the first American to die for his country's independence, the Corporation of Harvard College was bitterly protesting the seating of a Negro even in the gallery of the First Parish Church in Cambridge."[11] And in the South, the Presbyterian Synod of South Carolina and Georgia contended at a meeting in 1834 that "The gospel, as things are now, can never be preached to the two classes successfully in conjunction. The galleries or the back seats on the lower floors of white churches are generally appropriated to the Negroes, when it can be done without inconvenience to the whites. When it cannot be done conveniently, the Negroes must catch the gospel as it escapes through the doors and windows."[12]

In 1787, while the Constitution was being forged in Philadelphia, a small group of black Christians in that city were pulled from their knees while praying in the segregated gallery of St. George's Methodist Episcopal Church. While the divine expressions of the Declaration of Independence were dropped out of the Constitution, what came to be known as the black church was unceremoniously created. The very essence of the black church has been the freedom with which man was endowed by his Creator, considered necessary to fulfill the Christian's responsibility to achieve the highest potential of his humanity. The black church found symbolic gestures of man's superiority over man to be offensive to man and God alike, and

A Higher Law

at no time has this church denied its fellowship to a person because of his color.

A white slave owner built the first church for black worship in America near Savannah about 1773. Although building the church was actually against the law, the slave owner was converted to Christianity by the slave preacher who was its pastor. Before preaching by Negroes was outlawed during proslavery hysteria, many black preachers, slave and free, preached to white, black, and Indian. There were many active Negro churchmen. Henry Evans of North Carolina founded the First Methodist Church in Fayetteville, which became predominately white. Joseph Willis founded a mixed Baptist church in Mound Bayou, Mississippi, in 1805, thereby preaching the first Protestant sermon west of the Mississippi. John Chavis, educated at Princeton and at William and Mary, preached to white Presbyterians in Virginia and North Carolina; he also headed a prestigious academy for white youth and maintained a separate school for black youngsters at night.

The black church offered the only place where a black Christian could worship without experiencing overt discrimination. With its theme of freedom and dignity, however, the church was seen as dangerous to established white order; consequently religious observance became either forbidden or severely restricted by law until the Civil War. After the war divisions among the various white denominations pretty much reflected regional politics. Over the succeeding years, the subtlety of racial superiority survived and the white-black separation prevailed throughout the church. The black church exerted immeasurable influence as a symbol of hope and determination for an oppressed people. In my family, as has been true in so many other black families, religious faith enabled believers to endure even in the face of hopelessness and despair. From the early period in our nation's history when my father's grandmother, Pearlalee, and my mother's grandfather, Lewis, were held in bondage, the higher law prescribed in the Holy Scriptures has been devoutly fol-

A Certain Blindness

lowed. That my great-grandfather Lewis, my uncle Bookter, and my brother Lind were ordained ministers gave religion an added salience.

Besides being the center of spiritual and social development, the black church was the acknowledged source of organized leadership for the community, "as all roads converged at the Negro church," as Taylor Branch observed in his book *Parting the Waters;* the church "served not only as a place of worship but also as a bulletin board to a people who owned no organs of communication, a credit union to those without banks, and even a kind of people's court."[13] The churches operated in the best tradition of grass roots politics. For example, in the mid-1950s the black church in Montgomery, Alabama, had the influence and organization to direct the year-long bus boycott that resulted in a Supreme Court decision outlawing segregated seating.

The majority of white churches have failed to provide moral leadership in serving the reality of human beings in a nation under God, dedicated to liberty and justice for all. Immutable values so critical to human dignity have been ignored or compromised, and the church has become a replica of the society it has a mission to transform. These churches, including those of a more fundamental persuasion, are blind to the Scripture's message of justice for the powerless and oppressed. Although black and white Americans share many views, these don't include a common perception of Christian moral responsibility. An example of this is found in Jerry Falwell's 1987 book, *Strength for the Journey,* in which he revealed that while growing up he rarely thought of the "inhumanity or injustice" encountered by black people. He freely admitted that, even after graduation from Bible college and as pastor of his own church, he did not see "the irony that the white Christian church had been a keystone" in this "destructive and dehumanizing system." Falwell candidly stated that "if the church had done its job from the beginning of this nation's history, there would have been no need for the civil rights movement."[14]

Falwell denied he was a racist or a segregationist and explained how his attitude toward the struggle for equal rights was formed:

> I was just thirty-one years of age. I was born and raised in the deep South. I had grown up in a segregated society. I had been a Christian for less than a dozen years, and though my study of the Scriptures had left me with a growing restlessness with the traditional Southern position, I felt bullied and unjustly attacked by the army of white Northerners marching into the South, demanding that we follow their dictates in the running of our community and in the ordering of our lives. I was angry that suddenly the Supreme Court, the Congress, and the President had assumed rights once granted to the states, and I protested loudly the arrogant, disruptive, and often violent wave of demonstrators arriving daily in the South. I was determined to maintain the right to decide for ourselves how we would live together, black and white.[15]

As a Christian church leader, Falwell strenuously resisted legal efforts to secure racial justice, preaching, for instance, in 1958 that "if Chief Justice Warren and his associates had known God's word and had desired to do the Lord's will, I am quite confident that the 1954 decision [*Brown*] . . . would never have been made."[16] Falwell claimed: "The true Negro does not want integration. . . . Who then is propagating this terrible thing? First of all, we see the hand of Moscow in the background."[17] The fundamentalist minister persisted in issuing such absurd statements and from his pulpit attacked those ministers who participated in civil rights marches and criticized pending civil rights legislation, calling it "a terrible violation of human and private rights. It should be considered civil wrongs rather than civil rights."[18]

Falwell founded the organization Moral Majority in order to "speak out courageously on the great moral issues of the day." Never once in his 1980 book *Listen America!* did he list among "these great moral issues" the oldest and most persistently underlying moral issue America has faced—racial injustice. Racially determined values do deeply affect religious doc-

A Certain Blindness

trine, as the Mormon church, the Church of Jesus Christ of Latter-day Saints, strikingly reveals. The Mormon church was founded by Joseph Smith in Palmyra, New York, in the late 1820s. Among the books the church accepts as doctrine is the Book of Mormon, translated by Smith from certain gold plates revealed to him by an angel named Moroni in 1827.[19] Believed to be divinely inspired, the book states in Nephi 27:33 that "[The Lord] . . . inviteth them all to come unto him and partake of his goodness; and he denieth none that come unto him, black and white, bond and free, male and female; and he remembereth the heathen; and all are alike unto God, both Jew and Gentile." (When Smith declared himself a candidate for U.S. president in 1844 he proposed to free slaves by purchase with money obtained by selling public lands.)

The Negro Elijah Abel became an elder in the Mormon priesthood and in 1836 even succeeded in becoming a "seventy." Abel, one of the few black Mormons to join the cross-country trek to Utah, served his church another fifty years.[20]

When Smith compiled the Pearl of Great Price, a book of revelations of Moses and Abraham not found in the Bible, Smith enunciated racial views in sharp contrast to those expressed in the Book of Mormon. This book cast black people in an inferior light similar to the views strongly advocated in the South at the time. O. Kendall White, Jr., explained this transformation in the *Journal of Religious Thought*:

> When the Mormons settled in Missouri during the 1830's the established residents quickly accused them of "tampering" with their slaves and identified them as abolitionists who were "endeavoring to sow dissensions and raise seditions amongst them." Perhaps even more importantly, the Mormons were accused of inviting free blacks to become Mormons and to migrate to Missouri to help build the kingdom of God in preparation for Jesus' second coming. This early pro-black posture generated considerable hostility among the established settlers who initiated a number of persecutions that eventually led to expulsion of the Mormon community. Attempting to reduce these pressures from

antagonistic forces, the Mormons adopted a proslavery posture formulated in terms of the "curse of Canaan" motif of Southern Protestantism.[21]

Some scholars theorize that Smith's about-face was induced by external social forces. White explained that the proslavery attitude became the theological basis for denying the priesthood and other prerogatives to black members. (On August 17, 1949, an official statement of the Mormon church proclaimed that the denial of priesthood to black members was a "direct commandment from the Lord . . . founded on the doctrine of the church from the days of its organization.")[22]

The Utah state legislature, dominated by Mormons, also enacted racially discriminatory legislation, and the public sector followed suit. My brother Lind had difficulty finding public accommodations when the army stationed him in the area, and Nobel Peace Prize winner Ralph Bunche and concert contralto Marian Anderson experienced the same problems with Utah hotels. An article in the 1953 *Utah Law Review* noted that in Utah black people were barred from practically all night clubs, bowling alleys, and most of the better restaurants. That same year a field director of the National Urban League reported that in large areas of the state "discrimination is almost as severe as in the South." In 1963 an NAACP official in Salt Lake City declared that Utah had "potentially the worst race problem in the United States." The organization adopted a resolution accusing the Mormon church of maintaining a "rigid and continuous segregation stand" and condemned it for its indifference to widespread discriminatory practices in education, housing, employment, and other areas of life.

Defending racist practices, a Mormon-owned newspaper warned in 1921 that demands for full and immediate equality will "only intensify race antagonisms"; segregation was held to be a divinely sanctioned institution. Ezra Taft Benson, a Mormon apostle who served as secretary of agriculture under President Eisenhower, claimed in 1963 that "the civil rights movement in the South had been fomented almost entirely by the Communists"; a year later he warned that the "Communists were using the civil rights movement to promote revolution and eventual takeover of this country."[23]

A 1972 Louis Harris poll found that 70 percent of the Mormons in Utah opposed black priesthood in the church; a significant number believed the controversy "was part of a 'black conspiracy' to destroy the church." It was not until June 9, 1978, that the Mormon church reversed its prohibition against black priesthood, announcing that "every faithful, worthy man in the church may receive the holy priesthood . . . including the blessings of the temple,"[24] thus returning to the original teaching of the Book of Mormon. This was vital to black Mormons, because power and status in the church are only achieved through the priesthood. Unlike a parish priest in the Catholic church or a pastor in the Protestant church, the Mormon priest is not a pastor in the traditional sense. Beginning at age twelve every male, excepting black males, are ordained deacons, the first of six orders in the priesthood. No matter how moral or true to his faith a black Mormon was, he could not enter the temple or share meaningfully in church affairs without ordination. The prohibition had affected black women as well, since great emphasis is placed on the integrity of the family, and it is only through marriage to priests that women can receive the full benefits of the church.

Though I have discussed the Mormon church, I do not intend to criticize it—or indeed any specific group—but rather demonstrate that many Christian churches have absorbed the racially oppressive measures that prevail in our culture. These churches, in fact, came full circle, because it was by denying black men and women the freedom to worship with white Christians that they first established the policy of exclusion later followed by other institutions in society.

Just as Christianity has been diminished by racism, so the basic concept of the rule of law has likewise yielded to this distortion. Dating back to the constitutional convention, when the higher law precepts of the Declaration were abandoned, considerations of skin color have predominated among those who make, interpret, and enforce our laws. It is obvious that the founding fathers were pressed to subjugate Negroes legally, for some of the earliest congressional legislation was directed toward protecting the property rights of the slave owner rather than the human rights of the slave. It has been America's failure to shed this slaveholding image that continues to plague white-black relations. Yet America's constitutional heritage presents a different picture. In his notable essay "The 'Higher Law' Background of American Constitutional Law," Edward S. Corwin maintained that the Constitution *is* an "expression of the Higher Law," that it is in fact a "rendering of what Blackstone saluted [as] the eternal, immutable laws of good and evil to which the creator himself in all his dispensations conforms." This foremost historian of constitutional law declared, "Thus the legality of the Constitution, its supremacy, and its claim to be worshipped, alike find common standing ground on the belief in a law superior to the will of human governors."[25]

The constitutional amendments, federal laws, and Supreme Court decisions meant to benefit Negro Americans have not been interpreted and enforced with unbiased objectivity, and no offender has been so severely dealt with as violators of the Fugitive Slave Law. Injustice continues due to a lack of determined legal and moral effort for rectification. The observation of the late Pulitzer Prize-winning journalist Harry S. Ashmore, speaking on a related matter, is appropriate here: "It is true that the ultimate solution will not be found in laws, but in the dark places of men's minds and hearts. But it is also true that laws are the manifest of the national purpose, and when government is unwilling, or unable, to provide them, there is no standard to which the wise and just may repair."

In this regard the white church could play a crucial role, if it would take up the challenge. I recall an incident that took place in the early 1980s in Tuscaloosa, Alabama, where my great-grandfather had been a preacher one hundred years earlier. A

A Certain Blindness

black professor of religious studies at the University of Alabama and the black students in his class were barred from attending a nearby church. The class sought to observe services at different local churches but were rebuffed at the sixteen-hundred-member church as it "did not have integration." The group was told there was a "nigger" church around the corner. The professor was pained because he did not want his students to think the response was the "essence" of Christianity. To be sure, many churches have changed over the years and welcome all to worship without stipulation as to skin color, but in those churches where change has taken place, I have yet to hear a rational explanation for the changed Christian position for exclusion or inclusion one way or the other. Most certainly these churches have not been in the vanguard of groups actively pressing for a more just society. The American sense of justice has not been seriously influenced by the Christian church, which is neither willing nor able to appropriately address the ongoing moral issue of racial injustice. There is the need for a clear vision of religion and law and the relationship of the two in order to integrate belief and action, principle and practice, a first step toward establishing justice.

In recent times many are heard speaking critically of America's loss of traditional moral values due to one circumstance or another, but no one attributes the loss to our nation's denial of man's human worth and dignity and the ensuing consequences. This obscured vision has long afflicted our society. In 1831, when America was lavish in its praise of Polish rebels in their fight against czarist oppression, Nat Turner was condemned for leading a slave uprising a few weeks earlier. Nor was the highly praised Hungarian revolt against the Communist regime in the 1950s viewed in the same light as the Negro revolt taking place in the American South at that time; in fact, many Americans who participated in the highest tradition of Christian and democratic principles were vilified as Communists.

When he accepted the Republican presidential nomination in 1964, Barry Goldwater stated: "I would remind you that extremism in the defense of liberty is no vice! And let me remind you also that moderation in the pursuit of justice is no virtue!" To be sure, the millions who were stirred by such pronouncements were not inclined to equate them with the struggle for racial justice, which had been waged in their midst for so long.

On the fortieth anniversary of World War II, President Reagan went to Germany and placed a wreath at a cemetery where German soldiers were buried. The cemetery had been the German staging area for the bloody Battle of the Bulge and contained the graves of S.S. troops, Hitler's elite and most dreaded guard. The president's action sparked protest from veterans' organizations and Jewish groups, but Reagan explained, "While we remember the past with deep sorrow, we must look to the future with a firm resolve that it will never happen again."[26]

Looking back, I recalled President Roosevelt's wartime objectives of preserving our "democratic way of life" and "four essential human freedoms" (freedom of speech, freedom of worship, freedom from want, and freedom from fear). I could see how elusive these objectives have been for most black citizens. It can be said that America accomplished its objectives in wartime, but it also has gone full circle in its relationship with Germany since the war—from wartime enemy to providing for Germany's recovery through the Marshall Plan, and now paying tribute to German war dead. America has done much to serve a former enemy, yet so little to serve its own. Black Americans have fought in all of America's wars, but while peace and reconciliation have been established with all our enemies of past wars, full participation in the democratic way of life and equal justice have been withheld from America's loyal black defenders.

By the time World War II came to an end in Europe, the whole world had learned of the Holocaust. Six million European Jews were systematically murdered as part of Hitler's plan for Aryan supremacy. Plans have been made to create Holocaust memorials in Washington and elsewhere. Unquestionably the slaughter of millions of defenseless human beings, and the fail-

A Certain Blindness

ure of the rest of the world to do as much as it might to stop such horror, must not be forgotten. But since slavery ended over 120 years ago, most Americans have forgotten this horror and refuse to see that it plagues our nation still; both perpetrators and victims are cast in similar roles.

Like American slavery, the Jewish Holocaust was predicated solely on race. Hitler himself admitted: "I know perfectly well that in the scientific sense there is no such thing as race. . . . I as a politician need a conception which enables the order which has hitherto existed on historic bases to be abolished and an entirely new and anti-historic order enforced and given an intellectual basis. . . . And for this purpose the conception of race serves me well."[27] And Rudolph Hess once acknowledged that "we are very much like the Ku Klux Klan." W. E. B. Du Bois claimed that America's treatment of its black citizens taught the Nazis how to treat the Jews: "It gives rein and legal recognition to race hate, which the Nazis copied in their campaign against the Jews, *establishing it on American lines* of caste conditions, disfranchisement, mob murder, ridicule and public disparagement."[28] Writer Earl Conrad concluded from German publications that "our system of racial legality became the model for Adolf Hitler's regime."[29]

There has been no official act of the American government to memorialize slavery, nor has proper recognition been given to those who helped end it. Rather our society honors those who supported the system of man's inhumanity to man. Included are many leaders who renounced their citizenship and betrayed their oaths of office. They are compassionately remembered by memorials and statues, because race determines recognition in our nation, and not deed. What John Brown said to the court before he was sentenced to be hung remains pertinent: "Had I so interfered in behalf of the rich, the powerful, the intelligent, the so-called great, or in behalf of their children, or any of that class, and suffered and sacrificed what I have in this interference, it would have been all right, and every man in this

A Higher Law

court would have deemed it an act worthy of reward rather than punishment."

Here in the South, political leaders and statesmen are traditionally highly revered. But in 1956 virtually all Southern members of the House and Senate formed massive resistance against desegregation in their Southern Manifesto. Their example, as C. Vann Woodward observed, gave ordinary people "permission to hate." Under oath to support the Constitution and represent all the people, these powerful and influential men completely failed to lead in the face of the greatest challenge in their careers.

In 1979 movie actor John Wayne became one of the few Americans ever awarded a congressional gold medal for service to the nation. Apparently for the roles he had depicted Wayne was "loved and respected around the world as the symbol of America at its best." Yet Wayne had explicitly stated his belief in "white supremacy."

Relegated to a "place" in our society, black people have suffered enormous burdens, which have largely gone unnoticed, and have had to overcome the ever present debilitation of being made to feel inferior. Accordingly, any chronicle of a black person's success should include not only his worthy accomplishments but also the opposition he encountered and the courage he summoned to continue his struggle to achieve. I have noticed that the more effort to achieve a black American displays, the more effort the system exerts to show him he is unworthy. An open display of ambition and drive is sure to meet with blatant hostility. In many instances we are required to exhibit qualities superior to those shown to us. When Jackie Robinson was signed to play major league baseball, he was to exercise total self control and discipline. If he experienced abuse and insults he was not to respond in any manner.

Even children entering integrated schools for the first time have been required to exhibit perfect, civilized behavior—in sharp contrast to the taunting, cursing white adults. Inside the

A Certain Blindness

school these students had to endure insults, shoving, and being spat upon day after day, without complaint or response—while still being expected to get good grades. The imbalance is reflected early in life as the mortality rates for black male babies is nearly twice that for white males. The disproportion continues throughout a black man's lifetime, which lags behind white male life expectancy by 6.6 years (64.9 years compared to white male life expectancy of 71.5 years). In 1988 the Census Bureau reported that among all men only the median income of black men decreased during the 1986–87 period. Even with a college education he continues to earn less than a white high school graduate.

Steven Whitman of Northwestern University points out that "Dostoevsky once wrote that if you want to know about a society you should look into its prisons. When we look into prisons in the United States we see the reflection of a profoundly unjust society." In the May 27, 1987, *Washington Post*, Whitman declared that a look at our prison system reveals that, "most important, we are confronted with the undeniable reality that this society, built on a foundation of slavery and racism, is staying its course. The system of white supremacy has not been diminished but is in fact intensifying. . . . The only real question is whether we will pursue a humane society or a racist one." I am mindful of the thoughts of Victor Hugo who said: "Whenever there is darkness crimes will occur. But the guilty one is not merely he who commits the crimes but he who provides the darkness."

The reality of perpetual unfair treatment is not apparent to most Americans, but psychiatrists Grier and Cobb describe this underlying fact in their book *Black Rage:*

> For black and white alike, the air of this nation is perfused with the idea of white supremacy and everyone grows to manhood under this influence. Americans find that it is a basic part of their nationhood to despise blacks. No man who breathes this air can avoid it and black men are no exception. They are taught to hate themselves, and if at some point they are the object of this ha-

A Higher Law

tred, they are faced with an additional task, nothing less, for the imperative remains—Negroes are to be despised.

W. E. B. Du Bois observed that "throughout history the powers of single black men flash like falling stars, and die sometimes before the world has rightly gauged their brightness," a thought that brings my brother Arthur to mind. At an early age Art perceived the nature of the system. He could not accept the illusion that he was part of something that evidence around him showed did not exist. He understood that the society he was taught he shared in meant to permanently lock him out. As I came to adulthood I too was forced to unlearn much of what I had learned in textbooks in order to learn the truth about how success and heroes are actually determined. American history lent credence to Voltaire's assertion that history is a myth rewritten by each generation. Historians have largely reflected the prevailing myths. Historical accounts have been devoid of a true account of Africans prior to their arrival on the shores of the New World. Although I learned that Africa had been the seat of civilization, I was not taught that Africans, among other things, had discovered mathematics, invented writing, and developed sciences and medicine. Conventional history presented Africans as innately inferior and primitive and never mentioned developed African civilizations. School textbooks never acknowledged the scholarship that showed African schools were teaching astronomy at a time when western Europeans were living in caves and wearing animal skins.

As I learned more about my family background and the total spectrum of the black experience in America, I also came to realize how closely my experiences and views have paralleled the description Du Bois wrote of the Negro living in America—

> in this American world,—a world which yields him no true self-consciousness, but only lets him see himself through the revelation of the other world. It is a peculiar sensation, this double-consciousness, this sense of always looking at one's self through the eyes of others, of measuring one's soul by the tape of a world

A Certain Blindness

that looks on in amused contempt and pity. One ever feels his twoness,—an American, a Negro; two souls, two thoughts, two unreconciled strivings; two warring ideals in one dark body, whose dogged strength alone keeps it from being torn asunder.

"The history of the American Negro is the history of this strife,—this longing to attain self-conscious manhood, to merge his double self into a better and truer self," Du Bois declared; "he simply wishes to make it possible for a man to be both a Negro and an American, without being cursed and spit upon by his fellows, without having the doors of Opportunity closed roughly in his face."[30]

The lives of all black Americans have been affected by institutionalized racism, and this historical pattern of oppression is directly responsible for creating a separate group of virtual outcasts in America.

On the occasion of the one hundredth birthday of the Statue of Liberty we have been reminded that the statue has provided a vision of hope and the door to success for millions of foreign immigrants. This symbol is in stark contrast to those among us who are products of generation upon generation of the native born who have been exploited and deprived. These victims, in our highly technical age, are by present standards deemed expendable.

From the beginning, our nation's founders as well as later immigrants obtained economic, religious, and political freedoms. But as we have seen, African Americans were excluded from Adam Smith's free market system of economics. Smith said in his *Wealth of Nations* that there is "the uniform, constant, and uninterrupted effort of every man to better his condition," but black Americans have been denied this right. As a result, a large segment of native-born Americans now face economic crises.

This problem is particularly acute at a time when resettlement of indigents from foreign lands is national policy. The continuing nature of the discrimination faced by African Americans is confirmed by an alarming report by the University of

Chicago. This first national study to compare residential segregation patterns for African Americans, Hispanics, and Asians on the basis of education, income, and occupation was released February 8, 1989. It found that Hispanics and Asians were more easily integrated into residential neighborhoods regardless of education, income, or occupation.

The principal author of the study pointed out that "because of the persistence of strong barriers to residential integration, middle-class blacks are forced to live in neighborhoods of much poorer quality than whites with similar class backgrounds." This affords them less effective educational systems, poorer socioeconomic environments, and higher mortality risks. The author asserted, "The American dream of 'working one's way up' is not a viable option for blacks in the United States, at least in terms of residence." "The accumulated evidence . . . of segregation sugges[s] that progressive residential integration is possible, even likely, for all ethnic and racial groups except blacks. It is being black, not being non-white or non-European, that makes the difference."

If this situation exists regarding residential housing, so central to family, community, and essential living, how can it be otherwise in other areas of American society? Clearly some form of redress must be instituted to direct the "invisible hand" of Adam Smith's marketplace toward economic justice "to advance the interest of society."

The question remains whether America will prove capable of solving this dilemma it has created. Nothing less than a complete resurrection of the Constitution's Preamble to "establish justice" will solve America's problem. This principle must now be used to redress the inequities and produce a system that gives no preference according to color. Justice must become the overriding concern, justice that, in the words of Harvard professor John Rawls, is the first virtue of social institutions and human activities, for justice "does not allow that the sacrifices imposed on a few are outweighed by the larger sum of advantages enjoyed by many."[31]

A Certain Blindness

If Americans truly believe themselves to be a "Nation under God," they will respect and apply the Divine Law expressed by Jesus: "Therefore all things whatsoever ye would that men should do to you, do ye even so to them: for this is the law and the prophets."

Epilogue

As black Americans we share our humanity and aspirations with all this nation's peoples, but history and experience contradict that truth, and we continue to suffer from that contradiction. The principles found in the Declaration of Independence and in the Constitution have been neither completely accepted nor appropriately resolved. Instead further contradictions and inconsistencies have been introduced throughout our history, rendering our government practically incapable of perceiving the tragic results. Each time it appeared that racial barriers were removed by legislation or judicial rulings and that justice would prevail, some new obstacle would shatter our hopes. But our ancestors continued to imagine a better world and passed that vision on to succeeding generations.

Reconstruction after the Civil War seemed to offer my grandfather C. R. Wilson opportunities to realize his potential in the Deep South, but the prejudice and fear of the racial majority dashed those opportunities "like the baseless fabric of a vision."

Epilogue

Helping to tame the lawless frontier as a marshal gave my great-uncle Bass Reeves prominence in his own time, but when Oklahoma entered the Union it thanklessly declared itself "for whites only."

My father, Luck Brady, migrated north, hoping to realize his full potential, but found only small opportunity open to him. For my own part, I learned that the promise of advancement even in our nation's military was a cruel hoax. My cousin Nancy Todd discovered that having the Supreme Court vindicate her constitutional rights was no guarantee she was free to exercise those rights.

What we were taught about liberty, equality, and justice came from the Declaration of Independence and the Constitution, which white Americans wrote. We believe these documents mean what they say. What my family learned of this nation's Christian principles was learned from white Americans. We have accepted Christianity, but we have learned that we must be more forgiving than others. We have repeatedly demonstrated our commitment to this nation and to the rule of law—as when Uncle Bass was devoted to impartial enforcement of the law, when Aunt Cindy strove to change an unjust law, and when I strive to fairly interpret the law—yet as citizens we receive a lesser portion of liberty and justice.

As my ancestors sought a high purpose for their lives and never gave up their faith in God and country, they left a legacy of faith, courage, and endurance. In my time I have taken up their high ideals and have passed them along to my children. Laura, with a doctorate in pharmacology, and Paul, Jr., who proudly serves our nation in the U.S. Marine Corps, continue the quest for human dignity and justice, for as Scripture says, "The light is still shining in the darkness, for the darkness has never put it out."

Notes

Chapter 1

1. *Muskogee Daily Phoenix* (Muskogee, Ok., January 13, 1910).
2. Benjamin Quarles, ed., *Blacks on John Brown* (Urbana: University of Illinois Press, 1972), 61, 69.
3. Wendell G. Addington, "Slave Insurrections in Texas," *Journal of Negro History* 35 (October 1950), 408.
4. Ibid., 420.
5. Ibid.
6. Ibid., 424.
7. Ibid., 409.
8. Ibid., 418.
9. Ibid., 421.
10. Ibid., 419.
11. Peter Farb, *Man's Rise to Civilization as Shown by the Indians of North America* (New York: E. P. Dutton, 1968), 253.
12. Ibid., 253, 254.
13. William Loren Katz, *The Black West* (New York: Doubleday, 1971), 212.
14. Glen Shirley, *Law West of Fort Smith* (Lincoln: University of Nebraska Press, 1971), viii, ix.
15. Ibid., 63.

Notes

Chapter 2

1. Glen Shirley, *Law West of Fort Smith* (Lincoln: University of Nebraska Press, 1971), 28.
2. Jack Gregory and Rennard Strickland, eds., *Hell on the Border* (Muskogee: Indian Heritage Publications, 1971), 195.
3. Ibid., 196.
4. Ibid., 199.
5. Ibid., 188.
6. Ibid., 203.
7. Ibid., 27.
8. D. C. Gideon, *Indian Territory* (New York: Lewis Publishing Company, 1901), 115–16.
9. Ibid., 117.
10. Ibid., 108.
11. Ibid., 18.
12. *Indian-Pioneer History* (Indian Archives Division, Oklahoma Historical Society).

Chapter 3

1. J. W. Ehrlich, *Ehrlich's Blackstone,* Part One (New York: Capricorn Books, 1959), 70, 71.
2. A. Leon Higginbotham, Jr., *In the Matter of Color* (Oxford: Oxford University Press, 1978), 21.
3. Ibid., 53.
4. Alfred E. Cain, ed., *The Winding Road to Freedom* (Chicago: Educational Heritage, 1965), 18.
5. Higginbotham, 382.
6. Winthrop D. Jordan, *White Over Black* (New York: W. W. Norton & Company, 1968), 262.
7. Ibid., 263.
8. William E. Simon, *A Time for Truth* (New York: Berkley Books, 1979), 23.
9. Mary Cable, *Black Odyssey* (New York: Penguin Books, 1977), 90–105.
10. U.S. Constitution 1. Article I, Section 2 (the three-fifths clause). 2. Article I, Section 9, Par. 1 (the slave importation clause). 3. Article I, Section 9, Par. 4 (the capitation clause). 4. Article IV, Section 2, Par. 3 (the fugitive slave clause). 5. Article V (forbade amendment of the slave importation or capitation clauses before 1808).
11. William M. Wiecek, *The Source of Antislavery Constitutionalism in America, 1760–1848* (Ithaca: Cornell University Press, 1977), 74.
12. Loren Miller, *The Petitioners* (New York: Pantheon Books, 1966), 30.
13. Ibid., 29.
14. Mark DeWolfe Howe, *Civil Rights, the Constitution, and the Courts* (Cambridge: Harvard University Press, 1967), 35.
15. Miller, 33.
16. Ibid., 31.
17. Wiecek, 143.

Notes

18. Peter M. Bergman and Mort N. Bergman, comps., *The Chronological History of the Negro in America* (New York: Mentor Books, 1969), 225.

19. Robert F. Durden, *The Gray and the Black* (Baton Rouge: Louisiana State University Press, 1972), 7–9.

20. Ibid., 12.

21. Bergman, 245.

22. Ibid., 246.

23. Ibid.

24. Lerone Bennett, Jr., *Before the Mayflower* (Chicago: Johnson Publishing Company, 1982), 225, 226.

25. Ibid., 214, 215.

26. Bernard Feder, *What Was the Nature of Southern Reconstruction? Viewpoints: U.S.A.* (Cincinnati: American Book Company, 1967), 173.

27. Ibid.

28. George Sinkler, *The Racial Attitudes of American Presidents* (New York: Doubleday & Company, 1971), 162.

29. Ibid., 178.

30. Bennett, 277.

31. Miller, 114.

Chapter 4

1. J. A. Rogers, *World's Great Men of Color* (New York: Macmillan, 1972), 399.

2. Herbert Aptheker, ed., *A Documentary History of the Negro People in the United States*, Volume 3 (Secaucus: Citadel Press, 1977), 70–78.

3. Peter M. Bergman and Mort N. Bergman, comps., *The Chronological History of the Negro in America* (New York: Mentor Books, 1969), 404.

4. Victor G. Reuther, *The Brothers Reuther and the Story of the UAW: A Memoir* (Boston: Houghton Mifflin Company, 1976), 143.

5. James A. Geschwender, *Class, Race, and Worker Insurgency* (Cambridge: Cambridge University Press, 1977), 34.

Chapter 5

1. Mary Penick Motley, comp., ed., *The Invisible Soldier* (Detroit: Wayne State University Press, 1975), 23.

2. August Meir and Elliott Rudnick, eds., *The Making of Black America* (New York: Atheneum, 1971), 126.

3. Lawrence D. Reddick, "Blacks & U.S. Wars," *Atlanta Inquirer* (February 12, 1983), 14B.

4. U.S. Department of Defense, *Black Americans in Defense of Our Nation* (1985), 17.

5. Ibid.

6. Martin Robinson Delany, *The Condition of the Colored People of the United States* (New York: Arno Press, 1968), 76.

7. Ibid., 79.

8. Department of Defense, 18.

9. Ibid.

Notes

10. Ibid., 21.
11. George Sinkler, *The Racial Attitudes of American Presidents* (New York: Doubleday & Company, 1971), 71.
12. Robert F. Durden, *The Gray and the Black* (Baton Rouge: Louisiana State Press, 1972), 23.
13. Benjamin Quarles, *The Negro in the Making of America* (New York: Macmillan, 1969), 119.
14. Leon F. Litwack, *Been in the Storm So Long* (New York: Vintage Books, 1980), 70.
15. Department of Defense, 23.
16. Ibid., 29.
17. Reddick, 16B.
18. Motley, 13.
19. Reddick, 16B.
20. Motley, 12.
21. Ibid., 14.
22. Ibid., 13.
23. Reddick, 16B.
24. Morris J. MacGregor, Jr., *Integration of the Armed Forces 1940–1965* (Washington, D.C.: Center of Military History, 1981), 19, 20.
25. Roy Wilkins, *Standing Fast* (New York: Viking Press, 1982), 184.
26. Motley, 336.
27. Ibid., 339.
28. Ibid., 346.
29. Ibid.
30. Department of Defense, 34.
31. Motley, 157.
32. Ibid., 152.
33. Department of Defense, 35.
34. Peter M. Bergman and Mort N. Bergman, comps., *The Chronological History of the Negro in America* (New York: Mentor Books, 1969), 504.
35. Ibid., 509.
36. Motley, 26.
37. Bergman, 500.
38. Robert Lacey, *Ford: The Men and the Machine* (New York: Ballantine Books, 1986), 558.
39. Bureau of Naval Personnel 15092 (February 12, 1944).
40. Department of Defense, 23.
41. Lerone Bennett, Jr., "Chronicles of Black Courage," *Ebony* (October 10, 1983), 147, 150.
42. Department of Defense, 35.
43. MacGregor, 58.
44. Ibid., 317.
45. Ibid., 64.

Notes

46. "Navy Declares Itself Guilty of Racial Bias," *Atlanta Journal-Constitution* (December 20, 1988).
47. Ibid.

Chapter 6

1. Richard Kluger, *Simple Justice: The History of "Brown v. Board of Education" and Black America's Struggle for Equality* (New York: Alfred A. Knopf, 1976), 371.
2. Ibid., 376.
3. Ibid., 379.
4. Franklyn Peterson, "The Case That Started It All," *Cincinnati Enquirer* (February 24, 1974).
5. Kluger, 393, 394.
6. Karl Menninger, *Sparks* (New York: Thomas Y. Crowell Company, 1973), 159.
7. Kluger, 411, 412.
8. Ibid., 395.
9. Ibid., 404.
10. Ibid., 422.
11. Ibid., 540.
12. Leon Friedman, ed., *Argument* (New York: Chelsea House Publishers, 1969), 565.
13. *Brown v. Board,* On Questions Propounded by the Court, 2.
14. Kluger, 548.
15. *Topeka Daily Capital* (April 6, 1953).
16. Friedman, v.
17. Paul E. Wilson, "Brown v. Board of Education Revisited," *University of Kansas Law Review* 7 (May 1964), 507.

Chapter 7

1. Jack Bass, *Unlikely Heroes* (New York: Simon and Schuster, 1981), 151.
2. Loren Miller, *The Petitioners* (New York: Pantheon Books, 1966), 351.
3. J. Harvie Wilkinson III, *From Brown to Bakke* (Oxford: Oxford University Press, 1979), 64.
4. C. Vann Woodward, *The Strange Career of Jim Crow* (New York: Oxford University Press, 1974), 153.
5. Lerone Bennett, Jr., *Before the Mayflower* (Chicago: Johnson Publishing Company, 1982), 376–77.
6. Frank Freidel, *America in the Twentieth Century,* 4th ed. (New York: Alfred A. Knopf, 1976), 337.
7. Ibid.
8. Supplemental Memorandum for the United States in Brown v. Board of Education, filed April 21, 1955.
9. *Time* (March 26, 1956), 21.
10. Harry S. Ashmore, *An Epitaph for Dixie* (New York: W. W. Norton & Company, 1958), 29.
11. Wilkinson, 69.
12. *Time* (March 26, 1956), 26.

Notes

13. Ibid.
14. Walter Gelhorn, *American Rights* (New York: Macmillan, 1960), 162.
15. Charles L. Black, Jr., "The Lawfulness of the Segregation Decisions," *Yale Law Journal* (January 1960), 421–22.
16. Ibid.
17. Richard Kluger, *Simple Justice: The History of "Brown v. Board of Education" and Black America's Struggle for Equality* (New York: Alfred A. Knopf, 1976), 81.
18. Ibid., 654–55.
19. Gerald T. Dunne, *Hugo Black* (New York: Simon and Schuster, 1977), 316.
20. Ibid.
21. Kluger, 664.
22. Ibid., 662.
23. *Contemporary Authors,* Vol. 123 (Detroit: Gale Research Company, 1988), 443.
24. Ibid., 444.
25. Bernard Schwartz with Stephan Lesher, *Inside the Warren Court* (New York: Doubleday & Company, 1983), 81.
26. John Patrick Diggins, *The Proud Decades: America in War and Peace, 1941–1960* (New York: W. W. Norton & Company, 1988), 294.
27. Kluger, 749.
28. Taylor Branch, *Parting the Waters: America in the King Years, 1954–63* (New York: Simon and Schuster, 1988), 129.
29. Ibid., 121.
30. Bass, 150.
31. Ibid., 121.
32. Robert Frederick Burk, *The Eisenhower Administration and Black Civil Rights* (Knoxville: University of Tennessee Press, 1984), 168.
33. J. W. Peltason, *Fifty-eight Lonely Men* (Urbana: University of Illinois Press, 1961), 168.
34. Ibid., 169.
35. Burk, 175.
36. Peltason, 177.
37. Ibid., 188.
38. Reg Murphy and Hal Gulliver, *The Southern Strategy* (New York: Scribner, 1971).
39. Peltason, 195.
40. Burk, 183.
41. Ibid., 87.
42. Ibid., 263.
43. Ibid., 265.
44. Bass, 192.

Chapter 8

1. Arthur Keefe, "The Marble Palace at 50," *American Bar Association Journal* 62 (October 1982), 1227.
2. Jerold S. Auerbach, *Unequal Justice* (New York: Oxford University Press, 1976), 14.

Notes

3. *Georgia State Bar Journal* 20 (April 1984).

4. Auerbach, 264.

5. *American Bar Association Journal* (August 1977).

6. Geraldine R. Segal, *Blacks in the Law across the Nation* (Philadelphia: University of Pennsylvania Press, 1983), 121.

7. Harry S. Ashmore, *Hearts and Minds: A Personal Account of the Civil Rights Movement from Roosevelt to Reagan* (Cabin John, Md.: Seven Locks Press, 1988), 180.

8. Auerbach, 265.

9. Calvin D. Linton, ed., *The Bicentennial Almanac* (Nashville: Thomas Nelson, 1975), 384.

Chapter 9

1. Donald Dale Jackson, *Judges* (New York: Atheneum, 1974), 381.

2. Karl Menninger, *Sparks* (New York: Thomas Y. Crowell Company, 1973), 62.

3. Jackson, 381.

4. Ibid., 26.

5. Ibid., 366, 367.

6. Rose Matsui Ochi, "Racial Discrimination in Criminal Sentencing," *Judges Journal* 24 (Winter 1985), 7.

7. Bernard Schwartz with Stephan Lesher, *Inside the Warren Court* (New York: Doubleday & Company, 1983), 49.

8. Ibid., 78.

9. Jack Bass, *Unlikely Heroes* (New York: Simon and Schuster, 1981), 77.

10. Ibid., 81.

11. Ibid., 115.

12. Ibid., 112.

13. Ibid., 115.

14. Ibid., 119.

15. Ibid., 34.

16. Ibid., 69.

17. Ibid., 72.

18. Ibid., 50.

19. Ibid., 45.

20. Ibid., 46.

21. *Baltimore Sun* (December 14, 1969).

22. Bass, 106.

23. Ibid., 107.

24. Ibid., 332.

25. Reg Murphy and Hal Gulliver, *The Southern Strategy* (New York: Scribner, 1971), 2.

26. Ibid., 49.

27. Ibid., 62.

28. *U.S. News and World Report* (January 19, 1976).

Notes

29. Bob Woodward and Scott Armstrong, *The Brethren* (New York: Simon and Schuster, 1979), 38.

30. Ibid., 53.

31. *Report of the National Advisory Commission on Civil Disorders* (1968), 337.

32. *Commonwealth of Pennsylvania, et al., v. Local Union No. 242, International Union of Operating Engineers, et al.,* 388 F. Supp. 155 (1974).

33. J. Harvie Wilkinson III, *From Brown to Bakke* (New York: Oxford University Press, 1979), 20.

Chapter 10

1. Thomas Sowell, *A Conflict of Visions* (New York: William Morrow and Company, 1987), 173.

2. William M. Wiecek, *The Source of Antislavery Constitutionalism in America, 1760–1848* (Ithaca: Cornell University Press, 1977), 74.

3. A. Leon Higginbotham, Jr., *In the Matter of Color* (Oxford: Oxford University Press, 1978), 386.

4. Alfred E. Cain, ed., *The Winding Road to Freedom* (New York: Educational Heritage, 1965), 136.

5. Winthrop D. Jordan, *White Over Black* (New York: W. W. Norton & Company, 1968), 324.

6. Bernard Feder, *What Was the Nature of Southern Reconstruction? Viewpoints: U.S.A.* (Cincinnati: American Book Company, 1967), 173.

7. W. E. B. Du Bois, *Black Reconstruction in America, 1860–1880* (New York: Atheneum, 1979), 381.

8. Feder, 170.

9. Ibid., 173.

10. Sidney M. Willhelm, *Black in White America* (Cambridge: Schenkman Publishing Company, 1983), 10.

11. Whitney M. Young, Jr., *Beyond Racism* (New York: McGraw-Hill, 1969), 64.

12. Ira Berlin, *Slaves Without Masters* (Oxford: Oxford University Press, 1974), 217.

13. Young, 20.

14. Benjamin Quarles, *The Negro in the Making of America* (New York: Macmillan, 1969), 151.

15. Whitney M. Young, Jr., *To Be Equal* (New York: McGraw-Hill, 1964), 62.

16. Louis L. Knowles and Kenneth Prewitt, eds., *Institutional Racism in America* (Englewood Cliffs: Prentice-Hall, 1969), 118.

17. Ibid., 24.

18. Peter M. Bergman and Mort N. Bergman, comps., *The Chronological History of the Negro in America* (New York: Mentor Books, 1969), 88.

19. William Loren Katz, *The Black West* (New York: Doubleday & Company, 1971), 80.

20. Jackie Robinson, *I Never Had It Made* (New York: G. P. Putnam's Sons, 1972), 271.

21. Jules Tygiel, *Baseball's Great Experiment* (New York: Oxford University Press, 1983), 80.

22. Ibid.

23. Ibid., 84.

Notes

24. Ibid., 76.
25. Robinson, 287.
26. Tygiel, 337.
27. Leonard Koppett, *New York Times* (April 4, 1987).
28. Young, *To Be Equal,* 60.
29. Morroe Berger, *Equity by Statute* (New York: Octagon Books, 1978), 76.
30. Knowles, 46.
31. Ibid., 47.
32. Ibid., 49.
33. Jesus Garcia and Julie Goebel, "A Comparative Study of Black Americans in Selected U.S. History Textbooks," Texas A & M University, National Council for the Social Studies (November 1983).
34. *Atlanta Constitution* (April 22 and 29, 1984).
35. Allan Bloom, *The Closing of the American Mind: How Higher Education Has Failed Democracy and Impoverished the Souls of Today's Students* (New York: Simon and Schuster, 1987).
36. *Governing* 2 (February 1989).
37. *Wall Street Journal* (August 2, 1984).
38. Richard Willing, "A Face in the Crowd," *Detroit News* (December 5, 1982).
39. Richard L. Zweigenhaft, "Who Gets to the Top? Executive Suite Discrimination in the Eighties" (New York: American Jewish Committee Institute of Human Relations, 1984), 25–30.
40. Ibid.
41. Ibid.
42. Donald Dale Jackson, *Judges* (New York: Atheneum, 1974), 311.
43. Paul Seabury, "H.E.W. and the Universities," *Commentary* (February 12, 1972).
44. *American Bar Association Journal* 71 (April 1985), 33.
45. *New York Times* (February 13, 1983).
46. Geraldine R. Segal, *Blacks in the Law* (Philadelphia: University of Pennsylvania Press, 1983), 123.
47. *U.S. News and World Report* (May 11, 1987).
48. Joe T. Darden, "The State of Black Michigan," *MSU Today* (Michigan State University) 6 (Summer 1987).

Chapter 11

1. Ira Berlin, *Slaves Without Masters* (Oxford: Oxford University Press, 1974), 133.
2. Edmund L. Drago, *Black Politicians and Reconstruction in Georgia* (Baton Rouge: Louisiana State University Press, 1982), 152.
3. Theodore Cross, *The Black Power Imperative* (New York: Faulkner Books, 1986), 138.
4. Ibid., 131.
5. Talcott Parsons and Kenneth B. Clark, eds., *The Negro Americans* (Boston: Houghton Mifflin Company, 1966), 534.
6. Whitney M. Young, Jr., *To Be Equal* (New York: McGraw-Hill, 1964), 144.

Notes

7. Mike Royko, *Boss: Richard J. Daley of Chicago* (New York: E. P. Dutton, 1971), 135–36.

8. Young, 187.

9. *Atlanta Constitution* (January 11, 1985).

10. Ibid. (November 6, 1987).

11. Ibid. (May 1, 1988).

12. Louis Knowles and Kenneth Prewitt, eds., *Institutional Racism in America* (Englewood Cliffs: Prentice-Hall, 1969), 118.

13. *Atlanta Constitution* (March 28, 1983).

14. Ibid. (April 22, 1984).

15. Ibid. (October 4, 1987).

16. Ibid. (March 1, 1988).

17. Raymond Wolters, *The Burden of Brown: Thirty Years of School Desegregation* (Knoxville: University of Tennessee Press, 1984), 274.

18. David J. Garrow, review of *The Burden of Brown* by Raymond Wolters, *Reviews in American History* 13 (September 1985), 428.

19. Cross, 118.

20. Peter M. Bergman and Mort N. Bergman, comps., *The Chronological History of the Negro in America* (New York: Mentor Books, 1969), 368.

21. Lawrence Friedman, *The White Savage* (Englewood Cliffs: Prentice-Hall, 1970), 156.

22. Ibid., 160.

23. Herbert Aptheker, ed., *A Documentary History of the Negro People in the United States,* Vol. 3 (Secaucus: Citadel Press, 1977), 64.

24. Sidney M. Willhelm, *Black in White America* (Cambridge: Schenkman Publishing Company, 1983), 188.

25. *Bob Jones University v. United States,* 76 L. Ed. 2d 157, 176 (1983), cited in *Crisis* 91 (April 1984).

26. *Washington Post* (May 12, 1982), cited in *Ronald Reagan's Reign of Error* by Mark Grien and Gail MacColl (New York: Pantheon Books, 1983), 116.

27. *Civil Rights Cases,* 109 U.S. 3 (1883).

Chapter 12

1. Edward S. Corwin, *The "Higher Law" Background of American Constitutional Law* (Ithaca: Cornell University Press, 1955), 8.

2. Ibid., 15.

3. Winthrop D. Jordan, *White Over Black* (New York: W. W. Norton & Company, 1968), 433.

4. Ibid., 434.

5. A. Leon Higginbotham, Jr., *In the Matter of Color* (Oxford: Oxford University Press, 1978), 378.

6. C. C. Goen, *Broken Churches, Broken Nation* (Macon: Mercer University Press, 1985), 181.

7. Ibid., 166.

8. Ibid., 167.

Notes

9. Ibid., 10.

10. C. Eric Lincoln, *Race, Religion, and the Continuing American Dilemma* (New York: Hill and Wang, 1984), 25.

11. Ibid., 43.

12. Ibid., 31.

13. Taylor Branch, *Parting the Waters: America in the King Years, 1954–63* (New York: Simon and Schuster, 1988), 3.

14. Jerry Falwell, *Strength for the Journey* (New York: Simon and Schuster, 1987), 286.

15. Ibid., 291.

16. *Penthouse* (May 1983).

17. Gary Wills, *Detroit Free Press* (October 8, 1984).

18. Falwell, 290.

19. Newell G. Bringhurst, *Saints, Slaves, and Blacks* (Westport: Greenwood Press, 1981), 4.

20. Lincoln, 147.

21. Bringhurst, 148.

22. Ibid., 165.

23. Ibid., 170.

24. Lincoln, 151.

25. Corwin, 5.

26. *Atlanta Constitution* (March 14, 1985).

27. Earl Conrad, *The Invention of the Negro* (New York: Paul S. Eriksson, 1966), 207.

28. Ibid., 208.

29. Ibid., 207.

30. W. E. B. Du Bois, *The Souls of Black Folk* (New York: Fawcett Publications, 1965), 16, 17.

31. John Rawls, *A Theory of Justice* (Cambridge: Harvard University Press, 1971), 4.